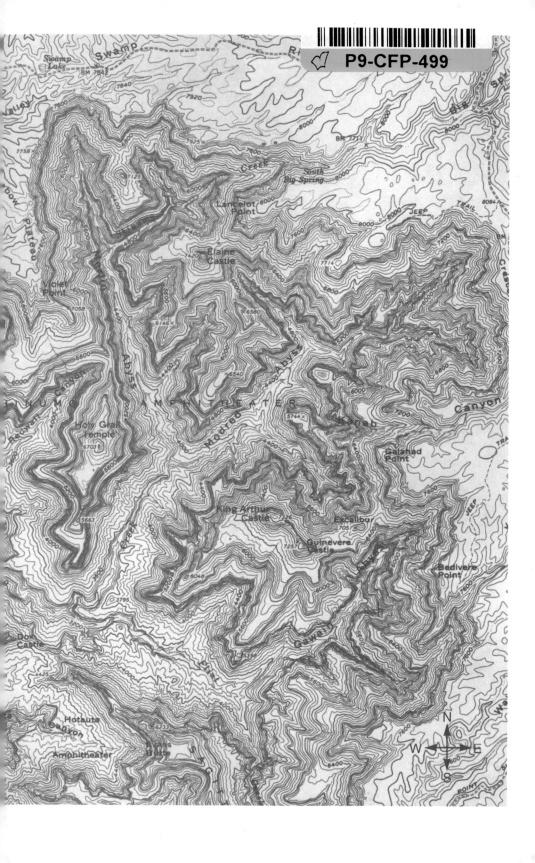

GRAND
CANYON
CELEBRATION

More praise for *Grand Canyon Celebration*

"*Grand Canyon Celebration* charts new territory where fathers and sons meet not in rivalry or combat but in mutual admiration and empowerment. It provides an initiatory key and an imaginal landscape where sons and fathers learn to bless each other."

Ted Tollefson
Codirector, Mythos Institute

"Enlivened by vivid nature writing and tense, dramatic encounters, this book will fascinate, move, and enlighten anyone who has struggled with the mystery of coming of age or the burden of fatherhood. Those who love wild places will delight in its celebration of the Grand Canyon; those who love their sons will find inspiration and wisdom in its candid, often humorous stories. . . . This is a wise and powerful book, written with uncommon grace, and suffused with candor. I felt the love behind it and admire the honesty with which it was written."

John Tallmadge
Former President, Association for the Study
of Literature and the Environment
Author, *Meeting the Tree of Life*

GRAND
CANYON
CELEBRATION

A Father–Son Journey of Discovery

Michael Quinn Patton

 **Prometheus Books**

59 John Glenn Drive
Amherst, New York 14228-2197

Published 1999 by Prometheus Books

03 02 01 00 99   5 4 3 2 1

Library of Congress Cataloging-in-Publication Data

Patton, Michael Quinn.
    Grand Canyon celebration : a father-son journey of discovery / Michael Quinn Patton.
        p.   cm.
    Includes bibliographical references.
    ISBN 1–57392–266–8 (alk. paper)
    1. Fathers and sons—Arizona—Grand Canyon. 2. Parent and teenager—Arizona—Grand Canyon. 3. Grand Canyon (Ariz.)—Description and travel. 4. Patton, Michael Quinn—Journeys—Arizona—Grand Canyon. I. Title.
HQ799.15.P37   1999
306.874´2´0979132—dc21   98–48764
                                                                         CIP

Printed in the United States of America on acid-free paper

To Brandon and Malcolm

Contents

List of Maps

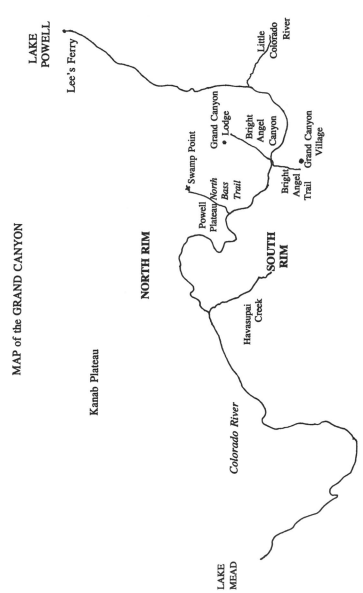

MAP of the GRAND CANYON

LAKE POWELL

Lee's Ferry

Little Colorado River

Grand Canyon Lodge

Bright Angel Canyon

Swamp Point

North Bass Trail

Powell Plateau

Grand Canyon Village

Bright Angel Trail

NORTH RIM

SOUTH RIM

Havasupai Creek

Kanab Plateau

Colorado River

LAKE MEAD

Distance from Lake Powell to Lake Mead is 278 miles

Preface

In the summer of 1991, I took my son into the Grand Canyon for an initiation experience. A longtime friend and experienced canyon hiker accompanied us. I wanted to do something to acknowledge and celebrate the coming of age of my firstborn, to engage in some kind of rite of passage. I was influenced in this desire by the Gourma initiation rituals I had come to know as a Peace Corps volunteer in Burkina Faso, West Africa, in the 1960s. I read about other tribal initiation ceremonies and explored both scholarly and popular literature on the subject. Somewhere along the way I began to see my inquiry as larger than the challenge of how to recognize and honor my own son's entry into adulthood. I discovered a crisis revolving around how youth in modern society come of age and a controversy surrounding various calls for a return to tribal initiation rites for contemporary young people, especially males. Reflecting on all this, and facing my own son's impending adulthood, I began pondering what the elements and processes might be for a humanistic rite of passage. That led, ultimately, to this Grand Canyon story.

I observed, recorded, and reflected on my son's initiation even as I participated in and helped facilitate it. This book tells the story of how what began as an initiation became a cele-

13

bration. Extrapolating from the particularities of our story, its unique canyon context, and the transformation I experienced personally, I have sought to understand the broader societal implications of what we experienced. As a result, I have come to view a humanistic approach to coming of age as quite different from traditional, tribally based forms of initiation.

In suggesting that this story offers a humanistic alternative to traditional tribal and religious initiation rites, I do not presume to be a spokesman for humanism. Indeed, humanists disagree about and debate the extent to which myths, fables, legends, and rituals can be incorporated into family life without encouraging superstition and mysticism. This book offers one family's experience at attempting such incorporation. We sought ways of tapping into and enjoying the rich creativity of human imagination while using our intellects to analyze myth and ritual, not least of all as a mechanism for accessing, experiencing, critically examining, and thereby understanding some of the emotional, social, and cultural dimensions of being human. So saying, I recognize that many will have a different perspective. I welcome that dialogue with fellow Titans as, in the tradition of Prometheus, we each work in our own way to steal fire from the gods in support of the development of humankind.

◆   ◆   ◆

My son Brandon, and longtime friend, Malcolm Gray, made this book possible, not only because we shared the ten-day adventure of this story in the Grand Canyon, but because they continued to journey with me throughout the years of writing that followed. They helped, first, by validating the facts of the story, making corrections as needed in places where my notes were inadequate or my memory failed. More importantly, they offered personal support and ongoing encouragement.

Malcolm has been my canyon guide and a close friend for years. He worked mightily to make the dialogue I wrote be true to and sound like conversations he had actually been part of, and he was relentless in keeping me infected with canyon fever. We have returned to hike North Bass Trail several times as I've worked at the ultimately impossible task of describing, for those who have not descended therein, what the Grand Canyon is like. We have also explored other canyon descents and rafted the Colorado River. The miles we've passed together have enriched me far beyond the majestic setting in which they occurred, to the point where I can no longer distinguish Malcolm's contributions from the canyon's, so intimately are they intertwined in my life.

While I worked on this book, Brandon completed four years of college, graduated, began a musical career, and put out a CD playing and singing his own compositions. He also helped with background research on the Grand Canyon. He returned with me to North Bass Trail five years after his own initiation to be part of his brother's coming of age in the canyon, adding to the ritual by hiking with and playing an Australian didjeridoo. Understandably, the eighteen-year-old depicted in this story seems to him at times like a slight acquaintance he knew for a while in his now distant youth. I take pleasure in assuring him that this was a person he once lived with and knew intimately. He takes pleasure in telling me it's my version of the story, not necessarily his. He has also acknowledged what I care about most, that the canyon experience holds a special and permanent place in his heart, and that he understands and experiences this writing as an expression of a father's love for his son.

I dedicate the book to Brandon and Malcolm.

Others who did not hike the canyon with us have nevertheless shared in and contributed to this writing venture. Some helped early in the journey, when I was searching for story cohesion and struggling to find that elusive thing called "voice." Nancy Boxill, John Bryson, Milne Kinter-Dee, Kristen Eide-Tollefson, Merle Fossom, Rodger Kemp, Diane Morehouse, Ted Tollefson, John Tallmadge, and Scott Walker read first drafts of early chapters and offered honest feedback about how far I still had to go, helpful advice about the direction I should take, and encouragement to continue the journey. Others joined as the book took shape, helping especially with what to leave out, what to keep, how to join the parts into a more coherent whole, and still more work on voice. I am grateful to Fontaine Belford, Angela Browne, Corrine Glesne, Susan Laughlin, Carter McNamara, Ricardo Millett, Michael Andrew Miner, Joseph Meeker, Clark Moustakas, Dan Odegard, Gregor Stark, and Eric Stevens for getting through full drafts of the book and guiding me in separating weeds from potentially flowering plants. Mary Bisbee-Beek, Kenneth Byers, Kay Lisch, Barbara Campbell-Moffitt, Herb Robertson, Arnie Shore, and Jennifer Thurman read different drafts at different times, each offering encouragement at a time when that was what was most needed. Nate Van Til, my son's friend of many years, and Karen Wilson, Brandon's mother, offered special and insightful feedback about his voice in the book. My siblings, Connie, Vanessa, and Tim, helped by reading the book, reflecting on my musings about our family, and sharing their own experiences in a way that gave me a still deeper understanding of the influences of family history.

Only Jeanne, my wife and fellow traveler throughout the canyon years, read every word of every draft. She brought her accomplished writing and editing skills to bear with a combination of affirmation and critical insight. Her words and notes were an added blessing on my good days; on bad ones, her love and presence offered sustenance to persevere. Our children, J.Quinn Campbell and Charmagne Campbell-Patton, provided understanding, support, and assistance with final manuscript preparation.

The illustrations throughout the book are reproductions from Mimbres pottery transcribed by New Mexico artist and potter, and Jeanne's sister, Barbara Campbell-Moffitt. I'm grateful to Barbara for the special work she did in preparing the illustrations.

◆   ◆   ◆

A passage from Edward Abbey's classic *Desert Solitaire* closes this preface. Brandon read Abbey as we traveled from the woodlands and lakes of Minnesota to the Grand Canyon desert. Years earlier, on my way to the Southwest for the first time, Abbey's images and reflections had introduced me to the desert. Thanks to him, once I arrived, I felt like I knew the place, at least a little. I would hope that this book might do a bit of that for those who have not descended the Grand Canyon.

It seems to me that the strangeness and wonder of existence are emphasized here, in the desert, by the comparative sparsity of the flora and fauna; life not crowded upon life as in other places but scattered abroad in spareness and simplicity, with a generous gift of space for each herb and bush and tree, each stem of grass, so that the living organism stands out bold and brave and vivid against the lifeless and barren rock. The extreme clarity of the desert light is equaled by the extreme individuation of desert life-forms. Love flowers best in openness and freedom.[1]

Michael Quinn Patton
Saint Paul, Minnesota
January 1999

Note

1. Edward Abbey, *Desert Solitaire: A Season in the Wilderness* (New York: Ballantine Books, 1968), p. i.

Day One

1. Vishnu Metamorphism

To see the enormity of the Grand Canyon you have to be orbiting the Earth. To feel it, you have to descend within. To learn from it, you have only to stay awhile and be present. At least that's what Malcolm had claimed when he first urged me to hike with him from Apache Point to Elves Chasm years earlier. And learn I had, about bloody blisters, debilitating thirst, and the importance of moving quickly when a rock ledge gives way a thousand feet above the canyon floor, especially if you're standing on it at the time. Modest learnings. But they left an impression. As did the depth and beauty of the canyon.

Malcolm had been bringing questions about his life to the canyon for years. And getting answers. I had gotten no answers on that first trip. But that, Malcolm explained, was because I had brought no questions. Fair enough. I had come for the hike and a chance to walk among the oldest exposed rocks on the Earth's surface.

But I did get an idea. Standing atop Mount Huethawali and staring across the Colorado River at Holy Grail Temple, I imagined someday hiking with my son, then just entering toddlerhood, and initiating him into manhood there amidst buttes named King Arthur Castle, Guinevere Castle, and Excalibur, and gorges named Merlin Abyss and

21

Modred Abyss. Malcolm called it a vision, which beguilingly transformed a passing notion into a quest, like framing a telephone doodle and calling it art. What better place for grandiosity than the Grand Canyon?

The gilt frame, however, didn't quite make it back with me to Minnesota. I realized that I lacked a few of the basic necessities for conducting an initiation. Tribal elders, for example. Hard to come by if you don't have a tribe. As are other essentials, like tradition, a sacred place, ritual, terrifying gods to appease, wisdom to pass on, and life-threatening tests for the initiate to pass (preferably ones that the initiator has successfully survived). From what I recalled of anthropology, strong gender identity would also be a prerequisite. That, however, might be conjured up. I had felt a vague sense of something while gazing toward Lancelot Point. Malcolm suggested that the canyon was putting me in touch with my masculine collective unconscious. After ten days in the canyon such things could be said without sounding absurd. Like eating freeze-dried food. It can taste gourmet scrumptious after a hard day hiking, but cooked at home, it's ghastly. So I found that my canyon initiation vision didn't reconstitute well mixed with urban fluoridated water.

But it also didn't evaporate.

Malcolm now smiles and says he never doubted. I, on the other hand, still find myself amazed that we actually did return with Brandon for an initiation experience. And, being a social-science researcher, I kept field notes. Not, I should add, because I had any premonition that they might reveal something important about a humanist approach to coming of age in contemporary society. I did it for family history and, I concede, out of habit. I had spent too many years in sociological observation to turn off that part of myself just because I had brought my eldest son into one of the most magnificent landscapes on earth after eighteen years of anticipation.

I considered leaving my scientific side behind. I even tried. Just be a father, I told myself. Just be in the canyon. Be present with Brandon. Don't analyze it while it's happening. Stay with the experience.

Or were those Malcolm's admonitions? Certainly, some part of me was intrigued by Malcolm's belief that he got answers from the canyon. And, unlike our first hike years earlier, this time I found I had come with a question, though I wasn't fully aware of it until our second night.

We were camped within the inner gorge, just short of the Colorado River, where White Creek flows out of Muav Canyon into Shinumo Creek. My aching body craved rest after two hard days' hiking, but Brandon's after-dinner questions about how different cultures define manhood had left me tossing and turning. He slept near enough for me to hear his slow, even breathing. As I studied him, he rolled from his back onto his side, pulling his knees up fetuslike, almost, but not quite, transforming his gangling, eighteen-year-old frame into a picture of innocence. He looked like the question he had asked over dinner.

He had adopted the tone of a teacher he and his friends loved to mock: "We're having a pop quiz today. I know you're all wellllll-prepared. How do I know? Because you're students. That's what students do. They read assignments and come to class prepared. So here you are. Enjoy."

With the same mocking tone he had observed: "So, this is my initiation. When do I find out about the manhood thing? I'm sure you two have come prepared with important insights. Might as well get on with it. I, your humble initiate, am all ears."

Our subsequent anthropological discussion about how different societies define manhood was rooted in cultural relativism as solidly as the large cottonwood that sheltered our campsite. The discussion had been serious, intense, and surprisingly lacking in satisfaction. Not for Brandon. For me.

As I gazed at Brandon sleeping, voices argued with each other in my head. What does a modern, humanist father tell his son about being a man? Some voices, recorded in my memory long ago, rasped repeatedly like a worn needle stuck in scratched grooves from the waxen days of graduate school. Others, more recently entered, played intermittently through the scratches. The messages from different eras competed to be heard, rising to a discordant crescendo, like being caught in a small gym between opposing fans and their blaring pep bands at a championship basketball game—exhilarating only if you know which side to cheer for.

Such imagery being incongruent with my peaceful environs, though I enjoy both debate and athletic competitions, I redirected my inner musings to the steady gurgle of nearby rapids and the chirping melodies of the canyon night. I quietly got up to stroll back and forth along the creek, pondering what I wanted to pass on to Brandon about the nature of manhood. I paused in the shadow of ancient rock and listened as Shinumo's rapids asserted the constant flow of the present. I tried out possibilities on a disinterested moon: metaphors of male incandescence and female florescence.

What was left to tell Brandon that he hadn't already heard from me ad nauseam? I could affirm that the moon is disinterested, that the canyon is rock, and that life offers many pathways for being a man and developing as a person, none of them certain. I could offer perspective and canyon-inspired metaphors.

Malcolm, in contrast, offered mystical connection, tapping into canyon consciousness, magical talismans, personalized totems, and the belief that we each have an ordained path with heart, that certain things are meant to be. I wanted to let Brandon experience Malcolm's mysticism before debating it. I harbored no fear that Brandon, having been reared with a solid humanist perspective, would ever succumb to the irrational claims of traditional religions, but some varieties of so-called New Age spirituality might prove more alluring given their pretense of being based in psychology, anthropology, quantum physics, Chinese medicine, Native American values, left brain/right brain neuroscience, holography, the Gaia hypothesis, and global consciousness, among others.

This trip, this "initiation," felt like a last chance. When, if ever again, would I have Brandon's undivided attention? Or at least some part of it? I was not quite so delusional as to believe I could attain the impossibly high standard of "undivided attention" with a member in good standing of the generation that grew up on channel-surfing. But I did have ten uninterrupted days and nights with Brandon. No outside influences. No competition from television, telephones, friends, or work. In his more than 6,600 days on this earth I had never spent ten uninterrupted days and nights with him. Never.

I had shared fully in his care as an infant and toddler. When his mother and I divorced, we shared custody jointly and equally, and he changed households on a regular schedule, adapted as he got older, and preferred longer periods at each place. He usually had a friend along for holiday events and summer trips. During his teenage years, full days of what has come to be called "quality time" became increasing scarce and precious.

Ten whole days with my son in the Grand Canyon. Ten days before he left home for college and the rest of his adult life. Ten final days. A last chance.

I returned to where Brandon slept and, gazing at him, considered whether it much mattered what I had to say—words, after all, being only words. But words matter in my world, as do answers. Thought matters. And so I thought some more until, under the influence of that elixir unique to the small hours when the body is exhausted and the internal dialogue worn down, I experienced at last a euphoria of analogical clarity. It came as I turned and peered into the dark gorge through which we had descended. That very afternoon, we had traversed the canyon's Great Unconformity, in one step passing through a gap of 250 million years across a space that had once been filled with massive mountains. Recalling that moment took me through what felt like a parallel unconformity, insignificant by standards of

Canyon time, but huge when measured on the modest scale of human evolution. Canyon metaphor offered sociological insight. Malcolm would later say the canyon had answered my question.

The Canyon's Great Unconformity had once been filled with towering Precambrian formations of Bass Limestone, Hakatai Shale, Shinumo Quartzite, Dox Sandstone, and Cardenas Basalts 800 million to one-and-a-quarter billion years old. They had been turned sideways and thrust up higher than the Rockies by monumental tectonic movements. During this churning, twisting, and thrusting, even more ancient rocks were exposed in places: hardened magma of Zoroaster Granites and the oldest rock in the Grand Canyon, the metamorphosed lava-black Vishnu Schist, 1.7 billion years old. Over millions of years these mountains were eroded until the space they once occupied was filled with sandstone deposited by encroaching seas.

When we arrived at the Great Unconformity, we joked about what it meant to arrive some place that isn't there. As we hiked on within the depths of the inner canyon, we marveled at the dramatic transition from sand and gravel to sculptured stone, its significance gradually penetrating with the cold feel of the marblelike rock. Now, inspired by the memory of that geologic gap, I contemplated the chasm that exists between modern society and ancient times. Many experience the gap as a painful loss. Lately, contemporary male elders have been trying to fill in the gap, build a bridge back, or at least make a connection. They hope a return to ancient initiation rites will help close the gap. I had been attracted by that possibility myself, but Brandon's reactions during our hike down said it wouldn't work, at least not for modern young people who have tasted choice, experienced the power of intellect, learned to value individuality and abhor control. The Great Unconformity impressed on me the gap between past and present when societal customs have been eroded to the point of vanishing. Our ancestral past will necessarily and inevitably remain a foundation, like the ancient Vishnu Schist, formed by 75,000 pounds per square inch of tectonic pressure and named for the Hindu god, the Preserver. The Tapeats formation now rises atop that preserved foundation, but is neither part of it nor continuous in time.

I imagined a contemporary coming of age journey that recognizes ancient foundations of human experience, but is separate and distinct in accordance with modern discontinuities and the great unconformity of human potential in our times—a coming of age process that does not require the societal equivalent of 75,000 pounds per square inch of pressure to assure conformity. Indeed, a coming of age process that does not even have

MAJOR STRATA OF THE GRAND CANYON

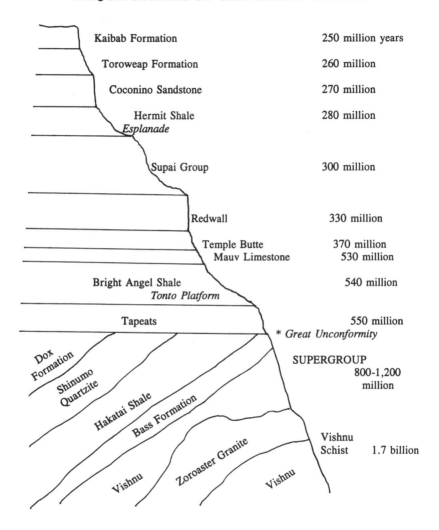

Kaibab Formation	250 million years
Toroweap Formation	260 million
Coconino Sandstone	270 million
Hermit Shale	280 million
Esplanade	
Supai Group	300 million
Redwall	330 million
Temple Butte	370 million
Mauv Limestone	530 million
Bright Angel Shale	540 million
Tonto Platform	
Tapeats	550 million
* *Great Unconformity*	
Dox Formation	SUPERGROUP
Shinumo Quartzite	800–1,200 million
Hakatai Shale	
Bass Formation	
Vishnu	Vishnu Schist 1.7 billion
Zoroaster Granite	
Vishnu	

conformity as its goal. That would be the greatest unconformity. A humanistic process designed individually for each young person instead of standardized by tradition; a process grounded in and honoring rational, scientific thought rather than mysticism and New Age spirituality; and a process of intergenerational bonding rather than separation.

In elucidating the role of traditional initiation for Brandon, Malcolm, my longtime friend and canyon guide, also an anthropologist and family therapist, had explained that initiation rites functioned to psychologically separate sons from parental domination in tribal societies with extended families where generations would live together in a confined village space. But in modern society, just the opposite is the case. Our children are separated from us by day care, schools, music, television, peer groups, and easy geographic mobility. The challenge of contemporary times is not to provide for the physical and psychological separation of children from parents. Society has evolved multiple mechanisms for detachment. Parents and children today are subjected to unprecedented centrifugal forces. The challenge now is to bond.

I thought I had come to the Grand Canyon for a ritual of initiation—recognizing and celebrating Brandon's manhood. But as we had descended into the inner canyon, the focus shifted for me. There, in the moonlight, I admitted why. He was leaving home and going off to college. We needed no ceremony to recognize his independence. It was not in doubt. Nor was his manhood. What I craved, that ancient rituals could not provide and had not been designed to arrange, was connection.

Abruptly, propelled by the force of illusory insight, I turned again away from the rapids toward Brandon and sleep. A piercing pain in my leg stopped me. I had connected with a prickly pear cactus. Examining the offending thorn, I heard my voice say: "Reality-check." Suddenly self-conscious, I looked around, then laughed out loud at the ridiculous figure I presented: pacing the canyon floor dressed only in the ephemeral threads of an emerging sociological paradigm shift.

2. First Glimpse of Temples and Gods

Malcolm yielded and pulled the car onto the shoulder just beyond the entrance to the park as I had requested. "We've always gone to the Grand Canyon Lodge first," he reminded me. "That's how we get ready to enter the canyon. Having Brandon along shouldn't change that."

Having him along changes everything, I thought, but said instead: "Why should his first look come squeezed in among thousands of cameras? If you go in alone and get the permit, we can begin more, ummm, seriously, away from tour buses and—"

"I can handle the tourist scene," Brandon interrupted, leaning forward from the back seat.

"I'm not trying to protect you," I insisted. "It's about getting focused and setting the right tone. I've imagined your first view coming at the trailhead, just the three of us looking out at Holy Grail Temple. We can sit here among the trees and get mentally prepared while we wait for Malcolm to return."

Malcolm put his hand on my shoulder. "Michael, going to the Lodge and the gift shop *is* how we get prepared." He looked back at Brandon. "We'll drive through the parking lot several times until a space opens up. We'll crowd among the tourists looking at the canyon.

29

We'll deal with the permit hassles. We'll even have a hot dog and fries. Then we'll really be ready to go in."

"You mean we'd like OD on civilization first," Brandon translated. "I can get into that."

"Overdosing on civilization was how it started," Malcolm mused, "but now it's something more. Over the years I've made my peace with the canyon meaning different things to different people. Some folks just want to take photographs. Some drive days to get here and then only spend an hour. I don't understand that very well, but it seems to work for them. By hanging around the lodge beforehand, I get centered on why *I* come."

Malcolm looked in the direction of the rim, still twenty miles away. "The canyon teaches me. Each time I'm here I discover something I need to learn—or relearn. Going to the lodge first begins the transition from busyness to openness."

"Don't the people bother you?" Brandon asked.

"Not any more. They're just there, part of the environment." He paused. "I stand there in the Great Hall looking out the massive windows toward the South Rim, protected from sun and wind, people oohing and aahing, cameras clicking, and it all takes me inside myself. Then I know I'm ready."

"You're right, I had forgotten your ritual," I said. Then to Brandon: "I want you to experience the canyon both Malcolm's way and my way. And then you'll come to your own way. Let me change places with you so I can nap until we get there."

Malcolm pulled back on the road behind a moving aluminum skyscraper. On the back of the Winnebago Brandon read aloud: " 'EVERYWHERE WE GO IS HOME.' Wasn't that one of your sixties' slogans?"

I bolted up, protesting: "No way!"

"No, really, like '*If you can't be with the one you love, love the one you're with*' and '*Everywhere we go is home*'—they're pretty much the same."

"He's all yours," I said to Malcolm and laid back. Cramped in the backseat of the car, I sighed deeply as I closed my eyes, wondering how Brandon would react to our effort at initiation. Facing the uncertainty of a difficult route we had never hiked down, I felt anything but confident. An awful lot of things could go wrong, and I wasn't sure what having things go right meant.

At Grand Canyon Village, we found a parking spot at the far end of the lot, behind dozens of empty buses, all with their motors running. We proceeded straight to the Great Hall and there, amidst the crowd, Brandon got his first look into the Grand Canyon.

"*Bue düden,*" he whispered.

"What?" Malcolm asked.

"*Bue düden,*" Brandon repeated, his eyes still on the canyon.

"He makes up his own words," I shrugged.

"Bue-due-den," Malcolm tried slowly, then added: "Bassdom."

"Bassdom," Brandon repeated, grinning at Malcolm.

"What made you think of Bass?" I asked, wanting Brandon to hear the story Malcolm had told me during my first look.

"We'll be hiking to the old inner gorge camp of William Wallace Bass. He and his wife, Ada, raised their family down there. They had a son, Bill. In his old age, he was asked what it was like to grow up in the Grand Canyon. He said he'd missed only one thing as a boy. Even as an old man he still felt the loss. He'd never had a first look at the canyon. All his life he'd watched others gaze into the canyon for the first time—and envied them that first look."

"Awesome," Brandon said softly.

We stood silently for a while, then Malcolm said, more to himself than to us, "It's one big hole." Each time I heard him repeat this, his canyon mantra, it reminded me of an astronomer I once met who, having devoted his life to studying the Milky Way, referred to it as "my little cluster of stars."

Malcolm led us out the side door to an asphalt path that guided us easily about a quarter mile to Bright Angel Point. With cameras aimed in all directions at the spectacular panorama, in a sea of domestic accents and foreign tongues, we waited our turn at the edge to behold the magnificent rock temples of Ottoman Amphitheater: Deva, Brahma, Zoroaster, and, in the distance, Thor. Each rises a half mile above the undulating grayness of the stark Tonto Platform defining the eight-mile descent of Bright Angel Canyon, a narrow slit hiding the inner gorge that looks like it had been drawn in black ink to outline the base of the temples. Each begins as sheer Redwall that forms a massive foundation supporting a series of sloping sedimentary rock terraces, the Supai. These sweeping terraces, spotted green with sparse desert vegetation, point upward like arrow feathers to a white sandstone pedestal, the Coconino. A dark red pinnacle of Hermit Shale uniquely crowns each temple. Eons of erosion have sculpted dramatic variations in every aspect save one: their common geologic history. I studied each separately, wanting to fix in my mind the differences between them, but the shared symmetry of strata melded them into a single, massive formation, a half mile high and many miles around.

Brandon wanted to know how so many canyon formations had come to have religious and mythological names, so I told him what I could remember of what I had read about Clarence Edward Dutton. Later, he, Malcolm, and I did further research. Dutton was a protégé of John Wesley Powell, the most renowned of the canyon's early explorers and the man credited with naming the Grand Canyon. Dutton had been part of a Powell exploration team in 1875. He returned in 1880 as a leader of the new United States Geological Survey, the result of which was the first important geological book on the canyon, *The Tertiary History of the Grand Cañon District, with Atlas.* He had been trained as a Christian minister before becoming a geologist. He had also studied oriental religions and combined this knowledge with poetic inspiration in attempting to capture the canyon's grandeur. He began naming templelike canyon formations and buttes after Eastern gods: Brahma, Vishnu, and Shiva Temples; the Tower of Babel; and Hindu Amphitheater. The area of the western canyon where we would be hiking was mapped in 1905 by Richard T. Evans and François Matthes. Matthes determined to continue the tradition of what he called "heroic nomenclature" begun by Dutton. Matthes added Krishna Shrine, Solomon Temple, and Wotan's Throne to the canyon's pantheon. He also championed the idea that the different parts of the canyon should have names consistently built around a central theme: Eastern gods in Hindu Amphitheater, great scientists in Evolution Amphitheater (Darwin Plateau, Huxley Terrace, Spencer Terrace), early explorers in Explorers' Canyon, and Indian tribal names along the South Rim. Most significant to us, he made the Arthurian legend the central theme of the area where William Wallace Bass had lived with his family, the area where we would make our descent beneath Holy Grail Temple.

"And is there a Jesus Temple?" Brandon asked when I had concluded the explanation of nomenclature origins.

"What would you guess?" I asked back.

"Probably too close to home. Might be viewed as sacrilege or something."

"Dead on," I affirmed.

We stood in silence for a while. I was surprised to find that the throng of tourists, far from being an annoyance, contributed to the impact of the temples. Their stony indifference to human presence accentuated our collective puniness. It occurred to me that their indifference and our puniness were but two manifestations of the same thing. Then, my experience of the temples was transformed, as if I'd been looking at a picture of a vase that turned into two silhouetted faces. My attention shifted from the massive forms to the surrounding emptiness. The temples, a moment ago so enormous, now seemed dwarfed by the much more vast, all-enveloping space. I saw the big hole.

Brandon's voice, telling me we were going, brought me out of my reverie. When I failed to respond, Malcolm said, "He's okay. He had just forgotten."

"Forgotten what?" Brandon asked.

"What Bill Bass couldn't have known, and what you're about to learn— that seeing the canyon for the first time isn't seeing it. There's too much to look at. You have to descend down through all the layers to really experience it. Then, away from the canyon, you think you remember, you think you have it with you . . . until you come back and see it again." He turned abruptly and headed back to the parking lot.

As we walked back, Brandon said: "I can see why someone named this Bright Angel Point. It's like a heavenly view looking down on earthly temples."

"Reasonable possibility," I confirmed, "but it didn't happen like that. I've been reading up on canyon history in preparation for this trip. The name 'Bright Angel' was first used at river level and had nothing to do with this or any other view."

"You mean somebody saw something they thought looked like an angel?" Brandon speculated.

"Captain John Wesley Powell came up with the name in 1869 before the temples were named—or much of anything else. We'll hike out on Powell Plateau, so you'll get to know the part of the canyon named in his honor. He led the first expedition through the Grand Canyon on the Colorado River. They barely made it, losing boats and men—only six of the original ten completed the trip. At one point all were believed lost. Powell became famous and controversial, including an ongoing dispute about whether he was really the first through the canyon by river."

"Who else could have been first? Native Americans?" Brandon asked.

"The evidence indicates that Southwest Indians didn't canoe or raft down the river, just across it in places. The competing version of who was first has one James White, a prospector, getting attacked by Indians, strapping himself to a raft to escape, and floating out the length of the canyon through the rapids without being able to navigate in any way."

"You sound skeptical."

"Pretty incredible story, but impossible to prove or disprove, so the debate rages on among canyon old-timers. Powell certainly conducted the first planned, scientific, and documented expedition. And that's where the name Bright Angel came from. Early in the expedition they stopped at a tributary that looked filthy from heavy sediment and smelled like a sewer because of sulfur emissions. One of the men called it the Dirty Devil and the name stuck. Later they came to a really clean, pristine creek. To balance the Dirty Devil, Powell named it Bright Angel, inspired by Milton's *Paradise Lost*."

"*Yebeday*," Brandon murmured.

"Exactly," I agreed, not at all sure what he meant, "and I can tell you that over the years a lot of places have been named Bright Angel, but there's only one Dirty Devil. And that only remains by the power of tradition. Powell tried to change it to Fremont River, but 'Dirty Devil' stuck."

"*Let's get on to the trailhead and start creating our own tradition,*" Malcolm urged. "I'm ready now to go in and," he put an arm around Brandon's shoulders and grinned mischievously, "I'm anxious as hell to find out what your father has planned for your initiation."

3. Ritual Beginning

North Bass Trail starts at the end of eighteen miles of deeply rutted dirt roads west of the park entrance. As we drove out, Brandon studied the topographic map. Our destination looked like a dense maze of brown, narrowly separated lines meandering amoebalike around and about through some fifty square miles north of the river. The forested North Rim, shown in green, stuck out at Swamp Point, our trailhead destination, as a protrusion surrounded on three sides by brown contour lines that gave the appearance of wind flowing around a jagged arrowhead thrown at Powell Plateau, a mile away across the open space of Muav Canyon. That's the dramatic imagery on the map. The actual drive along the ridge could have been in any forest: trees, standing and fallen; dense brush, rotting logs, large boulders, and occasional clearings, but nothing to suggest that nearby the earth fell away.

Backcountry park roads are no longer maintained, a policy decision that we experienced as the thud of a rock that felt like some underground giant had aimed his mighty fist to penetrate the car's exposed underbelly. After a couple more scrapes on exposed rocks, Brandon and I got out to lighten the load. Intermittent rain added mud to the road and tension behind the wheel. In many places Malcolm had to stop while we calculated if the bottom would miss a large jutting rock. I walked in front, directing the wheels above the deep ruts. Brandon watched the passenger side for protruding limbs, stumps, and boulders.

We persevered more than three hours in first gear, arriving at dusk, exhausted. More than physical weariness, I felt the crush of unmet expectations. My idealized moment of arrival, the three of us standing at the trailhead at sunset, would remain a vision. I recalled a quote about adventures just being inconveniences rightly thought about. Sure. And the Grand Canyon is just a big hole.

We tied our tarp to tree branches in what little light remained and fired up the stove to heat vegetable soup, racing against clouds so threatening we couldn't risk time to find the trailhead for a look down. After dinner, finally at the rim, we found too little light to distinguish formations or even identify Holy Grail Temple. Just as well, I thought. Better to experience the Grail in the glory of morning than a tired glimpse at dusk. As we peered into the darkness, a gust of wind snapped the tarp behind us. "Looks like a North Rim blowout's coming," Malcolm warned. "We'd better secure that tarp and get settled in."

"Wait," I said. "I don't want the hassles and weather to take over completely. Before we turn in, let's take a moment to affirm why we're here." I found myself acting on impulse born of months of anticipation and mental rehearsal. I took three votive candles out of my jacket pocket and arranged them in the center of the circle we made. Brandon's lean, six-foot frame was barely visible in the darkness. He stretched out on his side, his elbow on the ground, resting his head in his hand. His long brown hair was pulled through an opening in the back of his baseball cap to form a shoulder-length ponytail. The cap bore no insignia or logo, an expression of what he called his "endorsement policy." His demeanor, casual and relaxed as usual, told me he accepted my desire for some kind of ritual beginning, but I had best expect no more than indulgence.

Malcolm sat cross-legged, a stalk of grass in his mouth, projecting openness and warmth. I've heard him described as "teddy-bear huggable," which I can confirm, but if I were doing his caricature, I'd portray him as more walrus than bear because of the long gray moustache that curls around his lips. Before becoming a family therapist, he'd taught at Prescott College in Arizona, where he led students into the canyon in experiential courses. All totaled, he'd passed about a year and a half of his life in the Grand Canyon.

I fumbled to keep a match lit in the swirling wind, finally got a candle lit, and, using it, lit the other two. Instinctively we moved closer together to protect the small flickering flames. I took a deep breath, exhaled relief, inhaled determination, and began to speak.

"It's awkward being formal like this, but for months I've been imagining this night. It's gotten pretty big in my head. Still, this may come out stiff since, from the perspective of the ancients, we'd have to be considered ritually impaired."

"Ritually impaired," Brandon repeated ponderously, then grinned. "Yeah, I get it. You know, Dad, it's okay with me if we just do the hike. Really."

"We'll do the hike, don't worry. But let me tell you why I want to add a ritual context."

Brandon's reply was to relight a candle that had blown out. I continued. "Contemporary society does not provide, as former times did, a ceremony for recognizing and celebrating adulthood. Two months ago you turned eighteen and had a party, but that merely marked the passage of time. Two weeks ago you graduated from high school amid speeches about entering adulthood from people you didn't know and who didn't know you. That's not a rite of passage as understood and conducted by the ancients."

Brandon snickered in what I took to be an affirmation of the ridiculousness of trying to interpret his crowded commencement at the Saint Paul Civic Center as any kind of personal rite of passage. We stared into the candles and I felt as if I were reading the words I was speaking in the flames. A drop of rain urged me on.

"It's not possible for us to replicate tribal rites because, it's pretty obvious, we don't have a tribe. The canyon will be our surrogate tribal elder, connecting us to what has come before and to what endures, not in some abstract mystical way, but through its concrete physical presence and endurance."

"The first time into the canyon is an initiation in and of itself," Malcolm said. "The canyon sees to that. I don't know what all your dad has in mind, but what I urge is for you to be open to the canyon as more than just a place to hike."

"More in what way?" Brandon asked.

"You'll see," Malcolm replied smiling. "The canyon will show you."

"I hope you'll be open to both Malcolm's experience of the canyon— and to questioning it. In contrast to Malcolm's spiritual connection to the canyon, I'll offer you the path of skeptical inquiry. I don't think you'll find me different in that regard than you ever have, but the meaning of that path will perhaps be clearer and more dramatic because of this magnificent setting and Malcolm's deep connection to the canyon. This is the kind of place where religions are born, where humans seek answers to cosmic questions."

"That's literally true," Malcolm interjected. "For the Hopi people, the Grand Canyon is the place where human beings and animals emerge from the underworld and where, in death, they return to it. The Sipapu is the Hopi entrance to the underworld. It's located not far from here, in the Little Colorado gorge about four miles before it joins the Colorado. The Hopi still make pilgrimages there."

"Over the coming days and nights, Malcolm will tell you more about Hopi beliefs and the Anasazi who inhabited the canyon one thousand years ago. We may even come across one of their sites. We'll also discuss some European coming-of-age myths as a stimulus for thinking about what it means to be a man in today's world. We'll hike under and around Holy Grail Temple. We'll journey through layers of time descending to the oldest exposed rock on Earth. As we do so, if Malcolm is right, the Grand Canyon itself will conduct your initiation. I came across a passage in poet Robert Bly's book *Iron John* that, well, let me just read it."

I took out the folded pages I had carried in my pants pocket since we'd left Minnesota two days earlier. I tilted the page down and leaned over it to read in the candlelight.

We sometimes assume that contemporary initiation is accomplished by being confirmed, or receiving the Bar Mitzvah ceremony, or getting a driver's license. To receive initiation truly means to expand sideways into the glory of oaks, mountains, glaciers, horses, lions, grasses, waterfalls, deer. We need wilderness and extravagance. Whatever shuts a human being away from the waterfall and the tiger will kill him. *

As I refolded the page, Malcolm leaned in closer to the flames. "I like thinking of the canyon as initiator, as teacher."

"You make it sound like a person," Brandon said.

"You'll have to decide for yourself what it is," Malcolm replied. "For

---

*Robert Bly, *Iron John: A Book About Men* (Reading, Mass.: Addison-Wesley, 1990), p. 55.

me, it's . . . it's . . . I'd just say, be open to the possibilities." He pointed behind him into the darkness beyond the rim. "One possibility is locating a place of special power."

"What do you mean?" Brandon asked.

"I mean finding a place that connects you with the ancient origins of the Earth, a spot that will locate you personally in time and space. I can't tell you more than that."

"Do you have a place like that here?" he asked me.

"Malcolm believes that Mount Huethawali on the other side of the river is my special place. I experienced it on my first trip with him off Apache Point. It's where I first saw Holy Grail Temple and got the idea of conducting your initiation, when you were still just a babe. We'll tell you about it when we're in the canyon and you can decide if it merits the designation 'place of power.' "

Malcolm laughed. "A lot of initiation time gets taken up with stories. The whole thing's just an excuse for us old men to make you listen to our tales— but they're good tales, worth hearing, and some of them may even be true."

"Will we see Mount Whatchamacallit?"

"Withe-tha-wa-li," I repeated slowly. "Malcolm?"

"Not from here or the inner canyon. Maybe from Powell Plateau."

"Do you have a power place here?" Brandon asked.

Malcolm lifted both arms, brought his hands together, then slowly separated them, reaching out to the canyon in an all-encompassing circle that ended with his hands back together on his chest. "Your power place expands the more often you return."

With that as benediction, I held high a candle and let the wind extinguish it. Malcolm did likewise, then Brandon.

We sat for a few seconds while our eyes adjusted to the dark. Then the crack of the tarp flapping called us and we rose, without speaking, and went together to tighten the supporting ropes. As we finished, the sprinkling of rain became a downpour.

Afterward, cocooned within my sleeping bag against the fierce wind, I drifted into that vortex between wakefulness and sleep where, the body exhausted beyond reason, the mind's filters cease to protect from childhood imaginings. I turned over in my mind Malcolm's talk of the canyon as initiator. My academic self scoffed at this anthropomorphism turned to superstition, but some primordial part of me refused to yield. It knew the canyon as palpable—and ominous. This, I told myself, is how myths are created.

MAP of SHINUMO AMPHITHEATER

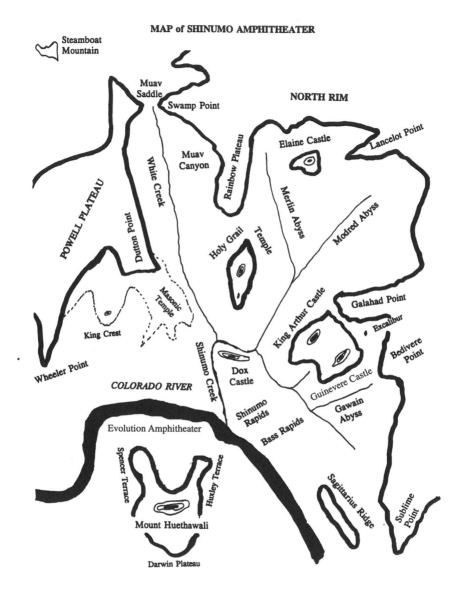

Claps of thunder, sounding rhythmic, called to mind tribal initiations I had read about. Among Australian aborigines, initiates lay awake terrified by angry spirits called forth as the elders swirl the sacred bullroarer. Papuan elders construct a monster called Kaiemunu and force the petrified initiates to enter its belly to experience ritual death and rebirth surrounded by terrifying sounds. Among the Pangwe in Africa a masked figure emerges from an excavated grave to haunt and terrorize the initiates. In tribe after tribe, culture after culture, the elders construct nightmares for the initiates, but never in all my studies had I come across a report of the elders having their own nightmares.

4. Anticipation

I awoke at first light, but stayed cuddled awhile in my bag, my arms wrapped tight around my knees, warm and dry against the surrounding cold and wet, letting anticipation build. I imagined having Brandon close his eyes, leading him to the rim with my arm around his shoulder, then intoning: "Behold, Holy Grail Temple." I would then tell him the special version of the Grail Quest that struck me as symbolically relevant to his initiation. It had a twist that I was sure would be new to Brandon and Malcolm. If it worked, it would help turn our hike into a modern quest, one that might actually be fulfilled without illusion.

In my youth, having devoured *The Boy's King Arthur,* I was enraptured by the Knights of the Round Table and their quest. Sir Thomas Mallory's archaic English felt familiar since my primary literature up to that time had been required study of the King James Bible. N. C. Wyeth's illustrations of knights in full armor, ladies in full gowns, and armies in full combat captivated me, but I found the portraits lifeless. In my imagination Guinevere radiated more beauty, Arthur exuded greater wisdom, and Lancelot projected more determination than Wyeth portrayed, so I covered all the bland faces with tinfoil to make them at least sparkle. I never saw a picture of Jesus I liked either, though my father cured me of coloring over his face after my Sunday School teacher complained. When I had told Malcolm of my youthful sacrilege, he observed that it foretold my becoming a sociologist—studying faceless masses.

Since Brandon and Malcolm were still asleep, I lingered in my bag recalling my first hike in the canyon fourteen years earlier. The feelings came back—the sense of wonder and awe, the strong sense of place—but I couldn't remember what Holy Grail Temple looked like, having seen too many other monuments in the intervening years. A compelling desire grew in me to rush to the rim and see it again.

I turned instead to the task of waking my companions and extracting a promise that they would not approach the rim until we were packed and ready to go, though Brandon expressed amused curiosity about the origin of my need to overdramatize things and Malcolm commented that I seemed inordinately animated for not having had even one cup of coffee.

"Is Dad always like this out here?"

"Not that I remember. Must be something different about this trip," he grinned.

We arranged the food and gear in three piles to distribute the weight fairly, about sixty pounds each once we added two days' water, not being sure if we'd find water in White Creek along the route of our descent. Brandon had a new backpack, a graduation present from me, that the man-ufacturer hyped as "very sophisticated in being adjustable to custom-fit your individual height, shoulder size and torso length." The store's technician had adjusted the load-lifter strap, fitted the waistbelt, calibrated the shoulder straps, then readjusted the load-lifters, positioned the sternum strap, and adjusted the mesh backband. Malcolm had a twenty-year-old Kelty expedi-tion-size pack, the red canvas faded to bleached pink and well-worn wher-ever metal met fabric. The only adjustment he had to make was adding duct tape at points of wear. My new pack already looked broken-in as a result of the hiking and training I'd done in preparation for this trip.

As we sorted and packed, Brandon picked up and looked into the small day-pack that contained medical supplies. "I'll carry the first aid stuff," he offered

"No can do," I said.

"Why not?"

"It's against tradition."

"What tradition?"

"The tradition that Malcolm carries the first aid kit."

"Why?" he asked.

"Why?! You don't ask why about traditions. You just observe them. That's what tradition means, something you do without knowing or asking why."

"You can carry the first-aid kit," Malcolm offered. "Just pack it where we can get to it easily and quickly. I could never trust your father with it because I was afraid he'd be off trying to find high ground somewhere when I needed it. I have a suspicion that you're going to be a real canyoneer, so you get the honor and responsibility of the first-aid kit."

"Watch out! When Malcolm starts breaking traditions as hallowed as this—"

"Did your father ever tell you how I first got him to hike the canyon?" Malcolm interrupted.

"You mean he resisted?" Brandon asked.

"Your dad was the evaluator for a wilderness program a friend and I ran. After a month of observing us in the woods, he imparted his feedback about what he considered improvements. He waited for us to be impressed. I was. I said: 'Patton, I have just one thing to say about your evaluation findings: You need to do the Grand Canyon.'

"He looked confused, as if my reaction was a nonsequitur, which, of course, it wasn't at all. His report was all about setting goals and accomplishing outcomes—which I admit we weren't much focused on. He tried to get through to us with analogies about climbing a mountain and reaching the summit. We were a tough sell. So, I took it upon myself to explain to him the obvious: If you want to understand the wilderness and the Earth and what it all means, you have to descend into it. You need to do the canyon."

"Malcolm will try to convince you that the path to enlightenment leads down rather than up," I countered.

"Has he convinced you?" Brandon asked.

I paused. Malcolm laughed: "Your dad won't admit to being convinced of *anything,* but you'll notice he's not taking you to a mountaintop for your initiation." Brandon grinned and nodded.

While Brandon was away stowing excess supplies in the car, I discovered we had neglected to include the rope in distributing the weight. We had 160 feet of inch-thick goldline rope and safety gear that weighed at least twenty pounds. "You want tradition," Malcolm said. "We'll make it tradition that the initiate gets to start off with the rope."

"We said we'd share the weight equally," I reminded him.

"It'll take a half-hour or more to repack. Give him the option. He's a strong young buck. We can repack at lunch. He wants to get going as much as we do."

I realized then that my conception of the trip included conflicting goals. In celebrating Brandon's coming of age, I expected he would get special attention. At the same time, I wanted him to have the experience of being treated as a man in his own right, equal in every way to Malcolm and me. Now I noticed the tension between these two forms of treatment: special versus equal.

When Brandon returned, we presented him the honor of the rope. Before I could complete what was obviously going to be a lengthy rationalization, Brandon cut me off with: "No prob."

We were finally ready for the rim. I led the way, brimming with anticipation. The vast darkness of the night had been transformed into a wide panorama of distant buttes, promontories, points, ridges, and peaks that cast purple shadows across layered cliffs and sloping terraces of gray and reddish-brown. The sheer drop below where we stood accentuated the long, narrow drainage of White Creek bordered by the four-mile-long wall of Powell Plateau to the west and the more jagged three-mile Rainbow Plateau to the east. Our route down Muav Canyon was revealed by a narrow band of green winding its way down to a funnel where the Redwall intersected the canyon floor. All this we took in as a surge to the senses, needing time for our brains to bring order to the infusion of stimuli much like the eyes have to adjust from dark to light. At least I thought such a mental dilation would suffice. It did not. Holy Grail Temple just wasn't there. It was blocked from view by Rainbow Plateau.

I felt like I'd just missed a long-anticipated meeting with an old, dear friend while passing through an out-of-the-way town and couldn't be sure when—or even if—I'd ever see him again. Malcolm offered hope that it might be viewed from an open Tonto expanse in the inner gorge. My own reading of the map left me dubious, but I decided to save the Grail story.

We lingered at the rim to sort out what we were seeing, comparing the map's abstract contour lines to the reality before us, the many peaks and points gradually becoming distinct and identifiable: Dox Castle, Sagittarius Ridge, Masonic Temple . . . by connecting names on the map with actual rock formations we began making the transition from general impression to the familiarity and intimacy of known detail.

As we returned to our packs, Brandon asked about the vegetation at Swamp Point: "Those look like oak leaves."

"They are," Malcolm affirmed. "Gambel oak."

"Are they trees or bushes?"

"A botanist might answer differently, but here's the hiker's definition. If you can walk under it, it's a tree. If you have to walk around it, it's a bush."

"A mere hint of the depths of wisdom you'll encounter in the days ahead," I added.

Thus encouraged, Malcolm sermonized on the virtues of canyoneering, especially starting off by going down, down, down. Ready at last, we shouldered the heavy packs amid groans and expletives, then Malcolm bellowed: "My backpack is my friend."

When Brandon didn't respond, we just stood there, staring at him. "What are we waiting for now?" he asked.

Malcolm eyed him expectantly. I patted his backpack. He looked at me, obviously puzzled, then brightened. "I get it. All right. My backpack is my friend."

Malcolm turned and led the way. Brandon followed. I brought up the rear.

5. Detox

The descent began at an angle down a rounded hilltop of gray Kaibab limestone, shallow sea deposits 250 million years old. I reminded myself to savor these opening moments when the trail is easy, the footing secure, and the pack does not yet cut into the shoulders and pound the vertebrae. I wanted to be mindful of the present moment, inhale consciousness, exhale tension, absorb the weathered terrain, and soak up the parched landscape. I admired the resilience of the scrub oak that had already made a comeback after a lightning fire that had swept across Muav Saddle two years earlier. I contemplated the surrealistic shapes of charred trees scattered across the hillside like abstract sculptures placed there to bemuse. I studied Steamboat Mountain, a massive island of rock rising from the floor of the Tapeats Terrace north of Powell Plateau. I slowed to take in the fragile loveliness of a purple cactus bloom.

But my efforts to immerse myself in the moment ultimately failed. Each glance around somehow segued back to invisible baggage I carried: phone calls not returned; money matters not attended to; weighing options on future decisions. The easy pace and clear trail offered insufficient distraction to halt the mental labor of driving life's never-ending rush hour.

49

I recognized this as the first stage of what Malcolm called "detox," an expression I first encountered hiking the Gila Wilderness of New Mexico for ten days as evaluator of Malcolm's wilderness program for college administrators. The most revealing experience for most came near the end during a two-day/one-night solo: thirty-six hours alone with nothing to do—no cooking, reading, or tasks to perform. That short period alone put us in touch with how the ceaseless banter of modern life pervaded our thoughts. As we departed the Gila, most participants reported hearing the wilderness silence, though some only got as far as knowing it might exist. We left feeling cleaner and purer than we had in years. We called this "detox." Like the drunk who is finally sober, we left the wilderness committed to staying clear of urban toxins.

Not one of us was prepared for the speed of retoxification. Three months later, as we drove from the Phoenix airport to the Kofa Mountains for the second phase of the program, we shared estimates of how long we'd been able to resist reentry poisons: a couple days to at most a week. Then the wilderness again salved us with its cleansing power. Most left the Kofas more determined than ever to resist retoxification, but the higher expectations only made the subsequent falls more distressing. Short of becoming hermits, we knew we would continue to be exposed to and eventually succumb to civilization's poisons. We became resigned to monitoring the level of toxicity in hope of having the good sense to get to the wilderness for detox when being poisoned started to feel normal. Since then, trips with Malcolm to the canyon had become my decontamination treatment of choice.

As we descended from Swamp Point, I recognized my mental frenzy as the first sign of detox. In an effort to be present in the moment, I studied the layers exposed on Powell's foundation and listened to the poetry of their geological names. Kaibab. Toroweap. Coconino. Supai. And the layers we'd find below, in the inner gorge. Temple Butte. Muav. Tonto. Tapeats. Vishnu Schist. Whispering them into the canyon expanse, I liked the way the names felt. I recalled what I'd read about the origin of these layers in the Middle Permian: the Kaibab, 300–500 feet thick; then the Toroweap, 250–450 feet and dating back 260 million years; about the fact that they were considered a single formation until McKee distinguished them in 1938; and about the subsequent subdivisions within each, the variety of their lithofacies, and the complexity of their paleontology. Poetry yielded to science and I felt both knowledgeable about the earth and intimate with it. I thought about how to share what I'd learned with Brandon. Then a voice within sounded a warning. "Naming something and knowing facts about it does not mean you understand. With all thy getting, get understanding—something worth passing on." I recognized my father's voice chiding me for relying on book learning to the detriment of attaining common sense about life.

Ahead of me, Brandon's backpack disguised all but his legs so that it looked like the pack was self-propelled. I wondered how having him along would affect my detox. And, perhaps even more intrusive, hiking with an agenda. Among other things, I intended to talk with Brandon about my father, something I had never done in depth. I had been thinking a lot about what my father, now dead, had to pass on through me to his grandson.

And would Brandon experience detox? Given his youth and easygoing temperament, I doubted that he had yet assimilated much poison. Then again, how would I know? Adult arrogance and our own poisonous saturation make us poor judges of the degree of youthful contamination. I knew that Brandon was prone to occasional periods of brooding, but his dark times seemed rare. I hoped exposure to the wilderness would help him build up resistance to the more insidious poisons of urban life. Then again, such exposure might make him all the more vulnerable to the toxins of modern society, just as newly discovered jungle tribes are especially vulnerable to civilization's diseases.

I came to another switchback, stopped, and looked south into Muav Canyon, Brandon and Malcolm out of sight around a turn below me. As I waited for them to come back into view, I resolved to just be with Brandon in whatever ways the canyon offered and trust that being in the wilderness would once again take me through detox. Brandon's initiation and my father's voice in my head must not become barriers; they might slow the process, but not stop it. This time, more than ever, detox felt critical, for I wanted Brandon to experience a detoxified father, something I had never known.

6. Harvey

"What's a cabin doing here?" Brandon asked.

We had reached Muav Saddle and found an old cabin nestled on its back side facing north. It had two rooms, an old iron stove, bed frames with broken springs, and a wooden table. Two shelves held old cooking utensils. A few plastic jugs left by hikers were strewn about.

"It was probably used by the construction crew that contoured the trail we just came down," Malcolm speculated.

"But that's my point," Brandon countered. "Why would they have done any work here? This is supposed to be wilderness."

"No, we're in a national park. The trail we just hiked was once maintained to provide easy access to Powell Plateau. Under the new policy, this trail, like the road to Swamp Point, won't be groomed anymore. From here on, it never has been. The wilderness starts here—and now."

Malcolm got out his tattered copy of Harvey Butchart's *Grand Canyon Treks*. "Harvey says the trail from Swamp Point to Powell Plateau was rebuilt in the thirties, probably by the Civilian Conservation Corps."

"I was just surprised to find a cabin," Brandon said.

53

"There won't be any more," Malcolm assured him.

"Is that a promise from you or Harvey?" I asked.

Malcolm smiled. He revered Harvey Butchart as *the* authoritative source on canyon hiking. A retired mathematics professor from Northern Arizona University, he was known among Grand Canyon folks as the "Flagstaff Flyer." Over forty-two years he had spent a thousand days in the canyon logging more than twelve thousand miles. Colin Fletcher had turned to him for help in planning his famous "walk through time" from one end of Grand Canyon National Park to the other. John Annerino's Sierra Club guidebook calls Butchart "undisputedly the father of canyoneering."

Whenever Malcolm began, "Harvey says . . . ," his tone conveyed genuine respect laced with a touch of jest. The respect was born of awe for the breadth of experience and depth of knowledge reported in Harvey's three books describing canyon treks, the only sources available for some remote areas; the hint of jest acknowledged that his directions range from terse to cryptic.

We'd relied on Harvey years earlier to make the descent from Apache Point to Royal Arch Creek: "Follow a deep notch on the very top of the pinnacle north of the trail"; it "loops below the pinnacle and then descends to the Esplanade on the east side." He then noted the existence of a "promontory" pointing to a natural arch near the lower end of the bed of Royal Arch: "The promontory pointing to the arch is the way down through the Supai from the west. The route is down the middle until stopped by a cliff. Then go northwest along the rim to a break behind a detached block of sandstone."

These three sentences cover a couple hours of hiking, much of it over rock with no trail. Malcolm and I had wandered about trying to figure out which of seemingly hundreds of promontories was the one Harvey meant and where exactly the middle might be in a nonsymmetrical landscape. After we found our way, Harvey's directions made perfect sense. His descriptions served to point in the right direction and assure that a way down existed, but didn't interfere with the challenge of personal discovery. All this we explained to Brandon at the cabin. Harvey would guide us, one terse sentence at a time, through the Redwall.

Brandon abruptly rose, went to his pack, and came back with Annerino's guidebook. He scanned a couple of pages and declared: "Annerino dedicates his book to Harvey. I thought I remembered the name from somewhere." He turned to the list of first ascents. "Yo, Harvey was sure into climbing temples. He's credited with first ascents of Apollo, Confucius, Deva, Diana,

Juno, Jupiter, Krishna, Rama, Solomon, and Venus—and a bunch of other points and monuments."

"My kind of hiker," I said, "going for the heights. But he didn't do Holy Grail Temple?"

"Not first, anyway. Trieber and Grubbs, 1976."

"King Arthur Castle?"

"Clubb, 1961."

"Excalibur?"

"Bain, Glen Rink, 1981."

"Guinevere Castle?"

"Score! Butchart, 1965."

"Harvey is credited with first ascents of forty-one of the canyon's 148 named buttes," Malcolm chimed in, "but that doesn't make him a heights man. That's only forty-one of more than a thousand days. Don't let your dad mislead you, Brandon. Harvey stands as the preeminent downhiller. All his treks are written from the perspective of the descent."

Malcolm recounted more of Harvey's accomplishments and then suggested that, in a world short of heroes, many considered Harvey worthy of such status. Brandon repacked the guidebook and said over his shoulder that he wasn't really into heroes. Malcolm suggested he withhold judgment until we got through the Redwall, then he'd be in a better position to evaluate Harvey's heroics in having pioneered 116 rim-to-river breaks through the canyon's most formidable barrier.

Our immediate task was to follow Harvey's instructions to a nearby spring where we could fill the empty bottles we carried. Malcolm read: " 'It takes only ten minutes to reach a good spring at the bottom of the Coconino east of the Saddle.' " He looked up and grinned. "If it took Harvey only ten minutes, we should be able to find it sometime in the next hour."

"Let's boogie," Brandon challenged.

I rose slowly, distracted, trying to make sense out of what I'd just heard. I felt certain that the spring must seep from the Toroweap on *top* of the Coconino, not below it. I said as much. Malcolm feigned astonishment. "You dare suggest that Harvey is wrong. We'd better go see."

Despite being caught up in ruminations about detox, I couldn't believe I'd missed hiking through the distinct white columns of the Coconino: petrified dunes blown into majestic swells by ancient desert winds 270 million years ago. In photographs of the upper canyon walls, the Coconino typically stands out as a sheer pearly wall, 100 to 350 feet high, set off above by the sloping layer of darker, lagoonal Toroweap and bordered underneath by the Hermit Shale's loose rock and chaparral vegetation. The upper North Kaibab trail, one of the most popular routes for mule rides into the canyon, is dominated by massive columns of white Coconino. Many of the buttes, crowns, and pinnacles that inspire the analogy to temples are Coconino, including Holy Grail Temple and Mount Huethawali, which in Havasupai means "mountain of white stone." Recalling these powerful associations, I was sure I could not have missed the Coconino on the descent from Swamp Point.

From the cabin we retraced the path past the junction to a hillside of fallen rock and loose shale from which we could look out over White Creek and our route down into the inner canyon. We were poised on the edge of a great valley almost 800 feet exactly below the view we had had from Swamp Point. Yet, because we were now in the canyon instead of on top of it, the perspective felt different: less spacious, more contained. We were no longer above the canyon; we were encircled by it. We could see each distinct layer from Redwall to rim along Powell and Rainbow Plateaus. From this vantage point the Coconino clearly towered above us. Harvey, of course, had been right.

When Malcolm pointed this out, I was ready: "Just part of Brandon's initiation to learn that his father can, on rare occasion, misread the lay of the land."

Brandon, too, was ready. "I'm crushed. Couldn't you at least have waited until the last day for such a devastating revelation?"

"At least you know the worst is out of the way," I replied.

"You've forgotten the Redwall," Malcolm warned. "I guarantee you, you won't miss the Redwall. It has its own way of revealing things about people."

As we hiked on, I figured out what had happened. Muav Saddle stands as the floor of a fault-line break in what had once been a rim-level connection between Powell Plateau and Swamp Point. As the gap opened, sediment and scree had covered over the transition between the Kaibab and Toroweap, and buried all but small outcroppings of the remaining Coconino. Our path down had not passed through anything like what I associated with Coconino, but we had descended below it. I had fallen victim to hardening of the categories. Having been studying graphics depicting the Canyon strata and their distinctive names, I had forgotten that the layers vary in width, composition, distinctness, and exposure.

As if to remove any doubt about our position *below* the Coconino and impress upon me my misperception, the path to the spring crossed a steep slope directly *under* a massive overhanging cliff of white sandstone. Suspended from sections of the rock ceiling hung cylindrical growths of thick green moss, like huge hornet nests, one at least five feet long. The route before us also would have wiped out any lingering question Brandon might have had about the difference between a maintained and a wilderness trail. We faced crossing a very steep rock slide. Though only fifty feet wide, a misstep would send one tumbling down a couple hundred yards of sharp, loose rock. One section, especially steep, required a quick dance across, awkward at best carrying cumbrous packs, with just enough challenge to focus awareness, stiffen the muscles, and generate a little warm tension in the back, neck, legs, and mind.

The spring was hidden within a cluster of lush green vegetation not far beyond the Coconino overhang. It took ten minutes to get there, just as Harvey had forecast. We unpacked the two-liter plastic soft-drink bottles we would use to carry water. Getting to the spring required crouching under dense vegetation. Within this small oasis the wall was wet and, upon close inspection, revealed a few thin rivulets of water. By trial and error we learned how to use leaves of seep willow to create a slow trickle running from the wet wall onto a leaf and into a bottle without also collecting chunks of dirt and moss. We began competing to see who could maximize the flow by arranging the tips of several leaves to converge. Brandon, positioned between Malcolm and me, was especially adept at this hydraulic engineering task. He launched into a running commentary like a radio sports announcer.

"Ladies and gentleman, Dr. Malcolm Gray has just located a beautiful leaf. It's all of four inches long and a full half inch wide. Looks to be just the thing. He carefully positions it under a glob of moss. Oh, no, sports fans, the whole glob has been dislodged in a great environmental tragedy. *Pleffd!*

"Let's check in on Dr. Michael Patton now. Aha, he has arranged three short blades to form a mighty waterfall that will probably fill his first bottle at least by nightfall. Oh no, another tragedy. The combined weight of the leaves and water has crushed the whole structure, toppling it hundreds of micromillimeters to the path below. He'll have to begin again.

"It is a battle of the generations here today, ladies and gentlemen. The elders are using mechanical techniques of old. The representative of youth, however, drawing on the technology of laser-induced virtual reality, has already filled a bottle while those veterans of bygone days are still getting started."

At first, Malcolm and I just smiled as his rapid-fire, hyperbolic descriptions of our ineptitude and the resulting catastrophes. Then I got drawn in. "The site for this year's water works competition was selected by that legendary canyon presence, the great Harvey Butchart. Too bad Harvey couldn't be here to offer his own color commentary, but he has assured us that this is a (quote) GOOD spring (close quote). Let this be a reminder to all you young listeners: What's 'good' to the goose may seem like a barely wet wall if you take a close gander."

Brandon picked up a small stick on the path and held it in front of Malcolm's mouth like a microphone. "Dr. Gray, you've journeyed all the way from Prescott, Arizona to Good-Spring-Below-Swamp-Point to represent Dr. Butchart. Would you care to comment on Dr. Patton's comments about Dr. Butchart's comments about this being a 'GOOD' spring?"

Malcolm responded, "On behalf of Dr. Butchart I am happy to explain that there aren't many places where there are dependable, year-round sources of water in the Grand Canyon. This is such a place and that's why this is a GOOD spring."

"Thank you. Now, then, as a public radio station, we, of course, don't have commercials, we just have very long announcements from our, ahem, supporters. This program is being brought to you by the Family Therapy Institute of Prescott, Arizona, directed by Dr. Malcolm Gray. We take a systems approach, so if your family needs systematizing, just bring it in and drop it off and we'll take care of it. But not this week. This week we're working on water systems instead of family systems."

As Brandon finished this mock announcement he also finished filling his second water bottle. "That does it for me. I'm going to see what's on the other side." He bolted up, squeezed past me, and disappeared through the vegetation portal. After a short while Malcolm remarked: "A teenager who listens to public radio. That's unusual."

"We often listen to Garrison Keillor's *Prairie Home Companion* during Saturday dinners. In Minnesota we say 'Garrison' the way you say 'Harvey.' "

"He's certainly got the style down."

"He and a couple of friends made a video parody of horror movies they called 'Killer Asparagus' and an action film on the adventures of a large pickle. During the Persian Gulf War they did a grim but hysterical parody of the military controlling a CNN broadcast. His fantasy is to write for *Saturday Night Live.* He faithfully watches the whole show—clicking back-and-forth to catch MTV, of course."

"I'm relieved to know he doesn't spend all his time listening to public radio," Malcolm remarked.

As we turned our attention back to the dripping water, I ruminated about parody as a major motif of our time and how our climate of irreverence contributed to my own feelings of awkwardness about incorporating rituals into our canyon hike. I knew Brandon would try to react seriously, but I also could picture him telling his friends about the trip in the manner of a *Saturday Night Live* "Weekend Update" commentary:

This week Brandon Quinn Tchombiano Patton was initiated in the Grand Canyon. In this picture he can be seen chipping away at the base of Holy Grail Temple.

Weekend Update has been assured by family therapist Dr. Malcolm Gray that even if Brandon can't wear the the million-ton rock around his neck, he'll carry it as a heavy psychological burden the rest of his life.

Coming out of my reverie, I glanced aside to gauge how near Malcolm was to finished and lost the point of leverage where I had carefully positioned the bottle to capture the drippings of three leaves. The bottle fell, splashing Malcolm.

"A little concentration problem?" Malcolm asked.

"Pre-detox distractions," I replied. "I realized as we were hiking that I've never before spent ten uninterrupted days and nights with Brandon."

"And?"

"And what?"

"It sounds like there's more."

I watched the water trickle slowly off the leaf and into the bottle, filling so slowly I could barely detect the level rising.

"I was wondering how having Brandon along would affect detox, whether I can really get inside your big hole this time because I have so many expectations, and I've come as a parent."

"Then don't."

"Don't what?"

Malcolm completed filling his second bottle and repositioned himself to sit on the path, groaning as he stretched joints grown stiff from squatting. "Don't parent. You'll always be his father. You don't always have to be parental."

"I know. I know. But that's a lot easier said than done. Accomplishing that transition is why I may need this initiation process more than Brandon."

7. Hermit Shale

The final ritual before leaving the spring was to consult Harvey. He described the way down through the Hermit Shale as a "scramble" which, given his hiking prowess, sounded ominous.

In reading about Grand Canyon geology, two things had particularly intrigued me about this 280-million-year-old layer of floodplain deposit we were about to descend. First, geologists consider "shale" a misnomer, though the name persists through common usage; it actually consists of siltstone, mudstone, and fine-grained sandstone from the early Permian period. Second, the Hermit layer, in keeping with its name, happens to be the least studied and poorest-known stratum in the Grand Canyon; it just hasn't attracted much interest. It was about to command my complete attention.

The largest cairn I've ever seen—assorted pinkish-gray rocks stacked over three feet high—marked the trail down. I soon lagged behind, struggling with the descent. I wasn't sure which was worse, the large, loose rocks that slid underfoot or the small pebbles that rolled. Had it not been for the manzanita bushes, whose brownish-red stalks proved sufficiently well rooted to grab hold of, I would have caught up with my companions by crashing down the hillside like a giant

61

sea turtle trapped helplessly on his back, my pack serving as my shell until it ripped apart on the sharp rocks and cactus stubble.

The bushes grew taller and thicker as we moved down a narrow ridge in the center of the slope. The surface changed from loose gray rock, droppings from the Coconino, to compacted red soil and pebbles, too hard to dig into for solid footing. Half stepping, half sliding added pressure on my ankles and cramped my feet, making them rub abrasively inside my boots. Brandon and Malcolm got so far ahead of me that I could just see the upper part of their backpacks now and again above the brush.

My legs began to feel tight, my knees weak. I tried stepping down so that my toe touched first before gradually flattening my foot as I felt the boot take hold. That just squeezed my toes more. I returned to stepping heel first, but bending my knee more. That didn't help either. A couple of times I fell, but managed to grab something before tumbling farther down, once grasping a thorn bush and tearing my hand.

I cursed and wrapped a bandana around the wound. My first Apache Point descent came back to me in full-bodied memory, how I feared and hated this kind of downhill terrain, steep like a ladder close against a wall, its rotted steps breaking under weight—or threatening to. And I was descending the ladder the wrong way, facing outward. I didn't feel out of control. I just didn't feel *in* control. I tried to distract myself by analyzing the difference. Instead I got another flash of crashing down the slope as a helpless sea turtle.

My back ached, my legs cramped, and my vision blurred, making it hard to calculate where to step down. Straining to see where I was descending, a thorny branch caught me in the face and scratched my forehead. I squatted down to creep under an overhanging branch, but as I moved forward, I was stopped. Not just stopped. Grabbed. The branch not only halted my forward momentum but, after first yielding, snatched the pack and pulled me backward. I turned and twisted to free myself, finally lunging in frustration and, as the pack tore loose, falling forward, my head landing precariously near a barrel cactus.

I got up on my hands and knees, breathing hard, but couldn't stand. I comforted myself with the knowledge that I didn't have to worry about getting lost. The only way down was down. I was just experiencing a little flare-up of my downhill curse.

I could see that I was surrounded by a forest of thorny locust and tangled manzanita. What I couldn't see was any evidence of a path or footprints from Brandon and Malcolm. My chest felt tight. It didn't seem possible. Could I actually be feeling claustrophobic in the Grand Canyon? Malcolm would have fun psychoanalyzing that. I sat back and released my pack straps, which instantly relieved the tightness in my chest. Faster and cheaper than therapy.

I leaned against the pack and peered up through the thicket to the distant rim of Powell Plateau far above me. That's where I wanted to be—on a pinnacle somewhere surrounded by open space, not a prison of thornbushes on a downhill slope. My Sisyphean hell would not be pushing a boulder uphill for all eternity, but carrying a heavy backpack down a steep canyon slope.

Studying the terrain, I saw that I was in an undulating section of wall that dropped sharply into a steep drainage. Bushwhacking through the dense thicket in which I found myself would be difficult and could further rip both me and my pack. I could see that I needed to move up and to the west to find the path, toward a ridge some fifty yards above, where I'd be able to get a better perspective on the way down.

I made my way slowly uphill by sliding the pack under the thicket ahead of me and crawling behind it. I spotted an opening along a shallow wash and pushed the pack there. Suddenly its weight shifted forward and I pulled back with all my strength. I crawled alongside it and found myself on a cliff edge a hundred yards above a side drainage. Across the chasm I spotted my companions ambling down a center spine. I had apparently missed a switchback and gotten sidetracked along a cliff ledge above a steep, densely foliated drainage. I started to shout, then thought better of it. My pack on again, I traversed along the open ledge and then bushwhacked across the drainage to the ridge, where I found the path down.

I indicted my downhill affliction with a string of expletives and felt better. I estimated that I had lost about fifteen minutes, long enough, perhaps, for Brandon and Malcolm to possibly get worried and come looking for me. I did not relish the idea of getting rescued the first half of the first day out on *Brandon's* initiation. Few emotions propel more powerfully than the desire to avoid shame. Downhill be damned, I would have to charge the rest of the way.

Once I got going, the hurried pace actually was a relief from my earlier one-step-at-a-time caution. I concentrated on my fitness, for I had trained hard to make sure I could keep up with Brandon. During the Minnesota winter I had worked out almost daily on a home exercise bike and rowing machine. In the spring I had jogged regularly and hiked a seven-mile loop along the Mississippi River weekly. Once, Brandon had jogged with me after I harassed him about needing to get in shape for the canyon. He didn't even breathe hard at my best pace of nine-minute miles, exuding an easy fitness and not my worked-at, ever-in-danger-of-slipping-away variety. I didn't harass him again about conditioning.

Nor did we have occasion to jog together again. He stayed busy with a multitude of senior year activities, including playing doubles on his high school tennis team. Our occasional games together were friendly but competitive. In his early teens, I consistently beat him. Then we'd reached a plateau where we played evenly, though our games were quite different: he hit harder, but my shots were more accurate; he excelled at charging the net, but I had the better lob. The big difference: his game was still improving and his best years lay ahead; I was struggling to maintain my game at its current mediocre level, knowing that someday he would consistently defeat me. That day had not yet arrived and I was determined to delay it as long as possible. Tennis had come to symbolize for me the transition between generations, a transition with both physical and psychological dimensions.

Like getting down the Hermit Shale. I had found no way to train for going sharply downhill in loose rock. My leg muscles weren't prepared and, apparently, neither was my head. As I neared the bottom of the V-shaped canyon, I stopped for a moment to compose myself before a final dash to catch up. My khaki pants were splotched brownish-red from crawling through the bush. I slapped away the dust and peeled off my tee shirt soaked in sweat and fear. I waved it back and forth in the dry air, then hung it on a nearby branch. I wet my bandanna and wiped the blood and dirt off my forehead to make myself as presentable as possible and thought about how I'd explain my tendency to struggle downhill to Brandon, a tendency he seemed not to have inherited.

Five minutes later I came out on a slab of smooth rock overlooking the dry bed of White Creek thirty-five feet below, Brandon and Malcolm sitting by their packs against a large boulder, studying the map. If Malcolm had been worried, he didn't say so. Brandon's behavior told me that Malcolm had given him no reason to be alarmed by my lagging behind. After all, I could have been taking a leisurely pit stop or meditating on a flowering cactus; then again, I could have stumbled across a rattlesnake; or I could have just missed a switchback and gotten entangled in the dense brush of a drainage. No one asked.

Malcolm looked up from the map and pointed out that where we had stopped marked as well as anywhere the transition between the Hermit Shale and the Esplanade, the topmost layer of the Supai Group. He explained how the layers of the Grand Canyon alternate as vertical walls and sloping terraces. The Supai Group is named after the village of the Havasupai Indians located along a wide Supai plateau at the end of an eight-mile descent that exposes exemplary traces of the Supai formation. Supai is a shortened version of the tribal name, meaning people. The Supai Group consists of four distinct strata, each containing deposits from retreating seas, dried rivers, and ancient swamps. Together they are 950 to 1,350 feet deep, the thickest layer in the canyon. The lower parts contain deposits of lime while the upper strata are more sandy, the residues of Paleozoic rivers that flowed through the canyon 300 million years ago during Pennsylvanian time. The names of the three layers below the Esplanade use Havasupai clan names to make geologic poetry: Wescogame, Manakacha, and Watahomigi. Each of these Supai strata is a complex formation in its own right with alternating slope and cliff units. In places the Supai Group includes additional divisions: Queantoweap Sandstone and Pakoon Limestone. Malcolm told Brandon how to distinguish the Hermit Formation from the Supai Group, and the Supai from the Redwall, but not even he could tell Wescogame from Queantoweap. Still, repeating the names gave us a sense of knowledge and intimacy.

The great variety of flora below us contrasted dramatically to the stark, charred descent from Swamp Point. Brandon wanted to know the names of the various plants so Malcolm, noting that we were traversing the same environment as that outside his home in Prescott, pointed out shaggy bark junipers, pinyon pines, mountain mahogany, creeping mahonia, New Mexico locust, banana yucca, and agave cactus. He explained that we were traversing typical Southwestern chaparral, a transition zone between the higher elevation pine forest and lower elevation desert.

Revived from our gorp break, I kept up as we hiked a mile or more down the dry bed of White Creek through the gently sloping lower terrace of the Supai, occasionally bouldering or hiking around small drop-offs. At places the weathered rock had eroded into a natural stairway of ledges. Set into a large boulder we found a round U.S. Geological Survey benchmark certifying the elevation as 5,691 feet and showing us exactly where we were. I was astonished to see on the map what a short distance we had come. During the break we had speculated that we might be approaching marker 5,175, a mile farther along. Obviously we were not "boogying." We determined to pick up the pace lest we get caught on the Redwall at nightfall.

A few minutes later we came upon water from a western drainage. Though only a couple of inches deep and wide, it flowed steadily enough to make a tiny waterfall where it sauntered over a ledge to moisten the dry creekbed in which we had been hiking. Malcolm bent over, backpack still on, and touched it. He looked up at Brandon and indicated with his head that Brandon should do the same.

"What are we doing?" Brandon asked.

"Running water's rare in the canyon. It'll probably disappear underground around the next turn. In the desert, you never want to be in such a hurry that you don't stop and sense any water you find. Touch, look, taste, listen, and, if you lean close"—he did so—"you can get the scent." He cupped some water in one hand, smelled and then tasted it. "You can carve a brain ravine, pay tribute, give thanks—do whatever comes up for you when you stop and sense the water—but you can't just rush by, not in the desert."

"What comes up for you?" he asked.

Malcolm looked around. "That water did all this. We're standing where there used to be an ocean. The Grand Canyon was carved by the Colorado River. This side canyon was formed over millions of years by surging water carrying tons of rock and debris: spring runoffs; flash floods; freezing and thawing. Everywhere the canyon reveals the effects of water, but few places offer even a drop to drink. We'll each need more than a gallon a day to survive. Nothing's more precious. That's what comes up for me." Kneeling on one knee, he splashed another handful of water in his face, then stood slowly under the weight of the pack, turned, and continued along the stream. Brandon and I imitated him.

The water stayed with us well beyond the next turn, then disappeared. One moment it flowed along the sand and gravel creekbed. The next it had gone underground. Malcolm speculated that it wouldn't reemerge until somewhere below the Redwall—or around the next turn—since this kind of flow is unpredictable season to season, year to year, and eon to eon.

Terraced Supai cliffs rose above us cutting off our view of the rim as Muav Canyon narrowed dramatically. A short time later water returned with an even stronger flow than when it had disappeared. It vanished and reappeared twice more as it led us to a gorge, perhaps five feet wide, that dropped precipitously through deeply creviced rock walls. We had reached the top of the Redwall.

We lunched on a ledge Brandon found, nicely shaded and just large enough for the three of us. Well below, perhaps fifty feet, a pool of water enticingly reflected the overhead sun. In the distance we could see the massive Redwall setting off the lower chasm of Muav Canyon. No break that would permit a descent was evident.

"I've never had sardines," Brandon said as I spread out food.

"Ah ha, your first canyon lunch," I exclaimed, in fine humor now that we had stopped. "Sardines top my list of things that taste gourmet wonderful out here and awful at home. Try one."

He popped a sardine-laden cracker into his mouth, gagged, and quickly washed it down with lemonade Malcolm had just mixed. "Truly delicious," he said, reaching for the peanut butter.

After lunch, I sat back against my backpack, breathed deeply, and let myself relax. "I noticed the way you glided down the Hermit Shale, Malcolm, that you were showing Brandon the joys of the descent."

He looked up from mining red peanut candies from the gorp. "He's a natural."

"His genetic predisposition should be uphill," I countered.

"I don't get this uphill-downhill thing you two keep bringing up," Brandon said.

"It's time you understood more intimately what your old man does for a living," Malcolm intervened. "He's a sociologist. They categorize and classify human experience. Uphill. Downhill. It's what they do."

"Right," I nodded. "It's also time you knew more about my affinities and infirmities, just in case you've inherited them. So, let me tell you about the dark side of hiking downhill, at least for me. On my first hike with Malcolm we took off from Apache Point through steep Kaibab that was a lot like the loose Hermit here. Because I struggled so much we had to proceed slowly. We ran out of water and had to suck chlorinated slime out of a rock hole somewhere above Royal Arch Creek. I blamed the problem on inexperience.

"Then, four years ago, we hiked down Hermit Trail on the South Rim in February. The trail drops 1,400 feet in about a mile and a half, with sheer drops along the side, and it was covered with snow and ice. Every step felt uncertain and I fell backward a couple times. My legs turned to jelly. I was shaking so bad by the time we got below the Coconino, where the snow ended, that we had to rest an hour before I could go on. Even then, my legs never fully recovered. The last hour I could walk only fifty yards at a time without pausing to stop quivering. We were trying to reach Hermit Camp. Malcolm would hike ahead around each corner and come back saying, 'It's just up ahead.' I knew he was lying, but the lie got me another fifty yards. My legs didn't hurt. They were just gone. It was dark when we finally made it. I thought my legs would never stop shaking, but the next morning I was fine. The body's recuperative powers are extraordinary."

"Why didn't you stop and camp on the trail?" Brandon asked.

"The weather was turning bad," Malcolm explained. "I knew Hermit Camp had rock overhangs where we could sleep protected. Besides, I had convinced myself it was just around each corner. I wasn't just conning your dad."

I picked up the story again. "On the way back up our roles were reversed. You haven't seen suffering until you've seen Malcolm hiking uphill, at least not since he broke his ankle a while ago. We hiked in a steady, cold drizzle, Malcolm's face a picture of pain. His feet bled through his socks and stained his boots. Above the Redwall it started snowing. His feet got so cold the bleeding stopped. I'd hike ahead, return to find him resting, then coax him along as best I could. So you see, our theory that the world is divided into downhillers and uphillers comes from years of personal research. Just like the rest of the world, we're perfectly willing to generalize from our own limited experiences. What do you say, Malcolm? Am I telling it true?"

"Close enough," Malcolm answered, "though I'd just as soon not talk about hiking up while some of us are still experiencing the joys of the descent."

"More joy to you. As for me, I'll probably lag behind again going down the Redwall, the same way I did this morning down the Hermit Shale. I struggled, I admit. I missed a switchback and found myself in a side drainage. My legs got pretty shaky. But I intend to revel in the hike back up and make sure Brandon sees the legacy he's rightfully inherited."

"I intend to fully enjoy both," Brandon insisted. "Your generation may divide into up and down subspecies, but mine has evolved into a higher-order life-form that excels at both."

"Does this new life-form honor rock lizard time?" Malcolm asked, leaning back and covering his face with his hat.

"I've been thinking maybe there are four categories of people," Brandon continued, unabashed. "Uphillers and downhillers, like you two, plus people who hate going up or down, which is probably most of the world, and finally, love-going-up-and-down types—a small, elite group."

"There are only two categories at midday," Malcolm grumbled through his hat, "rock lizards and those who disturb us."

"You may be right," I whispered to Brandon. "We'll see how you do going down the Redwall and then on the way back up before I accept your categorical revisionism." I winked at him, laid back, and was deeply rock lizarding in thirty seconds.

8. Redwall

Iawoke from my siesta to find Brandon reading Colin Fletcher's *The Man Who Walked Through Time*. I put my arms behind my head and peered over my feet at him, savoring being able to observe him unobtrusively. Soon he noticed I was awake.

"So we'll really get through the Redwall today, right?" he asked, his tone indicating both anticipation and respect.

I sat up. "You know, the Redwall isn't what it seems." I checked my hiking boots to make sure no little creature had sought them out as a place of midday shelter.

"What do you mean?" he asked.

"It's only red on the surface. It's actually gray limestone that has been stained by iron oxide from the Supai. The Redwall is the Grand Canyon's tribute to the modern world: a monument to surface appearances."

I regretted this as soon as I spoke, such vituperations a distraction from staying present to my surroundings. Yet I also understood the source; invectives against civilization often spew out in the early stages of detox.

Malcolm, meanwhile, was putting moleskin on his feet and explaining to Brandon the real significance of the Redwall. "The color isn't what makes it important. The Redwall separates the inner canyon from the upper canyon—a sheer, six-hundred-foot barrier about halfway between rim and river. What few breaks exist are hard to find and difficult to get down."

"Let's go do it," Brandon said, rising abruptly.

I winced as I stood up, feeling hot spots—areas of potential blistering—on the soles of both feet. We climbed off the ledge and out of the gorge with Brandon in the lead. He found the elevation benchmark we were looking for and the cairn marking the path up and around the gorge to the point of descent.

"It looks like we'll be heading uphill a ways from here," I said. "My legs will welcome the change. I'll take the lead."

"I'll take a piss and be right behind you," Malcolm said,

I hiked up the rock plateau and went the first few feet up the trail. Behind me I heard Brandon say, "That's really weak, Malcolm. After what you said about water this morning, I can't believe you'd do that."

I turned around so quickly that my pack threw me sideways a couple of steps. I regained my balance and looked back. Brandon was shaking his head disapprovingly as he watched Malcolm urinate in White Creek just before it dropped into the gorge. Malcolm finished and turned toward Brandon. "What's got your dander up?"

"You've got the whole canyon to piss in and you pick the one place that ruins the water. It's really gross. Now we have to drink your piss downstream."

I had seldom seen Brandon so agitated and never with a nonfamily member. Malcolm seemed disconcerted. "You're upset about my pissing in the stream?"

"It's not a toilet, you know."

"I'm sorry it's upset you and I'm glad you said something," Malcolm replied, switching unconsciously into a soothing, therapeutic voice, "but for me, it's okay to piss in running water at this particular place."

"No way!" Brandon countered, shaking his head.

"Let me explain," Malcolm continued calmly. "Urine is essentially sterile, but it does smell. To prevent odor building up on beaches along the river the Park Service requires that people urinate in the river. The same principle applies here. This is a natural stopping place for hikers. If everybody who stops here pisses around the water, but not in it, before long this place would smell like a toilet in a city park. *That* would be gross. Times of the year when the flow lessens through here, it would be wrong to piss in the stream."

"You could have waited until we climbed up away from the creek," Brandon challenged. "I need to piss too, but I'm waiting."

"That's fine," Malcolm acknowledged, "but think about this spot." He pointed to the flow of White Creek. "From here the water drops into a gorge too steep even for animals to climb in and out of. That water will flow through sand and gravel for a half mile or more before this stream reappears, if it does, below the Redwall. I wouldn't piss just anywhere. You're right to be concerned. The point is to read the environment and do what makes the most sense to preserve a particular place."

"I'm not arguing the philosophy," Brandon said emphatically. "It's how you practice it. I may give you this one, but I'll be watching," he cautioned, feigning sternness.

"You do that," Malcolm grinned back. Then he pulled his backpack upright. "Here, help me with this."

Brandon hoisted the pack up on Malcolm's back. A very nice touch, I thought, moved by their frank interaction.

Malcolm started up the path. Brandon, behind him, didn't move. When Malcolm reached me, he turned and looked back. "I'm watching you," Brandon shouted.

Malcolm and I laughed. When Brandon joined us, Malcolm winked. "Maybe I'll yield this one to you. I admit these old bones didn't want to hike up the hill in bladder pain when using the stream would do no harm. Watch me if you will, but don't miss the canyon. I'm not much to look at by comparison. Go on, your old man's waiting to strut his uphill stuff."

We left White Creek and headed up the west side of the Supai. Trying to find the path through the Supai vegetation, crisscrossed as it was by washes and ridges that could easily be mistaken for the path, proved much more difficult than hiking down the distinct bed of White Creek. I felt reassured to come upon a small cairn. After passing through a couple of small drainages, I stopped with Brandon to wait for Malcolm to catch up. "Have you been counting?" I asked as he joined us.

"Counting what?"

"I'm not sure if these up-and-down drainages are the 'parallel ravines' Harvey says we're looking for. Harvey says we have to go through *several* of these ravines. How do you calculate 'several' in Harvey math?"

"We aren't to the ravines yet. They'll be steep and deep and closer to the Redwall." He pointed across the chasm to the eastern canyon wall. "We aren't close to the descent yet."

"Okay," I said, trusting Malcolm's understanding of Harvey and the canyon. Brandon looked up from the guidebook he was studying. "Annerino says the route traverses three saddles."

"So," I concluded, "Annerino's saddles must be the humps between Harvey's ravines. And Annerino implies that 'several' means three. Having two guidebooks in the wilderness is like having two watches in the city."

Malcolm smiled, recognizing the ramblings of detox. Brandon looked confused. "Don't you know the old joke about a person with two watches not knowing for sure what time it is?" I asked.

"Nope. Does it take long to tell?"

"Never mind," I said and hiked on.

Not long thereafter the path dropped suddenly and steeply into a narrow cut sixty-five yards deep and twice that high up the other side. Getting down the ravine required half stepping, half sliding. At the bottom the ravine wall went straight back up, but there was no obvious path through the dense, thorny brush. After some searching I found a line of ascent. At the top I stopped for a mouthful of water, waited for my companions, and reflected on the difference between a hilly undulation and a Harvey-style ravine.

We continued through an even steeper ravine. I grunted with each labored step up, like a tennis player who puts his lungs into each swing. At the top we found ourselves on a sloping terrace crisscrossed by lines that looked like possible paths—rain drainages, natural ridges, deer paths, old burro paths, and bighorn trails. Malcolm speculated that we were at a congregating site for animals going through the Redwall. The problem was figuring out which path to take. Heading too far up would put us on a ledge above the Redwall, while the wrong down-sloping line could get us stuck on the edge of the gorge we had just left. We split up to reconnoiter the area. Malcolm stayed with the packs while Brandon headed up and I went down.

It felt good to move without the pack's weight, but I could find no sure route among the many faint, crisscrossing erosion lines that started and stopped along the steep hillside. I climbed back up, thinking I was retracing my steps, but couldn't find Malcolm and the packs. I called out and got no answer. I strained to see any kind of artificial color swatch among the scattered junipers, pinyons, desert scrub, and cactus. I thought I had paid close attention, but I couldn't find my own boot tracks or even tell how far up to go. Everything looked the same, but nothing looked familiar.

I wandered around at angles up and down the hillside, calling and listening, and finally hearing a faint response. I followed Brandon's voice and found him with Malcolm, sitting by the packs. "Did you turn up anything?" I asked Brandon.

"We need to go right along this fall line," Malcolm said pointing. Malcolm had been studying the map and rereading Harvey, extracting every nuance from his hero's parsimonious guidance. Carefully observing the surrounding topography, he had triangulated our location against the curvature on the other side of the White Creek chasm and located the ravines on the map.

I sat down by him, tired and appreciative. "I see you did your reconnoitering without even moving."

"I was just explaining to Brandon that finding an actual path isn't always the key. Knowing what direction to go, that's the key. Sometimes there's no path, so you have to make your own. Other times there are several paths, any of which will eventually get you where you want to go as long as you're clear about your direction and destination."

"My destination ten minutes ago was just to get back to where I started," I said, "and that proved no easy task. I was heeding the old adage that 'the map is not the territory,' thinking that meant I could just wander around the territory without the map."

"You've lost me," Brandon interjected before Malcolm could reply. "What's this map-and-territory stuff?"

"A little wisdom from our forebears. It's on the syllabus right after 'a man with two watches can't be sure what time it is.' That 'the map is not the territory' has been handed down from the first adventurers who got lost with map in hand."

"Watch the territory and the sky," Malcolm added, pointing up. "We need to push to get through the Redwall before dark."

He led the way. We hiked into a deep wash—or a shallow ravine. Following the flow of the terrain around a final slope, we found ourselves on a ledge beneath a bare wall—*just the way Harvey described it.* The ledge offered just enough width for cautious walking, wider than a plank but narrower than a sidewalk. Above rose a sloping rock wall, unscalable; below, the drop-off into the gorge seemed to have no floor. The gorge had widened to several hundred feet from its narrow beginning where we had lunched. Across from us a massive wall of red and gray rock, spotted with green vegetation, showed the kind of terrain we had to climb down. Beyond the wall we could see Coconino cliffs and the now-distant rim. It would be some time before we saw the rim again once we entered the inner gorge.

We made our way along the ledge, one portion of which was eroded so much that it was necessary to face the wall and move sideways for a few yards. Animal droppings revealed frequent use of the ledge by the canyon's permanent occupants. We passed a cave that had clearly served as a place of animal refuge. The ledge broadened into a sloping terrace of rock and brush dropping down to a precipice extending out into the gorge. The view from this precipice was the canyon's reward after the hike along the ledge. We dropped our packs and made our way to the edge of the precipice where a small platform offered just enough space to sit, study the map, and view the magnificent panorama all the way to the South Rim. For the first time we could see the inner canyon. The jagged spires of Dox Castle five miles away marked the junction where the precious water of White Creek flowed into the larger Shinumo Creek for its final journey to the Colorado River. Masonic Temple curved around toward us like a vertical highway to Powell Plateau, blocking any view of the river.

The late afternoon sun brought out an array of subtle hues to the south as purples, grays, oranges, deep reds, and pastel pinks accented the great line of Sagittarius Ridge. We had balcony seats, first row, to take in nature's late-matinee performance of changing colors and lengthening shadows within the gorge, throughout the lower canyon, and beyond to the haze-distorted peaks on the horizon. Hot gusts of painfully grainy wind offered a hint of how ten million years of sandblasting could change the face of things, one particle at a time. I said nothing to my companions about my deep disappointment that Holy Grail Temple still eluded our view. The reality of the canyon's erosion-layered twists and turns was thwarting my romantic presumption that the Grail would be readily visible. But then, that's not how it was in the original quest either.

Malcolm speculated that we were looking out from the point where Thomas Moran, who accompanied Major John Wesley Powell to the canyon in 1873, drew sketches for his famous Grand Canyon masterpiece that the U.S. Congress eventually purchased. His paintings are credited with introducing the American public to the magnificence of the Grand Canyon.

"Have you ever seen any of his paintings?" I asked Malcolm.

"Just reproductions," he answered. "Canyon purists disdain his works because he created montages that provide a feel for the canyon, but don't accurately depict any particular panorama—impressionism without an impressionist's style. Others find his paintings more real than a photograph."

"This spot is so awesome it should have a name," Brandon said. "How about Moran Point?"

"If every awesome spot had a name, you wouldn't be able to read the map through all the lettering. Besides," Malcolm continued, "it's been done. Moran Point is on the South Rim near the park's eastern border."

"I need to take a shit," Brandon announced abruptly, handing the map to me.

"That came on suddenly," I said.

"I thought I could wait until we got through the Redwall, but seeing it up close, I think I better not wait."

"Go back to where the ledge begins," Malcolm directed. "The slope isn't too bad just below there so you should be able to find enough loose soil to dig in. Find a strong bush to hold. If you slide down that slope with your ass bare we'll be picking thorns out of your cheeks the rest of the trip."

We sat quietly, enjoying the view, cooling in the breeze and mentally preparing for the descent. A few minutes later I heard what sounded like singing carried on a hot gust from up-canyon: "I'm sitting on top of the world." As he came closer we realized Brandon had changed the words.

> *"I'm shitting on top of the world,*
> *Just shitting along, My feces are gone."*

"I think it's time to get this young man off the ledge," Malcolm said.

"To each his own detox," I remarked.

"Since Moran Point is already taken, I'll dub this"—Brandon turned and shouted toward the river—"Release Point."

We laughed with his euphoria. As Malcolm pulled his pack on for the descent, he said: "I trust you're not planning on naming every place you take a shit."

9. Meeting the Wild Man

"**W**hat?! That's really weird, Dad. Like, I don't remember the Hermit Shale even being like a descent. *The Redwall was a descent!*" Brandon proclaimed. Malcolm nodded agreement, grinning.

"I'm not saying the Redwall was easy," I explained, feeling defensive, "but the really hard part was finding the break to get down. That's Harvey's genius. No denying the Redwall's a hell of a barrier, geologically and psychologically. But knowing that, I was prepared. Hermit took me by surprise. I just think the Hermit Shale deserves a little respect too."

Brandon and Malcolm looked at each other like they were listening to the rantings of a mad man.

"All right, you two, hear me out. The Redwall is so solid and steep, it's like walking down steps. Hermit is loose and slippery, and the brush thorny. So, for me, Hermit was harder."

"Your father has a very distorted sense of downhill reality, Brandon. Smile and nod, but don't take a word of it seriously."

"I hardly even remember the Hermit," Brandon said, "but the Redwall is *bue düden.*" He paused and looked up at the sheer wall, then back at me. "I don't get it."

"There's nothing else to get," Malcolm assured him. "The Redwall *is* boo-duden and, ummm . . ."

"Awesome," Brandon offered, grinning.

"Thank you," Malcolm nodded. "Say that to anyone who's ever hiked the Canyon and they'll instantly understand what you're talking about. Awesome, that is, not boo-duden."

"*Bue düden,*" corrected Brandon.

"Right. Actually, they'd probably understand that as well. Tell them the Hermit descent is awesome and they'll think you never made it to the Redwall. But, to each his own experience."

"And to each his own criteria for awesomeness," I added.

The descent had brought us back to the dry bed of White Creek. Above us towered eroded rock outcroppings like massive, gargoyle-topped columns guarding an ancient crypt. The gorge floor was littered with tree-sized logs and boulders of all sizes, many twice my height, evidence of a surging wall of water so powerful it swept along everything in its path above the Redwall before dropping into the inner gorge and leaving behind a debris-formed maze protecting entry into the catacombs ahead.

Something suddenly felt different, something unexpected that could not be explained simply by our entry into the inner chasm. My mind worked the comparisons. Bright to dim. Open to closed. Hot to cool. Dry to—musty! I spied an unexpected pool of water in a rock basin below a boulder, another in a depression near the edge. Only when the sun attained its daily zenith could its rays penetrate the towering walls and illuminate the inner canyon. The still air hung thick like a Minnesota basement after a summer rain.

About a quarter mile below the Redwall descent, White Creek emerged as a stream again bordered by large ferns. A shimmering canopy of cottonwoods and the evening sounds of frogs and canyon wrens drove out wearying thoughts of basements and catacombs with the refreshing notion that we had entered a semitropical oasis.

We made our way slowly, looking for a place to camp. We found an elevated ledge, about ten feet above the creek, with a floor of smooth, white sand just large enough for three sleeping bags. The ledge sloped slightly toward the creek, but not so much that we risked sliding down. Just below the ledge a small waterfall flowed into a shallow pool making access to water easy. A rock border along the ledge would serve as a dinner table.

We feasted on ramen noodles mixed with canned chicken, cooked on the same small campstove Malcolm had had as long as I'd known him. He coached Brandon in lighting the temperamental stove. He was undeterred when yellow flames burst forth nearly singeing his eyebrows. He worked determinedly, completely engaged through several failed attempts, until, at last, the flame burned blue and steady, eliciting from Brandon a broad, satisfied grin.

Watching, I considered how best to introduce the after-dinner ritual I hoped would let us talk about some things—about life and work and sex and his upbringing and similar modest and uncomplicated topics. This would be my last chance to find out how he thought about these things before he fell under the influences of dorm life, college instruction, and who knew what else. Asking Brandon to interpret a coming-of-age fable seemed to offer an appropriate vehicle for reflection and a provocative initiation challenge. Robert Bly's telling of "Iron John" suited my purposes, not the full book by that name, just his translation of the original Grimms' tale "Iron Hans," unencumbered by Bly's controversial interpretations. Recounting a boy's journey to adulthood, the story offered a menu of issues around which the three of us could engage.[1] That was what I wanted: engagement. Deep. Sustained. Meaningful.

After dinner, I announced that, in keeping with initiation traditions, it was storytelling time. Malcolm leaned back against the rock wall, barefoot. He sighed as he stretched out, his head tilted up, looking at the stars that filled the sliver of sky above the gorge walls. Brandon took off his boots and spread out in the sand along the ledge, propped up on his right elbow. I sat cross-legged. We listened in silence to the serenade of crickets and cascading water, and watched the Milky Way thicken as the last glow of light faded. At length, I began.

"I brought along a story that's believed to be twenty thousand years old. Over centuries, it's been recast in new languages, the images filtered to be interpretable in new places. The latest rendering, the one I want to read tonight, is Robert Bly's version. Do you remember hearing him read his poetry?"

"Sure," Brandon replied.

"Remember anything in particular?"

"It was called something like 'Fathers and Sons,' and that's why we went. You were surprised that it was about his father in old age rather than about, you know, a father your age and a son my age. He said something like fathers and sons can't really communicate until the son is fifty or so, and that seemed weird."

"Did he say why?" Malcolm asked.

"No. It was just, like, here's the way the world is: fathers can never give sons all they need; sons never get all they want; and they won't be able to talk to each other about their mutual disappointments until old age."

"Any other impressions of Bly?" I asked.

"He had long white hair and wore a colorful vest with an Indian design, and I remember him drumming and singing and experimenting with the words to some of his poems, seeing which way the audience liked them. And I remember that you leaned over to me about half way through and said, 'We may be in the presence of poetic genius, but his sociology sucks.'"

"I don't think those were my exact words," I protested.

Malcolm laughed. "Poets speak from their own experience and it comes out sounding like an overgeneralization. Sociologists generalize from others' experiences and bury their own."

"And therapists?" I asked.

"We work in-between," he smiled.

"At any rate," I continued, "Bly has become famous since then and the so-called Men's Movement has become controversial. We saw him before all that. I liked talking with you afterward about his poems. We haven't had a chance to do anything like that for a long time, so I brought along the story of 'Iron John' to see what you think of it. I'm curious to see what a young man who's just come of age makes of an ancient coming of age story. It's long, so I thought we'd read one short segment each night." Brandon nodded assent, so I read by flashlight the story's opening, which I've summarized here.[2]

The tale opens in a kingdom where the people are afraid of the surrounding forest because all the hunters who enter there vanish. After many years a stranger comes and asks permission of the King to hunt in the forest. When his dog is grabbed by a naked arm in a pool, the hunter gets help to empty the water. At the bottom of the pool, they discover a Wild Man. They capture and imprison him in the castle. The King's young son, while playing, loses his golden ball in the Wild Man's cage. In exchange for the ball, the Wild Man convinces the boy to steal the key to the cage from under the Queen's pillow and free him. Having done so, the boy realizes he must flee with the Wild Man into the dark forest to avoid certain punishment, for the King had commanded that anyone opening the cage would be put to death.

When I finished reading, I turned off the flashlight, waved my hand to scatter the flying insects it had attracted, and asked Brandon if anything struck him. "The Wild Man is like the Redwall," he said instantly.

Malcolm laughed heartily. "I'll bet that's not the answer you expected."

"I must protest, Dr. Gray. I had no expectations. Go on," I urged. "How's the Wild Man like the Redwall?"

"When they bucketed out the pool and found him, he was the color of rusty iron—like the Redwall. At lunch you said the Redwall isn't what it seems, you know, really red. It's gray limestone stained by iron oxide from the Supai, right?"

"Right."

"So the Wild Man is covered all over with hair and reddish-brown mud and looks dangerous, but underneath, I assume, he's . . ."

"What?"

"That depends on the rest of the story."

"But what makes you assume he's other than wild and dangerous?"

"He doesn't hurt the boy. Instead, the Wild Man takes him up on his shoulders and saves him."

"Saves him from . . . ?"

"The King had given orders that anyone who opened the cage would be killed."

"So you're saying the real threat to the boy was from . . . ?"

Brandon hesitated. I laughed. "Go ahead. Say it. The boy's afraid he'll be punished, maybe even killed, by his . . . ?"

"Father. But I don't think he'd kill his own son. He'd punish the boy, but it's not believable that he'd kill him."

"It's not what the King would actually do that's important," Malcolm said, "it's what the boy believes he might do."

"True," Brandon agreed. "At this point the boy's more afraid of his father than of the Wild Man."

When I didn't respond, Malcolm asked, "Michael, what are you associating the story with? Your father?"

"Maybe. But it's bigger than my relationship with my father or even Brandon. For weeks now I've been researching literature on fathers and sons and—"

"What literature?" Brandon interrupted

"There's always a literature," I intoned professorially. Then more lightly: "It's what we academics do when concerned about something. We 'search the literature.' I went through a lot of books about men looking for stories that might fit the canyon. They weren't very helpful. In fact, they left me depressed. And I just realized why. When you said, 'The father's the threat,' it was like the voices of all this stuff I've read shouting at once. Our culture is spewing forth great globs of venom aimed at fathers. Violent fathers. Absent fathers. Authoritarian fathers. Alcoholic fathers. Closed fathers. Angry fathers. Impossible-to-please fathers. Unloving fathers. On and on—and all leading to wounded sons. Father bashing makes great copy these days."

"You sound like you take it personally," Malcolm observed.

"I acknowledge that the fatherly record is heavily blemished. Men have inflicted a lot of pain and suffering on their children and wives. I don't want to make light of that or dismiss it. It's a central problem of our time. I'd just like a little balance, a little acknowledgment that not all fathers are bastards and abusers."

"It's not just our own time and culture," Malcolm commented. "As 'Iron John' illustrates, the tales of many cultures warn sons about their fathers. They help the son separate from his father so he can become his own person as an adult."

"You're saying the point of 'Iron John' is simply that a boy has to get away from his father to become his own man?" Brandon asked. "So then the Wild Man is, like, the boy's natural self that he has to find—and he has to escape his father to find it."

"That interpretation is consistent with similar stories in other cultures," Malcolm agreed.

"Give us an example," I suggested.

"Okay. The Hausa people tell—"

"Where are they?" Brandon interrupted.

"Niger and Nigeria. The story's been picked up by some of the men leading initiation workshops, like James Hillman, Michael Meade, and Malidoma Somé—"

"Leading what?"

"Weekend workshops for men who've never been formally initiated to help them find other ways of dealing with issues like male identity, masculinity, male roles—"

"Inadequate fathers, father-caused wounds," I added.

"So what's the story?" Brandon asked.

"A father who's a great hunter takes his son into the woods. The father climbs a tree to get honey, passes it down to his son, but tells him not to eat any. While the father's climbing down, the son eats the honey. The father becomes terribly angry and calls wild animals—water buffaloes, lions, and elephants—to punish the son, perhaps even kill him, for the father is in a great rage. But the son, being strong, kills all the animals. The father then sends the son to a nearby village for fire to cook the animal meat, but the villagers are cannibals. The son flees back to his father and climbs the honey tree to safety. The cannibals eat the father and all the dead animals, but the son escapes. He takes his revenge by burning the village and killing the cannibals while they're sleeping after their huge feast. He frees young people held captive in the village, being fattened by the cannibals. He becomes their chief and marries one of the girls. When his first son is born, he takes him hunting for honey as his father had taken him—and the cycle begins again."

"Let me see if I've got this," Brandon said, looking dubious. "The father wants to teach the son. The son disobeys. The father flies into a rage that almost gets the son killed. Then the father gets killed instead and the son becomes a chief. That's an initiation story?" he asked, his tone incredulous. "*Narlask!*"

"One of many where the son can't become his own person—can't become a man—until the father's out of the picture," I replied. "In 'Iron John,' the boy runs away. In the hunter story, the father is killed. Initiation is about separation: death of the child, birth of the man. And as near as I can tell, the father's presence always interferes with the rebirth, so he can't even participate."

"You didn't find any happy father-son stories?"

"Think about the stories you know. Do you remember the fathers and sons from when you were into Greek mythology?"

"Like who?"

"Try Zeus."

"King of the gods. He had a father?"

"Cronos."

"Right. Now I remember. When Zeus was born, his mother had to secretly give him to someone else to raise so that Cronos wouldn't devour him as he had his other children."

"A common motif in both old folktales *and* modern family therapy," Malcolm interjected sardonically.

"But then," Brandon went on, "Zeus was deposed by his son. Sons are just as much a threat to fathers as fathers are to sons, like in the Hausa hunter story, the father threatens the son, but the son ultimately triumphs."

"Until he's replaced by his own son," Malcolm pointed out.

"Who perpetuates what he learned from his father," I added. "Zeus escaped being eaten by his father, but Tantalus, a son of Zeus, inherited the male line's affection for making meals of sons. Tantalus gave a great banquet for the gods on Mount Sipylus. The main course was his son, Pelops."

"I can't believe how much you know about this stuff and how into it you are," Brandon said. "They're just stories."

"Just!? Perhaps, Dr. Gray, you'd be good enough to point out the significance of stories in passing on culture and religion, developing values, conducting initiations—"

"Ease up, Dad. I only meant that the old Greek stuff isn't directly applicable to today."

"Want to give him a spiel on the primordial and collective unconscious, Malcolm?"

"You want to get into Freud and Jung at this hour?"

"The Oedipus Complex," Brandon sneered. "In psych class we . . . umm, the boy stealing the key from under his mother's pillow after his father gave it to her could be interpreted as kind of sexual. Does the boy end up killing his father?"

"Freud's not about sons *actually* murdering their fathers and sleeping with their mothers," Malcolm interjected. "He focused on the guilt from even having such thoughts. From a psychological point of view, it's not so much the actual presence or absence of the father that matters, or even his behavior. It's how the son, or daughter for that matter, *experiences* the father. A lot of fathers are physically present, but emotionally unavailable."

"Odysseus!" Brandon exclaimed. "Odysseus and his son got along great."

"In the end," I said.

"That's all that counts," Brandon asserted.

"Maybe," I replied, "but remember, Odysseus was off warring and adventuring the whole time Telemachus was growing up."

"But then the kid went in search of his old man," Brandon continued, "found him, and they ended up happily ever after."

"The way I remember it," Malcolm appended, "Telemachus was guided by the goddess of wisdom, Athena, who took the form of Mentor, a lifelong friend of his father's. So the idea of having a mentor has come to signify a younger person's need for guidance from someone older or wiser."

"Which," I added, "although it doesn't sound like it yet, is what 'Iron John' turns out to be for the boy."

"So 'Iron John' *is* like the Redwall," Brandon concluded.

"Indeed," I agreed.

"Things aren't always what they seem on the surface," Malcolm added, "but you can't know that for sure unless you have some way of going deeper."

"Spoken like a true therapist," I chided.

"Spoken like a canyoneer," he countered.

"Whatever," I bantered back. "Let me try going below the surface. From what I've been reading, father-son relationships more often lead to sorrow than joy. That saddens me. Whether the father punishes the son or the son rebels against the father, or both, their relationship is usually characterized by conflict, competition, distrust, distance, or violence—even when they love each other. Abraham nearly slays Isaac to show God his faith and obedience. A thousand years or so later, God forsakes Jesus and subjects him to death on the cross. You convinced, or do you want more?" I asked.

"Convinced of what?"

"Convinced that the world's history, myths, fairy tales, religion, and literature combine to portray a pretty dreary picture of father-son relationships. Convinced that I have reason to be concerned about how you'll feel about your old man as you grow older."

"I'm convinced that you're convinced."

"But you're not convinced yourself?"

"It doesn't apply to me or to today."

"You don't have any friends who are having hassles with their fathers?" Malcolm asked.

Brandon laughed. "I don't have any friends who *aren't* having hassles with their fathers," he said emphatically. He paused, then added: "But that's them."

"I'm glad we don't have hassles—and pretty amazed," I admitted. "I've long lived in fear of some inevitable day when we'd become combatants, like my father and I were. I feel incredibly lucky that we've somehow avoided war. Quite the contrary. I marvel at how well we get along. I really do—and cherish it. But I also think about the warnings in stories and myths. You're about to leave home. We don't know what our future holds. I do know we're at a critical point of transition. None of what I've read provides guidance for that transition. Lots of warnings, but no real guidance."

"It sounds like you're asking if it's possible for you to stay a part of Brandon's story," Malcolm suggested.

"I suppose so. Our inherited wisdom says coming of age means the son must separate from the father. I understand that historically and sociologically. But, as a person, as a father, I'm looking for a way to recognize Brandon as his own person without the father disappearing, screwing things up, or getting killed off—though today I thought the Hermit Shale might solve the problem all together."

"I don't know what to say, Dad. I have trouble speculating about what's going to happen in the future. For me, the fact that we have a good relationship and are here now means the future looks good. I can't really go beyond that."

"Ah, the wisdom of youth," I sighed. "Where you are is where I'd like to be, once I get detoxed—here and now for nine more days. Of course, that might mean my not being a parent."

"Works for me," Brandon smiled.

"*The Wild Man is like the Redwall,*" Malcolm repeated. "I doubt I'll ever again look at the Redwall without remembering that line. *Well spoken.* Now I've got to get some sleep."

A few minutes later, as we settled in our sleeping bags, Malcolm's voice drifted to me from a ledge just above where Brandon and I had settled. "There's still a chance," he said.

"Chance of what?" I called back.

"The map shows an open plateau where this gorge opens out on the Tonto. Holy Grail Temple might be visible from there."

"Is that your idea of helping me stay in the here and now?"

"No, I just know how your mind works."

I drifted into sleep wondering what he meant.

Notes

1. Of the story Robert Bly said: "The Iron John story retains memories of initiation ceremonies for men that go back ten or twenty thousand years in northern Europe. The Wild Man's job is to teach the young man how abundant, various, and many-sided manhood is. The boy's body inherits physical abilities developed by long-dead ancestors and his mind inherits spiritual and soul powers developed centuries ago. . . . The metaphors in the Iron John story refer to all human life, but are tuned to the psyches of men." *Iron John: A Book About Men* (Reading, Mass.: Addison-Wesley, 1990), p. 55.

2. Each night in the canyon we read a segment of the "Iron John" story,

so I'll introduce each of those discussions with a summary of that segment. These summaries are meant to help the reader follow our subsequent discussion and use of the fable. However, this synopsis captures none of the literary style, rich imagery, and dialogue found in Robert Bly's translation of the tale or the original Grimms' fairy tale, "Iron Hans." See No. 136, "Iron Hans," in *The Complete Grimms' Fairy Tales* (New York: Pantheon Books, 1972).

Day Two

10. The Inner Gorge

Dimness foretold the day. A cottonwood across the creek pointed upward behind me in the direction of Holy Grail Temple. I wondered if the open plateau shown on the map would offer a view of it, thereby giving me occasion to tell Brandon what I had discovered about Lancelot and Galahad.

I got up and went to the creek to wet my bandana and wash sandy sleep from my eyes, then woke Brandon. "Top of the mornin'," I said, flipping the bandana at him in wet greeting.

"You're cheerful this morning," he grumbled, turning his back to the cold spray.

I roused Malcolm. He sat up and lit the stove next to him.

Having coffee while still bagged was a Malcolm detox ritual. As we prepared instant oatmeal, Malcolm proposed that we explore the Redwall gorge before continuing on. "Might even find a waterfall," he speculated.

"On the way down," I explained, "Malcolm loves hanging around at the bottom of the Redwall to savor having made the descent, but on the way back up we'll have trouble getting him near the Redwall. His polarity reverses."

"Will we get to the river today?" Brandon asked, studying the map. "We're only about a third of the way there."

91

"We're actually halfway down," Malcolm replied. "Look at the map lines above and below the Redwall. The terrain's not as steep today. Yesterday we hiked *down* farther than we came *in*. Today we'll go *in* farther than we hike *down*. Check out the elevation markers."

"Umm, 7,517 feet at Swamp Point and . . . 5,006 above the Redwall . . . and it looks like about 4,400 where we are now. So we came down about half-a-mile to the top of the Redwall, then 600 feet in the descent. That's about 3,100 feet down yesterday."

"Now, find an elevation marker near where White joins Shinumo."

"There's a marker at 3,160 about three lines above where they come together, so that's about a 1,300-foot drop from here."

"And at the river?"

"Let's see, it's 2,266 at Bass Rapids. So it's only about 2,200 feet down from here to the river and we did about 3,100 yesterday, so we're more than halfway in."

"We're more than half DOWN, but not yet halfway IN. Remember, the erosion from the North Rim is longer from rim to river because of drainage into the canyon. The South Rim's distance from rim to river is only half as much."

"So it all depends on where you are in relation to where you want to be. I understand the philosophy," Brandon said with a hint of sarcasm. "The here-and-now question is, do we want to get to the river? I do."

"I wasn't suggesting that we wouldn't get to the river," Malcolm said reassuringly. "I was just emphasizing that we don't have any place we *have* to get to. The river's not our destination. The canyon is. So we've already arrived."

Brandon looked at me questioningly. "Malcolm has arrived as soon as he's below the rim."

"And you?"

"I'm just beginning detox. I'm not sure what arrival will mean for me this time."

"Let's do it," Malcolm said, reaching for his boots. "Let's explore. I have a feeling about this place." Then, punching Brandon lightly on his arm: "And we'll get to the river—at some point—probably."

"What happened to wanting to get down and see Holy Grail Temple?" Brandon asked me.

"Like the river, it'll be there when we get there, if it's visible at all. I didn't really mean to make it such a big deal."

"What are the odds?" Brandon asked Malcolm.

"Hard to say. Depends on terrain. But if you don't see it, you'll have a reason to come back and see it from across the river, the way your old man did."

"Then let's boogie," Brandon urged. "Doesn't really matter which way we go. It's all new to me."

We made our way back up through the boulders we had climbed down the evening before. Past where we had descended the Redwall, the gorge separated into two sections of narrows. We explored the right channel, climbing up sometimes smooth, sometimes terraced rock walls. Large boulders that the night before had been barriers became guideposts—natural cairns marking the former descent of great torrents. No path commanded where we stepped as we enjoyed the freedom of maneuvering without cumbersome weight.

At the end of the channel our ascent was blocked by a smooth wall three times our height. Barely perceptible rivulets trickled down its slick, mossy green surface. Malcolm insisted his hope for a waterfall had been fulfilled. Brandon pretended belief. I demurred. We scaled the water-wall by using a side crevice for leverage and ascended to be swallowed by a huge, circular amphitheater completely enclosed by towering Redwall. Near the top, morning sunlight accentuated two great concave indentations, one with splattered whitewash over a background of browns and grays, the other mostly red, streaked with black. Splotches of mossy green peeked out of long columnar crevices. The angular rays integrated nuances of color and texture giving the impression of a monumental stained glass window illuminating an upper balcony. An outcropping sloped down to a crystalline platform, perfectly located to be the focal point from all directions.

We lingered awhile watching the light descend down the wall. I studied the myriad stone formations and enjoyed watching Brandon whir from boulder to boulder like a hummingbird searching for nectar.

A raven appeared overhead, circling, descending lower with each turn, then abruptly disappearing toward the river. Malcolm took out a small pouch and sprinkled something on the ground.

"What's that?" Brandon asked.

"Corn pollen I acquired from the Havasupai."

"What's it for?"

"An offering to the raven clan. Most life here is restricted to a narrow zone. The Grand Canyon rattlesnake prefers inner ledges. The white-tailed Kaibab squirrel lives only in the ponderosa forest on the North rim. Tamarisk thrives near the river and in lower riparian zones. But the raven occupies the whole canyon, so offering corn pollen or sometimes maize to the raven clan gives thanks to the whole canyon. The offering draws on several different traditions, something I've come to over the years." He put the pouch away and we returned to our campsite. Before we resumed hiking, he sprinkled some more corn pollen on the sand ledge where we had slept.

I was surprised that Brandon didn't ask Malcolm more about his reference to "raven clan." I presumed it was because he was anxious to get hiking and didn't want the delay that might come with more storytelling. I made no comment, biding my time, certain that we had not heard the last about Malcolm's chosen totem. Having become accustomed to Malcolm's canyon mysticism, I was content to let Brandon experience it for himself.

Hiking in the full light of morning and at the slow pace imposed by carrying weight, we had time to absorb the close intimacy of the narrow lower gorge. By the time we reached the opening onto the wider plateau of Muav Limestone, the heavy packs had settled familiarly into sore shoulder and back muscles. As we walked out into direct sunlight for the first time, it illuminated a section of wall that showed the geological transitions from Redwall to Temple Butte to Muav Limestone. We crossed the plateau, wound around turns where White Creek had carved a route through the limestone, and stopped at a narrow cut of greenish-gray rock that had eroded in thinly layered serrations, like a huge honey-dipper. We then descended down pinkish-gray marblelike corridors where the smooth, hard floor rounded gently upward in tiny steps. The water-polished rock led us down and around through narrow channels that had the feel of palace corridors. Guards in medieval armor lining our route would not have felt out of place.

Being well below the Redwall gave us a new perspective on the strata through which we had passed. We didn't yet need a rest break, but mentally we needed time to experience the transitions. At least I did. Like a diver who risks getting the bends when ascending too fast from the ocean depths, a too-fast descent would deprive me of the intellectual oxygen I needed to breathe deeply of this place.

We took off our packs and Brandon got out Annerino's guidebook to study the canyon's middle strata. "This drawing makes the layers appear very distinct," he said, "but when I look back they blend together."

"I read some in a geology text on the canyon," I offered, "all about intrusions, transgressions, regressions, intertonguing, intraformational undifferentiated juxtaposing. I quickly got the idea that actual canyon formations are a lot messier than the diagrams."

"Temple Butte Limestone is one of the hardest layers to detect," Malcolm explained. "It's not very thick and gets overwhelmed by the Redwall. The lower ten feet of the walls along there look more purple and textured. That's Temple Butte, though it blends quickly with dolomites that overlie the Muav Limestone."

"Do you know where the names come from?" Brandon asked.

"The geologist who first identifies a distinct layer usually names it for a place where he's found a good example of it. That place is then known as the 'type locality.' Temple Butte Limestone gets its name from Temple Butte in the eastern canyon. Bright Angel Shale was named for exposures along Bright Angel Creek. Muav Limestone was identified here in Muav Canyon. The names got adopted around the time of World War I when the Shinumo quadrangle, right where we are, was mapped."

Brandon read the description of how each layer was formed. Temple Butte Limestone accumulated in shallow seas some 370 million years ago. Below this layer a discontinuity of 160 million years has eroded away. The evidentiary record picks up again with Muav Limestone, the upper layer of the three-tiered Tonto Group, the other two strata being Bright Angel Shale and Tapeats Sandstone, all formed by sea deposits during parts of the Cambrian period 530 to 550 million years ago. This sandstone-shale-limestone sequence was named for the Tonto Apaches. Brachiopods, trilobites, fragments of sponges, primitive mollusks, echinoderms, and ancient algae are fossilized throughout the Tonto Group.

When Brandon finished reading the scientific descriptions, he placed his open hand on the canyon wall and looked at it.

"You're spanning a million years," Malcolm remarked.

We did what humans do under such circumstances. We tried to find analogies to make canyon time comprehensible. We failed, recognized we had failed, and, surrendering, found satisfaction in our failure. Brandon put the guidebook away and we passed the final few minutes of our break in silence.

As we shouldered our packs to continue on, Malcolm alerted Brandon that we were about to traverse the Tonto. Canyon hikers have acquired the habit of referring to the horizontal platform of Bright Angel Shale as *the* Tonto even though, technically, it is only the middle layer of the Tonto Group. Malcolm described long, hot days hiking from side canyon to side canyon across the Tonto, following trails made by wild burros before their arrest and expulsion by the National Park Service. Along the way he had developed a strangely deep affection for this intensely hot inner desert shelf. He began reciting its virtues: open panoramas, distinct trails, solid footing—

"Don't bias me," Brandon interrupted. "Let me get to know it myself."

"One can no more know the Tonto in a couple of hours than one can know another person from a brief conversation." He looked downcanyon. "You have to be on the Tonto for a full day or more to adjust and then, the next day or day after, in the middle of the afternoon heat, everything around you shimmering, you give in and become enveloped. Then you can . . . you hear the sun's silence. You're forced to stop hiking and just listen. You can't move. The silence stops you. You have to stop and be part of it." His shoulders and head shivered as he returned to the present. "We'll just be passing through it now, but someday you'll need to do several days on the Tonto if you want to know the inner canyon."

We hiked at an easy pace, gently descending, then mounting a contour rise. On the other side we came out on an open expanse of sparse vegetation. Each small bush, clump of dry grass, or cactus—none more than shin high—claimed a distinct territory. Midday heat radiated off the stark, flat surface of pebbles and sand. Brandon turned to Malcolm, bowed, and with a sweeping gesture said: "Welcome back to the Tonto."

"Thanks," Malcolm replied grinning. "It's good to be back."

Somewhere beneath us the water we'd parted from at the Bright Angel narrows continued its journey, safe from the evaporating effects of the Tonto heat. Or so we thought. Ten minutes farther along the small stream reappeared. Malcolm bent over and touched it reverently. "Water on the Tonto," he said. "But I wouldn't count on it from July on."

Twenty minutes later it was gone again. A bit later we came upon a terraced drop-off where, in a shallow pool at the bottom, small greenish-brown toads, otherwise perfectly camouflaged, revealed themselves by diving. Playfully unpredictable, water appeared, disappeared, reappeared, surprised, and, most of all, refused to be taken for granted.

Around a sharp jutting wall we passed along a cliff that suggested some great cataclysmic event, purple Temple Butte intruded into the greenish Bright Angel Shale pushing it sideways—a tortured, twisted monument to tectonic power. Beyond this geological turmoil White Creek became a pastel rock garden of pebbles from all the upper layers: pink stones, light gray, black, reddish brown, dark brown, tan, and deep red. We speculated that floodwaters rushing down the canyon slowed and dissipated on this long, flat stretch to deposit tons of pebbles and sand, the larger boulders having already been left behind in the sievelike gorges above.

To the west we could see all the way to the rim of Powell Plateau. Overhanging cliffs blocked the view to the east, but we could see where they stopped. The opening ahead would be the last possibility that Holy Grail Temple might be visible. Involuntarily, I picked up the pace, stepping ahead of Brandon and Malcolm. I stumbled over a rock trying to look up while I walked. I leaned forward like a sprinter reaching the finish line and peered out beyond the gorge wall.

11. Quest

"So that's it!" Brandon exclaimed as he came alongside and followed my gaze. He patted my shoulder. "Feel better now, Dad?"

Before I could respond, Malcolm joined us, putting his hand on my other shoulder. "Is that how you remember it?"

"It's strange, but I don't have a specific memory of what it looked like. From the other side of the river it was more an idea than real stone. It's so close here."

"*Vujà dé*," Brandon declared.

"*Vujà dé*," Malcolm repeated. "I'll have to remember that, but I won't if we stand here frying our brains. Let's find some shade for lunch."

As we resumed hiking Brandon remarked, "I thought you'd be more excited, Dad."

"Me? Excited about a rock? No way! I told you this morning I thought we'd blown it out of proportion. Excuse me a minute."

I turned aside a few steps, faced Holy Grail Temple, thrust my fist in the air, and shouted: "Yes! *Vujà dé!*" Then I turned back and rejoined them, my face as placid as I could make it. "As I was saying, just another pretty rock. Whatever the canyon offers. No expectations . . ."

Brandon grinned broadly in what I took to be his pleasure at seeing me exuberant. I real-

99

ized that I liked having him see me openly excited. Detox. Lifting the heavy burden of calm detachment. I did feel euphoric. More than I had been willing to admit to myself, I had developed strong expectations around the symbolism of telling the story of Lancelot and Galahad while gazing at Holy Grail Temple. I liked the symbolism. It was central to this being a different kind of initiation ritual. And I wanted to show Brandon that it was possible to enjoy myths and symbolism, use them and learn from them unabashedly, both rationally and emotionally, without crossing over into mysticism, whether of the New Age or older varieties.

As we followed the parched creekbed through shimmering heat looking for a lunch spot, I studied the details of the Holy Grail Temple formation, gradually letting its specifics blend into an impression of the whole: a distinctly crown-shaped pinnacle adorning a massive tower of Redwall that rises like a castle rampart from the shimmering Tonto plateau. As high as a fifty-story building, the great concave foundation runs even wider than it is tall. Distinct vegetation-draped terraces slope back gently above the sheer Redwall suggesting a protective awning over a great inner courtyard. A pedestal of deep-red Hermit Shale emerges from the center of this Supai canopy. On the pedestal sits a white Coconino tiara, as high at the pinnacle as it is wide and extending well beyond the pedestal at each end. Balanced and symmetric, its great mass seems deliberately sculptured to contrast with and draw attention from its huge island foundation.

We arrived at the edge of a sloping stone floor where White Creek dropped precipitously into the Tapeats gorge. In the western cliff wall just before the drop-off, we spotted an indentation where a major section of mudstone had collapsed. It offered a narrow ledge of shade. We accepted.

We scrambled up into an alcove as high and wide as a large cave, but only ten feet deep. One of many slabs of mudstone bored through with fossilized wormholes served as a lunch table. Enough different kinds of dried animal droppings littered the ledge to be a scatologist's paradise. Below the ledge a pool of slimy green water was alive with frogs and water bugs.

Peering at Holy Grail Temple out the picture window of our alcove, we devoured peanut butter, slimy cheddar cheese, and crackers. Brandon mixed lemonade and passed it around. As our ravenous pace slowed, Malcolm leaned back on his elbows and commented that what struck him about the Grail was the rarity of a natural formation so perfectly proportioned.

"But it's shaped wrong," Brandon said. "I mean, it's awesome, but it's not shaped at all like a chalice."

"Don't be so literal," I chided. "It's Holy Grail *Temple,* a memorial to, but not revealing, the Grail. When the Grail appeared over the Round Table it emitted a wondrous light, but it was covered by a samite cloth. The knights never saw it."

"What's sammy cloth?"

"Sa-mite. The finest medieval cloth interwoven with gold and silver. You do remember the story of the Grail?"

"What a question! I am culturally literate," he declared.

"I'm greatly relieved."

"In senior English a friend and I got very into cultural literacy. This one book listed everything the guardians of Western civilization thought we should know. We went through and disputed every item. Then we realized we'd been had. By going through all that crap to reject it, we ended up learning it. Score: Western civilization 1; radical youth 0. Major downer."

His banter filled the alcove and drifted out onto the Tonto with our laughter. "But when it comes to THE Grail—the holiest, grailiest of quest-inspiring goblets—I'm more than merely culturally literate. I've read *The Once and Future King* and *The Grey King.* I've seen *The Sword and the Stone, Camelot,* and *Excalibur.* I've sought the Grail playing *Dungeons and Dragons.* And, are you ready . . . ?"

"Ready!" we assured him in unison.

"Really ready? Cause this will impress you."

"Really ready."

"I've even been to Holy Grail Temple in the Grand Canyon. I'll tell you about it some time. It's awesome but, to tell the truth, it doesn't look at all like a chalice. So, yeah, to answer your question, I know the story of the Holy Grail."

"You left out *Indiana Jones and the Last Crusade.* Are *you* ready? Choose the right chalice from among hundreds or this alcove will cave in," I challenged, pointing up.

"No problem," Brandon declared, holding up a stone. "This plain, ordinary goblet, not those beautifully jeweled ones." He looked up. "See, I was right."

"You've done better than you know. In some early versions the Grail *was* a stone, the philosopher's stone, *Lapis Exilis,* an ordinary, undistinguished, run-of-the-rockpile stone."

"I've heard of that. Had something to do with alchemy, didn't it? Turning lead into gold or something."

"You're on the right track. In the German version of the Quest written by one Wolfram von Eschenbach in the twelfth century, the Grail was a stone brought to earth by angels who stayed neutral when Lucifer and God had their little falling out. It held the secret of perpetual youth, provided everlasting nourishment, healed the sick, contained knowledge from the original tree, prophesied like an oracle, resurrected the dead, and bore the names of God's chosen. One Grail for all human quests. A rock!"

"How'd it go from being a stone to a chalice?" he asked.

"That's a matter of considerable scholarly debate."

"I detect another 'search of the literature,'" Malcolm grinned.

"Ancient Celtic folktales got Christianized," I replied, ignoring Malcolm.

"Just like that?" Brandon asked.

"Over a couple of centuries. In terms of canyon time, you could say it was 'just like that.' "

"What do you mean, 'Christianized'?"

"Talismans with magical properties appeared often in British folklore. Old legends told of a cauldron of plenty or a platter guarded by virgins in a castle. Everyone in the castle lived off the Grail. It healed them when sick and restored them to youth as they aged. As Celtic tales got combined with Christian themes, the Grail became either the cup Jesus drank from at the Last Supper or the vessel in which Joseph of Arimathea collected Christ's blood."

"I'm confused about the timing," Brandon said. "When did the official version of King Arthur and the Round Table get written and when did it get mixed up with Christianity?"

"Are we keeping you from rock lizard time?" I asked Malcolm.

"This is what you've been waiting for," he smiled. "Don't let all that research go to waste."

I nodded and turned back to Brandon. "A Welsh poem from the sixth century alludes to a great warrior leader named Arthur, though scholars disagree over whether a real, historical Arthur was the inspiration for the later legend. In the eleventh and twelfth centuries different versions of the Arthurian story appeared, a French one by Chrétien de Troyes and the German version I mentioned before. Sir Thomas Malory wrote his account while in prison during the fifteenth century. The adventures of the knights of the Round Table became a popular subject for paintings, which helped spread the legend, since few people read. Interest waxed and waned over the centuries, almost disappearing during the Renaissance, then revived in the Victorian nineteenth century with Wagner's operas and Tennyson's *The Idylls of the King*. Literary scholars started doing research on the various

versions of the legend after that, then T. S. Eliot wrote *The Waste Land,* and
T. H. White popularized the story in *The Once and Future King.* Broadway
picked it up, then Hollywood, and new versions are still coming out, like
Marion Zimmer Bradley's *The Mists of Avalon* told from the point of view
of Morgaine. End of literature review—but by no means end of the literature. We could spend our whole time here reading scholarly papers and still
not make a dent. International societies devoted to the legend are debating
origins and symbols even as we speak."

"Sounds like religious zealots arguing," Brandon remarked.

"There are definite similarities. When Malcolm suggested this area for
your canyon initiation, mainly because of the challenge the route offered, I got
caught up in the symbolic possibilities and began looking for the most
authentic or definitive version of the legend—the one worthy of being retold
here in the canyon. I knew vaguely that different versions existed, some fea-
turing Sir Gawain, some with Perceval as hero, and some with Galahad as the
greatest knight. I should have known better than to think scholars would have
arrived at a consensus, but some lessons have to be learned over and over."

"A consensus about what?"

"There is not and cannot be a definitive telling of the tale. Each version
reflects its author's values and the issues of the times. The earliest versions
are unfinished and confused. Later versions go in all directions, some filling
in historical gaps, some trying to resolve inconsistencies. I got frustrated by
the discrepancies and turned off by the religious interpretations. Then I discovered that not only had the legend been fantasized and Christianized, it
has suffered an even more invidious and demeaning influence in modern
times." I sighed deeply, feigning distress.

"Well?" Brandon asked.

"I wish there were some way of cushioning the blow, but you're a man
now and must know the truth. Like everything in our time, the Grail legend
has been . . . ," I sighed again, "psychologized."

Malcolm laughed. "Sounds like you stumbled into Jung."

"Stumbled into? More like run over by. His disciples are everywhere."

"Your father appears upset that no sociologist has written a great treatise
analyzing the Holy Grail. Have you heard of Jung?"

"We covered him a little in school. Collective unconscious. Archetypes.
Animals."

"*Anima.* The unconscious feminine side of man. And animus, the masculine side of woman," Malcolm explained.

"Hey, I only claimed to be culturally literate, not an expert."

"From a Jungian perspective, we're all experts when we tap into our unconscious. The Grail legend helps us do that. Emma Jung worked on it for thirty years. Robert A. Johnson, another Jungian analyst, has done several short books on masculine and feminine psychology. I like his work analyzing Perceval's quest the best. There's a lot of *anima* in Perceval."

"I detect a literature review coming on," I warned Brandon.

It was Malcolm's turn to ignore me. "If you were going to be limited to just one story as a Jungian, the Grail legend would do quite nicely because it exudes archetypes."

"Are you a Jungian therapist?" Brandon asked.

"Not in a pure sense, but I draw on Jung's work. I'm what you might call eclectic," Malcolm replied.

"Meaning he's pragmatic and utilitarian," I interjected. "Whatever works. The issue then, Dr. Gray, is which legend works best here in the canyon."

"I take it you've made the appropriate selection," he said.

"I haven't. The canyon namers have." I handed Brandon the topo map. "Read the names in this area."

He used a bit of straw to locate each name: "King Arthur Castle . . . Guinevere Castle . . . Elaine Castle . . . Modred Abyss . . . Merlin Abyss . . . Excalibur . . . Lancelot Point."

"And?"

"Further down there's Dox Castle."

"And?"

"Up above are Emerald and Violet Points on Rainbow Plateau."

"And?"

"There's something on the crease, but the lettering's worn."

"Let me see that." Brandon shrugged and handed me the map.

"Prevaricating beneath Holy Grail Temple. You could be in for big trouble." I handed back the map. "Read it."

He scrutinized it painstakingly. "Oh, you mean Galahad Point."

"Thank you. And do you see any Perceval Point, Ridge, Castle, Mount, or Butte?"

"Can't say I do."

"So the canyon namers have chosen."

Malcolm laughed. "He's got us, Brandon."

"Left on my own, I would probably have chosen the Perceval version to retell in deference to my therapist friend here. But the canyon mercifully intervened, for which I am sociologically grateful."

"Okay, the canyon has Galahad Point. So what?"

"Glad you asked. I've found out some things about the Galahad version that make it especially appropriate for your coming of age celebration here. At least I think so. We'll see what you think."

Brandon looked calmly at me, attentive but not riveted, waiting. His pants were so brown from the dust that he seemed joined to the ledge. A small, dried turd was squashed into the waffled center of his boot. The straw he had used in looking at the map clung to his knee. He seemed a natural part of the place, solidly grounded. I exhaled slowly and asserted: "The Galahad legend is a poignant father-son story. Perceval, in contrast, never knew his father."

"Heavy," Brandon said. Malcolm winked at me.

"So what's the story?" Brandon asked.

"Before I tell it, let me explain why it's important beyond my own interest as a father. Jessie Laidley Weston was one of the greatest of the Grail scholars. Working at the turn of the century, she translated different versions of the legend and wrote several books analyzing origins and story variations. After a lifetime of study, she concluded that the three major Grail heros—Gawain, Perceval, and Galahad—constitute a sequence that represents three stages in the development of initiation rites and, more generally, the development of humankind."

"A modest proposition," Malcolm remarked, his grin taking the edge off his mockery.

"Wait till you hear the specifics," I continued, undaunted. "Weston concluded that Gawain's story was originated by ancient nature cults, essentially sun worshipers. His heroics were celebrated as a rite of spring because he broke the winter spell and brought the vegetation god back to vitality. But Gawain was more a mythical being than a man. Having no human failures, he didn't need initiation or salvation.

"Then along came Judeo-Christian mythology and separated humans from nature with expulsion from the Garden. God was no longer the concrete sun, but the abstract everything. The sun was dependable. Yahweh was arbitrary. Sun rituals were celebrations and thanksgivings. Judeo-Christian-Islamic rituals have become confessions of sin—supplications and genuflections of the weak before the almighty. So the pagan hero, Gawain, first of the Grail winners, was deposed by Christian monks and replaced by an idealized innocent, Perceval, trying to make his way in an evil world while struggling to decipher God's intent and fulfill God's will."

"Major bummer for Gawain," Brandon remarked.

"Weston would have agreed. She decided that, in the end, Perceval was an unsatisfactory hero because he lacked intelligence. He was a simpleton—a *dummkopf*—incapable of assimilating and profiting from his experiences. He happens on the Grail castle before he even knows a quest is underway. He sees the Grail at a banquet for the Grail king, but doesn't understand its import. He's a naive fool who doesn't know what's going on around him or to him. His misadventures provide lots of grist for the Jungian mill of opposites—light and dark, masculine and feminine, virtue and sin—and he does heroic things, but his obliviousness keeps him from being a satisfying or fulfilling hero."

"And Galahad?" Brandon asked.

"He supersedes Perceval in every respect, but especially intelligence. Galahad displays confidence, courage, and determination from the beginning. He never wavers or fails. Unlike Perceval, he doesn't just wander aimlessly around falling into adventures. He seeks challenges. He chooses a path—as opposed to having it chosen for him by God or fate—and lets nothing stand in his way as he follows it."

"Galahad's intelligence and determination were obviously due to having a father to instruct him," Malcolm quipped.

I leaned forward in a bow. "That would not be for me to say, Elder Gray, but nothing in Weston disputes that conclusion, though I don't recall her saying it with such forceful insight and clarity."

Brandon began turning his head this way and that, sniffing loudly. "Anyone else notice that all these little dried lumps suddenly smell really strong?"

"I'll tell you what Weston sniffed out. She was initially perplexed by Perceval's anointment as the Grail hero after Gawain. After painstaking research and scholarly contemplation, she concluded that it was precisely because Perceval was fatherless that he replaced Gawain, and then Galahad superseded Perceval in part because of his father."

"I don't get it," Brandon said.

"Perceval was originally known as *le fils de la veuve dame,* meaning 'son of the widow,' a common designation for initiates. In mythic terms, the widow is the earth in winter bereft of the sun, so Perceval is a son of the earth who has lost his father, the sun, and that's the connection back to Gawain."

"Father Sky, Mother Earth," Malcolm interjected sitting up. "They're central to Native American mythology in the Southwest."

"A common theme," I affirmed. "So Perceval had a heavenly father, but no earthly one. The Galahad version brings the earthly father back into the story and gives him a significant role in preparing his son for the Grail quest. The downside is that Galahad's story also gets mired in medieval Christian morality, especially the notion that his resolute virginity was what made him worthy of attaining the Grail."

"Did Perceval ever have sex?" Brandon asked.

"Yes, a consummation of great passion and love that brought with it lands and castles."

"Let's see that map. You sure there's no Perceval Point?"

"I'm sure," I grinned.

"Galahad's father obviously wasn't a virgin," Malcolm observed.

"Not even close. Lancelot was Galahad's father."

"Lancelot! Of course. Now I remember," Brandon said.

"Lancelot conceived Galahad with Lady Elaine under enchantment, thinking she was Guinevere. Most popular renditions of the legend focus on Lancelot's passion for Guinevere and his betrayal of Arthur. Galahad is largely ignored. He's so perfect, he's not very interesting. I didn't pay attention to him either until after I realized Perceval wasn't on the map. Then I started probing beneath Galahad's boring, unidimensional appearance. Galahad and Lancelot have the most positive father-son relationship I found in all the myths I came across."

"Positive how?"

"King Arthur dubbed Lancelot the greatest knight in the world, but Lancelot knew he was blemished. Galahad was knighted by Lancelot — essentially initiated by his own father in violation of all known traditional initiation norms—and then went to Camelot to take the *Siege Perilous* which identified him as the greatest knight in the world. Son replaced father, and the father not only didn't resist, he celebrated. After the veiled Grail appeared above the Round Table, Lancelot and Galahad separated because the knights decided that it would be inappropriate to quest as a group, for each had to find his own path and prove himself worthy. However, after a number of separate adventures and battles, Galahad and Lancelot encountered each other, though neither recognized the other. They fought long and hard, jousting furiously, until Galahad finally unhorsed Lancelot, the first time he'd ever lost, and the most exhausting engagement Galahad had ever known. Then, each revealed by his courage and strength, they recognized each other and embraced. The next day a ship appeared from nowhere. They boarded it and spent six months sailing together. What happened during that time is not reported. It was their first and only extended time together. After six months they drew near to shore and a white knight called Galahad to come forth. He led Galahad to the Grail castle. In some way not revealed in the story, that six months completed Galahad's preparation for fulfilling the Grail quest."

"That's it?" Brandon asked.

"Not quite. Lancelot returned to Camelot. King Arthur wanted to hear all about his quest adventures, but all Lancelot wanted to talk about was his six months with Galahad on the ship. Lancelot had found something that meant even more to him than the Grail. He told Arthur that being with Galahad had been the best time in his life and changed him forever."

"*Ramsperd dudicious,*" Brandon declared in his own language.

I looked at Malcolm for his reaction. He was staring out at the Tonto, his arms folded across his chest, his head resting peacefully on his pack. His countenance appeared placid, merely hinting at lips indecipherable beneath his long moustache. When Malcolm showed no sign of responding, Brandon looked back at me with raised eyebrows.

"That's his quixotic look," I explained. "It's an old rock-lizard camouflage. Rock lizards take on a look of deep serenity to disguise the fact that they're in a state of trance, oblivious and therefore vulnerable. It's an evolutionary adaptation to—"

"Quixotic?" he interrupted. "I've come across it, but—"

"I withdraw the word. We've already got the Arthurian legend and Iron John with us. Let's leave Don Quixote out of it for now."

As I laid back and drifted contentedly into rock-lizard time, I heard Brandon say, "Galahad probably had great sex during those six months they were off adventuring. That's what got him ready for the Grail."

12. Totem

I sensed something different as I emerged from rock lizard time. Human intensity mingled with the alcove shade, disturbing its calm. I tried looking out across the Tonto plateau, but the bright light hurt my eyes. I raised up on my elbows and squinted through the shimmering heat. A low "shhhh" greeted my movement. I followed the sound and found a likeness of Brandon transformed from boogie-ready energy to sculpturelike stone. Hunched forward, arms wrapped around legs, his silencing "shhhh" was barcly pcrccptiblc through motionlcss lips. I turned my head slowly to follow his gaze and, seeing nothing, sensed that he had become stone to avoid attracting attention.

The alcove wall riddled with bore holes; the only shade on the Tonto; heavy mudstone slabs; dark, recessed corners. The evidence mounted. Rattlesnake. The canyon's famous pink rattler. While we'd been making noise it would have stayed hidden, but in the quiet of rock lizard time . . .

I turned slowly toward Malcolm. His floppy felt hat hid his face. I watched his chest and stomach gently rise and fall, saw nothing on or around him, and turned back toward Brandon. He remained transfixed. I tried to remember what the field guide said. Did it always rattle before attacking? Could it bite more than once? What was the latest thinking on treatment? Of seven thousand people bitten annually, how many had died? I vaguely remembered being impressed by the smallness of the number.

Brandon showed no fear, only stillness. How long had he been sitting like that? How long could he keep it up? Maybe it was only a black widow or a scorpion.

"Where?" I whispered, forcing the sound from my throat through still lips.

"Shhhh" came back insistently, but his head seemed to nod forward ever so slightly.

I followed his nod down, lowering my eyes as much as possible without moving my head so I could peer just below the ledge. Malcolm stirred. "Shhhh," Brandon warned. Malcolm reached for his hat and rolled on his side, propping himself up on one elbow. "What's up?" he whispered. "You boys seem tense."

"Shhhh," I replied.

Again Brandon nodded slightly. This time some movement on the Tonto caught my eye. I squinted out, but couldn't detect anything. Fighting the temptation to ask what he saw, I scoured the wide, rounded ridge on the far side of the dry creekbed where I thought I'd seen the movement. The reddish brown terrain was spotted with clumps of dark green and boulders of white above the pinkish-gray floor. The blend of light and landscape played tricks on my eyes, like looking through a window that has a reflection on it and not being able to distinguish what's the reflection and what's outside the window. The canyon changed before my eyes as my perception shifted from two-dimensional postcard to three-dimensional world. What at first appeared as a single, rising slope gradually separated into a series of undulating terraces and hills. In that newly detected world, poised atop a lower escarpment, I finally found what Brandon saw.

I felt pressure in my chest and realized I was holding my breath. Exhaling, I lost him and had to begin all over again the process of focusing to lift his camouflage. I found the horns first, two thick arches curling up and back, crowning a head that might have seemed burdened if not for the strength and power declared by his ready stance and angled body. His front legs were positioned higher than the back so the line of his body projected upward to the neck which, sloping more steeply still, accentuated the spiral horns. His thick wool was so saturated with the colors of the Tonto that he appeared from the distance as a grayish-white boulder.

He took a few steps and stopped, then a few more and brought his hind legs down even with the front until he was turned sideways, though his head seemed not to move as he kept his eyes focused in a steady gaze at our shade. He continued approaching a few steps at a time and I noticed for the first time that he was following a faint trail along the eroded hillside. When he got within half a football field we could see him quite distinctly. His horns appeared rough like a seashell, his wool carried bits of bush and matted dirt, and his eyes—large, gleaming marbles on either side of his head—seemed to penetrate into the rock behind us. What I lacked in knowledge, I supplied with speculation. I imagined him to be a fully mature male surveying his territory.

As he continued slowly in our direction I whispered: "Do you see more than one?"

"Normally, they're in groups, but he seems alone," Malcolm replied softly.

"Normally?" I repeated, finding it impossible to associate that concept in any way with this extraordinary desert apparition.

"Shhhh," Brandon hissed.

In the silence that followed, the bighorn approached until no farther away than a neighbor's yard. He looked to the left, then to the right, then stared directly at us. In slow motion I reached inside a side pocket of my pack for the small camera I was carrying and brought it up to my eye.

"Dad, don't!"

I aimed and snapped. The bighorn stiffened, but did not retreat. Brandon shot me a dirty look. "That's enough," he declared parentally.

I put the camera down and settled into observing where he directed his attention: directly at Brandon. Brandon and bighorn seemed locked in mutual contemplation for some time. Then, abruptly, the horns turned away, head and body followed, and he proceeded northeast along the hillside, up canyon, in the direction from which we had come. Every so often he stopped and looked back. We watched until he disappeared up Redwall Canyon moving toward Holy Grail Temple.

"That's very rare," Malcolm said, "very rare. In all the years I've been hiking the canyon, I've never encountered a lone bighorn up close."

"I was reading *Desert Solitaire* on the way out here," Brandon said. "Abbey wrote that in all his time in the Canyonlands and Grand Canyon he never saw a bighorn. It was like a real gap for him. He'd probably be annoyed that I got to see one my first time out."

"You think he was looking for water or shade?" I asked.

"He has too many options for water and shade to have kept coming that close to us," Malcolm asserted. "He knew we were here from the time he stopped on that first hill."

"What then?" I asked.

He turned to Brandon. "That had the makings of a totem encounter."

"Really?! Meaning what?"

"A totem animal connects you to the Great Mystery. It represents the ancestral spirit from which you're descended. When you acknowledge your totem and accept it into consciousness, its characteristics and power become available to you. You can learn about yourself by studying its nature and habits. In time of trouble or danger, it can be an ally offering you the survival solutions and strategies it has used for centuries."

"It sounds . . . religious. I'm not exactly a believer."

"In what?"

"God."

"Do you believe you just saw a bighorn?"

"Sure, but I've also seen ants and lizards and birds."

"Did the ants and lizards and birds walk up and look you in the eyes?"

"No, but—"

"Did you feel a special connection to any of the ants and lizards and birds?"

"What do you mean by 'connection'?" Brandon asked.

"You're right. Language isn't adequate." Malcolm paused. A far-off look came over his face. "A few years ago I was hiking alone along Clear Creek Trail going from Bright Angel Canyon toward Zoroaster Canyon. A raven flew over me and landed on a rock about as far ahead of me as the bighorn was from you. I stopped to watch him and he watched back. After a while I started toward him. He flew off and landed again farther ahead. All afternoon he stayed with me, sometimes flying high overhead, sometimes disappearing above the cliffs, and often stopping ahead and waiting for me to catch up.

"I didn't think much of it at first, but after a couple of miles, I started feeling . . . a connection. I liked his company. He never squawked or cawed, he just stayed with me. At some point a thought popped into my head and wouldn't leave: 'This bird is choosing me.' I tried talking to him, but he never made a sound and never let me get too close. I finally said something like, 'Okay, have it your way. It's your canyon. I'll shut up.'

"Suddenly, in late afternoon, just before I reached where I planned to camp, he circled around, flew up behind me, and let out a single screech.

QUORRKKK . . . the sound reverberated in waves like a rock hitting hard against the gorge wall. Then he vanished across the river. As I hiked on, I knew—I had this sense—that I'd been chosen."

"Then what? Do you have to accept being chosen?"

"First, I needed to learn more about the raven's characteristics. I talked to a Navajo elder and did some reading. The raven plays the trickster in a lot of Southwest Indian legends. He schemes and uses magic or cunning to get what he wants. While most birds have a dominant flying pattern, he uses them all—rolls, dives, circles, makes steep ascents, glides, soars, flies long distances, does short aerials, whatever. And, of course, the raven is black."

"Evil and death," Brandon joked.

"Only among white men," Malcolm retorted instantly. "He scavenges large game so he's often associated with death in European tales, but for many Native peoples, black represents mystery, especially raven black. It's a changeable black—deep purple or blue—and when the sun hits it just right, it becomes phosphorescent white. Instantaneously, just for a second, it shows its white, then the light shatters into a spectrum of color, is absorbed, and returns to black. Trickster black. Raven black. The color of the void from before time began. The raven was present at creation, in some legends is the creator. As a medicine totem, raven presides over the healing circle, bringing the power of creation from the void of the Great Mystery to change consciousness and infuse life energy. Raven, flying without boundaries, moves between worlds so he can carry messages to and from higher powers the ancients, Father Sky, Mother Earth, the Great Spirit or transport understanding from one's unconscious to consciousness."

"Sounds like the perfect totem for a therapist," Brandon mused.

Malcolm smiled.

"But I still don't understand," Brandon continued. "Did you ever do something to, I don't know what, acknowledge it somehow, I mean, to accept the totem? Is there some kind of ceremony?"

"No, but ravens began appearing in my dreams. Once, I dreamed that I was a raven, but flying high over a seacoast, not the canyon. Flying felt wonderful. Not like being in an airplane. I was unbounded, soaring, free . . . a raven. I was amazed at flying. Afterward, it didn't feel like I had dreamed I was flying. I had actually flown. I knew I had flown.

"The dream stayed with me, the raven feeling grew with each dreaming, but I was puzzled by the seacoast. Then I came across an Australian Aboriginal myth, from their tribal dreaming, that explains fresh-water mussels. It tells of a raven who picked up a mussel from the coast and dropped it inland. Then I understood that the raven wasn't just available to me in the canyon.

"I continue to learn about ravens. Just last year a field biologist, Bernd Heinrich, published his studies of ravens in the wild. He dedicated the book "TO ALL THE RAVEN MANIACS WHO ANSWERED THE CALL." I know what he meant. I have a feeling of belonging to ravens. I wake up joyful from raven dreams, even when they should be scary, like a dream where the raven's as big as a house and watching me piercingly with one eye. Not menacingly, but piercingly. It feels good to be watched. . . .

"I want to return as a raven. I think they're a higher-order existence. When one is flying in front of me, I know I'm headed in the right direction. And I know one more thing . . ."

We waited. Brandon looked at him questioningly. Malcolm stood and stepped behind Brandon, put his hands solidly on his shoulders and massaged them. After a while, he spoke, his words deliberate and measured. "Raven reality . . . totem power—these are but names for imagination. Whatever we call it, however we name it, from the outside, subjected to analytical scrutiny, it will appear mystical and unreal. And it is unreal—constructed reality . . . emotional and irrational. Once that was an obstacle for me. Now it's freeing because I don't have to fit it into some intellectual framework. From the inside, it's about *feeling* connected. The feeling, the lived experience, is real enough. So you start with the physical reality of the bighorn—we all saw him—and see where he touches you, where he leads. It looked like he offered a connection, but only you can know for sure because only you can know what you feel . . . he won't impose."

"I'm still not sure what you do to accept."

"I accepted the raven by paying attention to my dreams, being open to his company, and drawing on his power when need be. You'll have to figure out what the bighorn means and, if you choose, how to let him know you accept."

"But he's gone."

"Only if you let him be gone." Malcolm patted Brandon playfully on the head and resumed sitting cross-legged.

In the silence that followed I considered how to respond. The specifics of Malcolm's account were mostly new to me, but not his overall mystical orientation. I was ready to counter his eclectic spirituality with scientific skepticism, pointing out how he had attached supernatural meaning to quite ordinary, explainable, and natural occurrences. I was tempted to discard my silence as one would throw off a black cloak in the desert sun, not to undercut Malcolm, but to make sure Brandon heard the contrary evidence. At the same time, I didn't want to get in the way of Brandon asking his own questions and making up his own mind. Malcolm had indulged me in the telling of the Grail legend. I would indulge him, for the moment, in his totem tale and study how Brandon reacted. Like the bighorn's slow, careful approach to our alcove, I decided to approach slowly and observe more carefully before deciding whether to charge into debate or wait for a better time. I was brought out of my reverie by Brandon: "Say some more, Malcolm, about totems as connections."

"Okay, take the bighorn. Prehistoric peoples honored bighorns in pictographs. The pottery of the Mimbres people, relatives of the Anasazi, was often decorated with bighorns. The tribal logo of the Havasupai people in the western canyon prominently displays the bighorn. These images connect." He turned to Brandon. "Think about your totem as a memory aid—a kind of mnemonic. It can remind you of your connection to nature, to the universe, to the Great Mystery—however you want to think about it. It can help you recall characteristics you want to cultivate and power available to you. It can offer a point of reference in unmapped territory. Or, when you find yourself cruising along some busy thoroughfare bombarded by neon poisons, your totem will send you a warning. And when your mind is jumping hither and yon as if someone was flicking you with a remote, the bighorn can be a focus for meditation, channeling your thoughts . . . for we all become what we think about.

"Any time you return mentally to this place and look again into the eyes of the bighorn, he'll be with you. He's not gone unless you drive him away or let him wander off through neglect. What is true of the mind, body, feeling self, and spirit is also true for your totem: Use it or lose it. That's the universal law."

I had never heard Malcolm speak so forcefully. When he spoke of returning mentally to this place, he turned away from Brandon and looked out over the Tonto as if fixing it in memory. Brandon stared in the direction the bighorn had gone. After a short silence he continued speaking, not to Brandon, not to me, not even to the raven, but to the canyon.

"Not a day goes by that I don't come here. I fly to Apache Point and swoop down through Royal Arch Creek to Elves Chasm. Or I may glide along Phantom Creek, circle Deva Temple, buzz Brahma Temple, and come to rest atop Zoroaster Temple. On hectic days I may only have time for a quick flyover, but not a day goes by that I don't come here." He paused. "And I sleep here most every night."

I looked away, feeling embarrassed, as if I'd happened on someone making love. After a while Brandon turned toward me. "What'd you think, Dad?"

"Malcolm's affection for the canyon is so deep it's sometimes hard to tell where metaphor begins and ends. I was thinking of asking him to fly us up on top of Holy Grail Temple to get a closer look."

"Sorry," Malcolm replied. "No passengers. You'll have to learn to fly yourself. And Brandon will have to climb, like the bighorn he is."

"I wasn't asking what you thought about Malcolm's totem," Brandon explained. "I want to know what you think about my having a totem, about the bighorn."

"You'll have to decide that for yourself. If you're going to have a totem, the bighorn seems quite serviceable. It's not bound to an existing trail, so it goes wherever it chooses. And it climbs or descends with equal ease and agility—an uphiller and downhiller. Seems a pretty good fit—if you're going to have a totem."

"Do you have one? Before coming to the canyon I never heard you say anything about totems."

"Totems have always struck me a bit like sports mascots. You may have noticed that calling themselves the Timberwolves hasn't helped Minnesota's pro basketball team win many games. I have trouble imagining that calling yourself a bighorn will change who you are. But it works for Malcolm, so you have to decide. For my part, I quite like your logo-less cap."

Brandon turned to Malcolm. "I guess Dad won't be coming with us to the top of Holy Grail Temple tonight," he winked.

"Good idea," I said. "Put your new bighorniness to the test. Let me know what you discover. And take my camera with you. I'd like a shot from the top of the Grail."

13. Tapeats

Before we departed the Tonto alcove, Brandon got Harvey from Malcolm's pack. "There's something here I want to be sure we do. We should come on it pretty soon." He read Harvey.

> Go down to the bed below the Tapeats through a ravine. To the north there is the deepest and narrowest fissure in the Tapeats in the park. A huge boulder is lodged between the walls 80 feet up just as it was when the Kolbs photographed it sixty or more years ago. (p. 61)

We climbed down from the alcove moaning as our stiff joints protested being on the move again. Brandon headed right for the drop-off into the Tapeats. The sudden opening looked like a serrated storm sewer leading into the center of the earth. Malcolm explained that we'd have to hike around to a less steep point of descent. We lingered there studying the rough pancakelike layers of pinkish-brown sandstone while he explained their origins, pointing out how the weathered cliffs revealed long periods of buildup followed by exposure and erosion. Over centuries the ebb and flow of turbulent coastal waters wore away coarse-grained sand

117

dunes deposited 550 million years ago. Shallow tides heavy with sediment scoured the dunes leaving behind a herringbone stratification. These diagonal crossbeds gave the appearance of shallow layers of sand deposited one after the other on top of each other when, more likely, we were looking at the top of a 300-foot-high dune that had been worn away and cut into by abrasive tides. In many places the lower foundation had eroded away creating a precarious and impassable overhang at the top.

"Why's it called Tapeats?" Brandon asked.

"The geological type locality is Tapeats Creek, which flows from Tapeats Spring around Tapeats Cave and empties into Tapeats Rapids below Tapeats Terrace in Tapeats Amphitheater," Malcolm responded, the series of Tapeats rising like a symphonic crescendo as he added increasing emphasis to each repetition.

"But where does the word 'Tapeats' come from?"

"It means white men don't understand Indian culture."

"It does?!"

"That's what it means to me. It's actually named after a Paiute Indian, Ta Pits, who showed Major John Wesley Powell what Powell subsequently called Tapeats Creek. Powell reported that Ta Pits claimed to own the creek and surrounding drainage. My guess is that Ta Pits said something like, 'This is my place.' "

"What do you think he meant?"

"That he had some special relationship to that place. Maybe he'd been initiated there, or had a vision, or received his totem there, or just felt connected with the Earth there. What he didn't mean was that he held deed and title as his personal property. Only white men seem to have to own something to feel able to say, 'This is my place.' "

"Heavy," Brandon said.

Malcolm led the way around the drop-off. We moved sluggishly after lunching and rock lizarding, but the bypass along the edge of the Tonto Platform took us to a path that descended easily through the upper Tapeats back into the dry bed of White Creek where we hiked through low cliff walls. The pack straps and belt soon settled snugly into my shoulders and hips, and I fell into the rhythm of afternoon endurance, caught up in watching my shadow seep out of my boots. I looked up to find Brandon well ahead, excitedly waving at us to hurry, a gesture entirely incongruent with the still landscape. He had discovered, only ten minutes below our luncheon alcove, the narrow fissure described by Harvey.

We were never in danger of missing it. The dry creekbed led right up to the fissure, a slit in the earth a hundred yards long but just wide enough for a person to fall through, a black crack in the otherwise omnipresent illumination of midafternoon sun. The darkness below accentuated the great globe of solar heat above, radiating so white that a glance skyward inflicted instant pain. Brightness overwhelmed details of the landscape, making it seem like we had wandered into an overexposed photograph. I wore two layers of sunglasses: dark clip-ons over my prescription shades. Still, my head ached from squinting.

Staring into the darkness below brought relief from the desert glare, but revealed no details within the subterranean chamber that had once been a sea cave. In contrast to its searing skin, the Earth's innards looked cool, protective, and inviting.

"It's changed since Harvey and the Kolbs were here," Brandon asserted. "Harvey described only one boulder in the fissure."

Suspended over the mouth of the opening, fifty yards apart, two boulders were lodged below the lip of the fissure, each denied access to the depths by no more than six inches.

"That crack doesn't look like it will hold for long," I speculated. "In no more than a few million years it'll be worn away enough for the boulder to drop through."

"Then we'd better hurry to see what's below," Brandon urged. "Where do we go down?"

"Probably at the end down there."

But it wasn't that simple. We had to climb above the Tapeats and hike over a ridge on the Tonto to find a way around the crack and down into the gorge where the lower ravine of Redwall Canyon joined Muav. "Take your last look at Holy Grail Temple," Malcolm advised. "Once we get inside the Tapeats cliffs we won't see it any more until we come back out."

At the bottom of the ravine we came out on the floor of the Tapeats gorge. We left our packs and climbed up into the cavern that led back below the fissure. The reddish-brown mudstone walls contrasted markedly with the pink and gray pebbles that crunched beneath our feet. A trickle of water along one side and small pools of mud collected dampness from the seeping walls. Though cooler than seemed possible only eighty feet below the blistering desert, I was more surprised at how much light pierced the fissure. What had seemed impenetrable darkness from above appeared as a slice of luminous blue from below.

We stopped directly beneath the first suspended chockstone. Brandon had black-and-white film in his camera to take what he hoped would be Ansel Adams–type artistic shots of canyon formations. He deemed the natural tiger's-eye overhead the first real challenge to his artistry. He paced back and forth, peering through his hands, as he tried to determine the best angle.

"Have you read about Adams?" Malcolm asked.

"Why?" Brandon asked back.

"To understand the values that informed his approach to photography."

"I've seen his photographs," Brandon responded. He stopped and took a single shot. "Done," he announced.

He noticed Malcolm look at me quizzically and my return shrug. "I brought one roll of twenty-four exposures. I don't like taking a hundred shots of something and picking the best. I allow myself one shot. It either works or doesn't. No big deal."

As Brandon moved on to the far end, I lingered and took several shots from different angles with my camera, musing that photographic aesthetics did not appear to be genetic.

At the north end, the narrows ended in a small grotto twenty feet above the floor, hollowed out and arched at the top like a sarcophagus. Rust-colored lines of water flowed down from the opening across horizontal streaks of pinks, grays, and whites. Deep-green moss and long, draping maidenhair ferns framed the entrance. Brandon managed to scale the smooth surface and climb into the alcove. He stood on his tiptoes and stretched both arms upward as if trying to measure the height of the opening. He touched one side, then the other. He spun around on one foot and faced inward, his arms stretched out in a V. I had expected him to look out of place—for any live human presence to seem out of place in that open tomb—but his youth blended with the ancient cavern in a natural continuum of time.

He stood motionless, seemingly fully absorbed, until suddenly spinning back around. He looked directly at me and turned visibly self-conscious in a startling transformation of countenance. From youth at one with nature to gangly teenager aware of parental scrutiny, his contemplative expression turned into a mischievous grin. He cupped his hands to his mouth and shouted at the top of his lungs: "*Yebiday.*" Then again: "*Yebiday.*" He listened a moment, then called to us: "Stir up some sound. Maybe we can shake a boulder loose if we all shout at once." He blasted his vocal trumpet— "*YE . . . BI . . . DAY . . .*"—but the sound came out muted as if absorbed before it could bounce. He looked surprised, tried a few more blasts, but failing to enlist our help, gave up and jumped down. "Let's make for the river."

We returned to our packs and descended down White Creek between ever higher Tapeats cliffs, stained in long streaks of sometimes brown, sometimes white residues. We stepped back and forth across a narrow but steady stream as it meandered through the pebbled creekbed. Bright-green maidenhair fern grew abundantly under and out of the gorge walls. Every so often we'd come to a lone cottonwood tree straining to get what sunlight it could in the narrows, leaning and curved to form an arch across the creek. I stopped beside one arched specimen growing at an angle over a cut in the eastern wall, an opening so narrow and indistinct that had it not been for the cottonwood I'm sure I would have missed it. I leaned against the trunk, impressed at how solid it felt despite being partially uprooted. I lingered to study the survival niche it had found: the stream near its roots, leaves perfectly positioned to capture the morning rays of sunlight. I moved to sit on a nearby boulder, looked up through the cottonwood's arch and was startled to see Holy Grail Temple framed perfectly by the opening, like looking through a keyhole into another world. The brilliant light above the gap washed out the Temple's foundation so that the Coconino crown appeared suspended in a phosphorescent fountain. The cottonwood's deep green leaves framed the upper part of this picture providing living contrast to the Tapeats brown, red Hermit Shale, Coconino white, blue sky, the ephemeral light above, and the dark shadow in which I stood.

"What in the world are you looking at?" Brandon called, starting back.

"What've you boys spotted?" Malcolm asked, following Brandon back. "Ah hah, so we hadn't seen the last of it."

I took off my pack, rested it against the cottonwood, and sat down. "It's kind of soon for a break, isn't it?" Brandon wondered, his question a statement.

"I want to show you how rituals are created," I replied. "It'll only take a couple of minutes."

Brandon looked at Malcolm quizzically. Malcolm shrugged.

"Take off your pack," I directed, "and squeeze in that cut. See if you can climb up to that first overhang."

"Why?"

"Just humor me."

He did as I asked. "Back in and up just a bit. . . . That's it. Now turn and look up. . . . Hold . . ." Slowly I chanted "*Ye-be-day. Ye-be-day.*" I motioned to Malcolm to join me.

When we stopped, Brandon climbed back down.

"You didn't take a picture," he observed as he approached.

"I wasn't trying to get a picture. I was trying to get at ritual."

"How so?"

"Rituals are born by ascribing special significance to some occurrence so that it can be remembered, repeated, and memorialized. We thought we'd seen the last of Holy Grail Temple, but, by accident, I happened to glance up at just the right time to catch this unusual framed view. You two passed by without noticing. It's a small step to attaching mystical significance to my sighting."

"Like sighting a bighorn," Brandon grinned. "But what's the ritual?"

"The ritual significance comes from imprinting the event in our minds, our collective consciousness if you prefer Jungian lingo, by associating it with some legend or story. So I sight Holy Grail Temple through this unusual crevice, with the afternoon sun illuminating it perfectly, and suddenly I remember a scene from the Grail legend. Seems pretty magical, doesn't it."

"What scene?"

"The night after Lancelot unknowingly jousted with Galahad and was defeated, and before they boarded the mysterious ship, Lancelot had terrible nightmares, including a vision of the Grail procession and a voice telling him that he'd never attain the Grail because he was 'harder than stone, more bitter than wood, and more naked than the fig tree.' From that moment forth, he knew he'd never attain the Grail, meaning he'd never hold it in his hands, never touch it, never possess it, never be able to take it back to Camelot to King Arthur. He came to realize that his betrayal of Arthur through his love for Guinevere made him unworthy. But, unexpectedly, he did get to see the Grail. When Galahad was called forth from their ship by a white knight, Lancelot followed from a distance. He came to a great castle guarded by two lions. Lancelot's sword was useless against them, but when he set it aside, they allowed him to enter. He went from chamber to chamber, finding all the doors open but all the rooms empty, until he came to a final closed door. He forced it open and was blinded by light. Once his eyes adjusted he saw Galahad with the Holy Grail. He tried to enter but some force hit him like a blast from a furnace and knocked him into a coma for twenty-four days. When he awakened, he was being cared for in another castle. Once he overcame his surprise at being alive, he proclaimed that his quest had been fulfilled after all. He had seen his son with the Grail." As I finished, I pointed up toward the Grail Temple through the crevice where Brandon had just been. I took a swallow from my canteen and passed it to Brandon. He drank and passed it to Malcolm. "And with that shared drink from the same canteen we bring liquid significance, water of life, to the ritual of the father seeing the son with the Grail. Ommmm," I chanted.

"Being in the canyon makes you weird, Dad."

"You've just never seen me detoxed before. Besides, why pass up a chance to reflect on how a place like this, a place seemingly beyond human comprehension, would give rise to religion, superstition, and ritual."

"You might even communicate with ghosts here," Malcolm added in a tone ambiguously between mocking and serious. "You're looking at William Bass's tomb up there. His will stipulated that his cremated remains be scattered over Holy Grail Temple. This was his trail in life. It's still his place after death—and not just because the trail's named for him."

"Who took the ashes up there?" Brandon asked.

"They were dropped from a plane."

Brandon lifted his eyebrows in surprise. Malcolm chuckled. "Yes, planes were already flying over the canyon in the 1930s."

Brandon thought for a moment. "That means some of the ashes could have fallen down here."

I jumped to my feet. "I'd give it a high probability rating, I would. Knowing this spot was here, Bass would have calculated it that way. This is holy ground. I didn't glance up by accident. Bass must have stopped me here on purpose and made me glance up. Then he implanted the idea of the ritual in my mind. Wow. I'm been having a mystical experience. Quick, Brandon. Look up the height of Holy Grail Temple in Annerino."

While he did so I got out my notebook.

"6,703 feet."

I spoke out loud as I wrote. "When William Wallace Bass chose the 6,703-foot-high Holy Grail Temple as the place for his remains to be spread over the canyon, he knew that some of him would fall to a precise point on North Bass Trail, the only point of direct exposure from Grail to Trail in the Tapeats gorge. Those who pass by when the light is just right and are attentive enough to spot the opening may wish to stop for a moment of ritual remembrance. A lucky few may even commune with the ghost of Bass." I put the notebook away. "There. We've added to Bass's legend. Now all we have to figure out is how to get the word out."

"You can't just make up stuff like that," Brandon objected.

"You can't?" I asked, eyes wide.

As we continued our descent down through the Tapeats, I thought about how the many and varied versions of the Grail legend epitomized the human capacity, perhaps even the human need, to add to, change details of, and otherwise alter stories and their meanings to fit emergent beliefs, new circumstances, and successive generations. Much of the conflict in history, whether political, religious, or cultural, could be interpreted as power struggles over which version of a legend would prevail.

We didn't stop again in the Tapeats. It had taken us about a half day to traverse the twenty million years of geological history from the Bright Angel Shale below the Redwall down through the Tapeats. But that was nothing compared to the millions of years we were about to cross with a single step. We had arrived at the Great Unconformity.

14. The Great Unconformity

The Great Unconformity spans 250 million years, once massive mountains now vanished below the Tapeats. Unconformities of smaller scale, called disconformities, include a gap between Muav Limestone and Temple Butte Limestone of 125 million years; another between the Supai Formation and the Redwall of 25 million years; four minor disconformities that distinguish the layers within the Supai Formation and mark its boundary with the Hermit Shale; and a recent disconformity, a very minor one, between the Toroweap and Kaibab formations. The "Greatest Unconformity"—450 million years, the equivalent of 10 percent of Earth's existence—*nonexists* between the Vishnu Schist and the Bass Formation. Taken together, the two unconformities and multiple disconformities account for 900 million years, more than half the span of canyon time. If all these layers remained, the Grand Canyon would be twice as deep—two miles from rim to river.

As we hiked we had a leisurely discussion about the scientific detective work involved in discerning unconformities. Brandon was fascinated by the idea of studying something that's not there. He made a leap to theology. We considered the parallels, which offered an opportu-

125

nity to consider what constitutes evidence, and concluded that if one has to believe in something that doesn't exist, better the Great Unconformity than God. At least we know it was once here and why it's gone.

I felt exhilarated by this conversation. It was precisely the kind of lengthy, leisurely dialogue on matters of fundamental importance that were difficult to have in the busyness and separation of modern life. What seemed like a hundred other possibilities came to mind, subjects I wanted to discuss with my now-adult son, man to man. I thought about what other metaphors the canyon geology might offer and speculated about what focus would emerge in the segment of "Iron John" we would read that night, anticipating learning what Brandon would find in it.

Below the Tapeats the flow of White Creek gathered force with frequent deep pools and small cascading falls. The creek cut through a gorge whose walls got higher and steeper as we descended. As the iron-bearing Hakatai Shale became predominant, White Creek offered a kaleidoscopic display of multicolored, varietal rock. Columns of dark brown streaked with black, white, and tan supported undulating walls marbled purple, orange, and red, and occasionally permeated with textured intrusions of pink and gray. Through this section, we hiked not just with our feet, but with our hands—clutching and holding onto the rock.

No sunlight reached the inner gorge in late afternoon to mellow the hard blackness of the Vishnu Schist, the oldest exposed rock on earth. Streaked through a wall of gray, it looked more like a vein of melted ebony than metamorphosed lava from ancient volcanos. Mixed with the sediments of Proterozoic seas, it had been reinterred as the earth's surface churned from colliding internal plates.

Then, around a turn in the gorge, an open plateau commanded our full attention, like a sudden surge of dramatic music in an epic film. On the left, shoulder-high reeds marked the flow of Shinumo Creek, a larger stream than White, which itself poured out of the gorge into a sandy-bottomed expanse fifteen feet wide and two feet deep. Beyond this quiet, slow-moving interlude, we could hear the rapids where White flowed into Shinumo for its final journey to the Colorado.

We crossed just above the confluence and found ourselves on a sandy beach just large enough for three sleeping bags, not much by Caribbean standards, but in the Grand Canyon, idyllic. Bushes framed the border while cottonwoods formed a canopy. To the west, a rocky hillside rose to a point, drawing attention to Masonic Temple. The jagged turrets that gave Dox Castle its name towered to the southeast.

As soon as we dropped our packs, I peeled off my sweat-drenched T-shirt and felt the delicious chill of evaporation. My back was dry by the time I got the shirt hung on a thorny bush. Malcolm and Brandon sat on stone seats removing their boots. "What do you think?" I asked. "Do we set up camp first or cool off in the stream?"

Brandon peered at me as if dumbfounded that I could think there was something to discuss. Malcolm leaned over and whispered something in his ear.

"You're right to take your time and confer," I continued. "There's a lot at stake since your answer will reveal your basic philosophy of life: work-before-play . . . or go-for-the-gusto and live-for-the-moment."

Brandon ignored me, hummed quietly to himself, and proceeded to undress. Completely nude, he headed for the stream, tested the footing, hobbled slowly to midstream, sat down, and leaned back on his elbows, like he was sinking into fluffy pillows on an old, familiar couch. With eyes closed, still humming, he let his head drift back as if pulled by the weight of his ponytail as it dipped in the current. I couldn't help but smile as he took his pleasure. When I stepped into the water to join him, gasping at the sudden cold, he opened his eyes, stopped humming, and asked sarcastically: "Were you saying something?"

"Thank you for noticing. I was saying something and I intend to speechify as befits an elder. There's a third approach, a particularly modern philosophy: act like you're *here,* but really be worrying about *there*—preoccupied with work left undone, the ultimate form of toxification laced with deadly stress and stifling guilt. Malcolm's profession depends on, indeed thrives on, this approach to life. If we were to choose this third alternative, choice being merely a figure of speech since these are more matters of habit than choice, we'd find ourselves sitting in this stream, acting like we were completely caught up in the pleasure of the moment, yet all the while thinking about getting unpacked, starting dinner, and feeling guilty about the fact that Malcolm is doing just that, goddamn him."

Brandon closed his eyes, let his head fall back again, and said softly, "Do I look like I feel guilty?"

I stood just a couple feet into the stream, the water at midcalf. "No you don't, but maybe you should. Maybe I haven't taught you to be responsible. Maybe we should both go help. He's getting the stove out to boil water for soup."

"You aren't helping him by trying to guilt me. He told me to try out the water and he'd join us in a moment. He's cool. Sit down and get yourself detoxificated."

"Detoxed."

"Whatever. Show some sixties cool, man. Chill out. Let Malcolm do his thing." With that he closed his eyes and leaned his head back, his hair once more dipping in the water.

I looked at him closely. Who was this person? I felt pride, shame, elation, confusion. I felt parental and childish. I felt naked. I was naked.

Brandon opened his eyes. "You still standing there?" A menacing grin took over his face, like a Stephen King character possessed. "You need to be initiated," he pronounced. As I opened my mouth to rebut his audacity, a wave of cold water hit me followed instantly by hands grasping my shoulders, pulling me forward under the water. As I came up splashing for balance, I spied his lowered head coming at me. Back under water, I sputtered like an expiring balloon. Gasping for breath, I resurfaced only to be dunked again. And then again, my head like a basketball in his surprisingly strong hands. My sentient world reduced to the last gulp of air I had managed, I ceased struggling and lifted my hands in surrender. He let go. My whole body reduced to gasping lungs and pounding heart, I gave in to leaning back and chilling out, as my son had commanded.

Not easy, but if one can't do it in a cool stream in the inner sanctum of the Grand Canyon after descending through the Great Unconformity, then one probably can't do it anywhere. I came close. For a few seconds I may have stopped the internal dialogue and experienced a discontinuity of the mind. Not a great unconformity, just a small discontinuity, what I imagine a Zen master means by a lotus-blossom smile. Not in some ephemeral soul, but in purity of nonthought—consciousness of consciousness suspended. Presence of mind. Emptied. And in being emptied, acknowledged. Celebrated. Renewed. Detoxed.

Malcolm joined us. "You boys finally settled down enough that an old man can take a quiet soak?"

"Sure. I was just telling Brandon how you were demonstrating the responsible principle of work before play. He accused me of trying to guilt him. Can you imagine?"

"Lighting the old stove for hot drinks and soup after a full day's hike isn't work or play. It's ritual."

"We were engaged in a bit of that ourselves."

"How so?" he asked.

I looked to Brandon, who answered for me. "Just performing one of many duties that fall to a son. I had to initiate him."

"It's about time," Malcolm laughed. "How was it?"

"Like I imagine it was for Lancelot to be unhorsed by Galahad." Thus saying I ducked under, held my breath, and stayed completely immersed as long as I could to further numb my head, the opposite of mind over matter.

Afterward I indulged in the luxury of clean socks, but the pants were the same cotton khakis I had been wearing for two days, pants that now showed evidence of Coconino, Hermit Shale, Supai, Redwall, Tonto, and Tapeats I had encountered along the way. But no Great Unconformity. That had attached itself elsewhere, in some deep cerebral crevice.

15. Iron John's Test

"Tonight I want to know what Bly thinks," Brandon announced.

Coffee and hot chocolate in hand, we had just gathered for the evening reading of "Iron John" after scouring with sand residues of tuna macaroni from our fine metal dinnerware. "We never got around to Bly's interpretation last night. I want to know who he said the Wild Man was."

"I didn't bring his book, just the story."

"Come on, you know what he said."

"He says lots of things. For example, he goes on for several pages about the significance of male hair."

"Okay. Start there. What's with the hair?"

"He says hair falling out of our heads is like thoughts coming out, which may explain my mental acuity these days. And a mustache is the way a man shows his pubic hair to his mother. Since Malcolm's mustache predates mine—and is much longer and less trimmed than my beard—I take it he is the greater exhibitionist. Want to hear more?"

"He really says that stuff? That's lame."

"Freud lives," Malcolm pronounced. "A Freudian would interpret the Wild Man as the id, you know, the center of the boy's sexual

131

urges and animal emotions which have to be repressed by society if the boy is to become a productive adult."

"Bly, on the other hand," I interjected, "urges us to be in touch with our Wild Man, to neither suppress him nor let him take over. But I'm afraid if we get into Bly's stuff before you've heard the whole story, it will color your own interpretations."

"I don't think it has to be either-or."

"Bly interprets the story in relation to the symbolism of ancient myths and classical literature. So every time a color is mentioned, he analyzes it at length. If you don't have his extensive knowledge of the cultural, religious, and literary meanings of colors, then from Bly's perspective you miss a lot. For me, however, the real test of the timelessness of a story is what we make of it now. If you have to have studied world mythology to interpret a story, it's not powerful in its own right.

"We might also want to keep in mind," I continued, "that we're dealing with only one version. Just like the Grail legend, there are multiple accounts of 'Iron John.' A professor at the University of Minnesota[1] has accused Bly of using a faulty translation and then distorting the original—called 'Iron Hans'—and of ignoring the fact that the Wild Man in many versions was the devil tempting the boy, not saving him."

"Hey, I recognize that version," Brandon quipped. "The boy rejects Satan when he finds the Holy Grail in a witch's house made of gingerbread and candy."

"You already know the ending!" I exclaimed.

"In the version I grew up with," Malcolm said grinning, "he finds the Grail under Little Red Riding Hood's skirt."

This launched Brandon into a raucous improvisation of Cinderella in which Iron *Hands* crushed Cinderella's glass slipper as he fumbled to slide it on her foot. Brandon bent over and stared in mock dismay at Cinderella's bleeding foot. He pleaded for Cinderella to forgive him in-between screams for a doctor as he fumbled to apply a tourniquet to her gushing wound.

I waved like a referee stopping play for a football penalty. "Such sacrilege!" I scolded, trying unsuccessfully not to laugh at his distressed expression as he gazed unfalteringly at Cinderella's injury. "But if we're going to read any of Bly's 'Iron John,' we're going to have to do it soon. I'm fading fast."

"Go for it," Brandon assented, instantly feigning a serious demeanor. So I read the next segment.

After their escape from the castle, the Wild Man took the boy to his forest home, explaining that he'd never see his parents, the King and Queen, again, but assuring him he'd be taken care of if he did everything he was told. The boy was then ordered to guard a golden spring, making sure nothing touched it. The first day the boy dipped his injured finger in the water and it instantly turned to gold. He was forgiven by the Wild Man, who always knew what had happened despite the boy's attempts to hide his failures, and warned to do better. The second day a hair from his head fell in the water and turned to gold. Again he was scolded and forgiven, but warned that if the spring was contaminated again, he'd be forced to leave. The third day he accidentally touched his head to the water while looking at himself in the spring's reflection and his hair turned golden. He was banished because, the Wild Man explained, he hadn't made it through the trial. He was told to go into the world and learn about poverty, but assured that if he was ever in trouble he could return to the forest, call the Wild Man's name—Iron John—and he'd be helped because Iron John was both powerful and wealthy.

"It's about the preciousness of water," Brandon declared. "Last night the Wild Man was found in a deep pool. Tonight, he's the guardian of the spring, teaching the boy the value of water. He was instructing him not to piss in the water," he concluded, smirking at Malcolm.

"If he'd pissed in the spring, he would have been giving gold instead of taking it out," Malcolm retorted.

"All right, let's not turn this into a pissing match," I entreated. "What do you make of the gold, Brandon?"

"If gold represents whatever is most precious, then water is what is most precious. I remember when we were up in Duluth people were predicting that Minnesota would soon be exporting water from Lake Superior the way the Middle East now sells oil."

We could hear the rapids just below us as we talked. Did it make any difference that the water in the story was a spring rather than a river? Brandon didn't think so. Malcolm reminded us of how the spring below the Coconino connected to the Colorado River through White Creek and Shinumo; that all routes into the canyon were carved by water; that the layers of the canyon were deposited by seas.

I asked Brandon if anything stood out to him in the story.

He rocked back and forth rubbing his hands hard up and down his thighs, agitated, the buildup of energy palpable. "Their relationship sucked."

"Define 'sucked,' " I requested, taken aback by the ferocity of his reaction.

He became perfectly still, then slowly worked his head from side to side as if releasing tension. Before answering he stretched out, resting his head on his elbow. "I'll wait till I hear the whole story. I don't want to sound like I've made up my mind about it already."

"Yeah," I agreed. "Why don't we wait until the age Bly said sons can finally talk to their fathers, say your fiftieth birthday. We'll get together and you can tell me what sucked about the story. I'll be, let me see, I'll be seventy-eight and you'll be fifty. We'll do it then."

I glared at Brandon, trying to read his reaction to my sarcasm. He looked back at me calmly, almost serenely, revealing nothing in his expression. Where, I wondered, had he learned to feign such tranquility? Did playing *Dungeons and Dragons* require a poker face?

"All right you jerk-offs," Malcolm burst out. "You two may be able to wait thirty years, but I could croak hiking to the river tomorrow. Let me die in peace, Brandon. Please answer your dad's question for me, if not for him. What sucks?"

"As your elders we command you to speak," I said in a mockingly authoritarian manner.

"That's it, that's exactly it," he charged, bolting up and leaning forward, his serenity vanished. "What sucks is Iron John. He orders the boy around all the time. 'You can stay with me if you do exactly as I say.' 'Make sure nothing falls into the spring.' 'You have to leave here now.' 'You failed the test.' He's mean and authoritarian and . . . judgmental . . . and totally controlling."

"The boy didn't seem to mind," I suggested.

"Then he failed the real test," Brandon asserted.

"Real test?"

"Yeah. The real test wasn't guarding the water. The real test was whether the boy would put up with letting someone tell him what to do all the time. He was better off leaving the forest if Iron John was just going to order him around and control his life. By failing Iron John's tests the boy passed the real test of maintaining his own identity."

"But the boy wasn't trying to fail the tests," I countered. "It's not like he decided to rebel against Iron John's commands the way you rebelled against guitar lessons because they interfered with your creativity. He just failed. In that sense, he wasn't being his own person. He bought into the tests. He just couldn't pass them."

"That's true. It would have been better if he had failed on purpose. But I still think he was better off, whether he wanted to fail or not, because he got to leave the forest and get out from under Iron John."

Malcolm howled. His shoulders and head shook with laughter. Wave after wave burst forth overwhelming the night. Even the frogs momentarily stopped croaking. I'd never witnessed such an uproarious outburst from Malcolm. Startled, I watched intensely for some sign of what he was up to, perplexed at not knowing, waiting for a chance to reassert my own order and control.

As his howl quieted to a chuckle I jumped in. "You just scared the shit out of every living thing in Muav Canyon, Malcolm. Ignore him, Brandon. After you've met a few therapists, you'll come to appreciate their sudden, inappropriate bursts of laughter. It's a helpful reminder that underneath the facade they're all basically maladjusted. Go on."

"I want to know what Malcolm found so hilarious."

"I'm sorry, Brandon. I wasn't laughing at you or what you said. I was laughing because you reminded me so much of someone."

"Who?"

"Your old man."

"Dad?"

"Not to take anything away from you expressing your own thoughts, but you might as well know. Your issue with Iron John is also your dad's issue with the world."

"What do you mean?"

"Over the years down here we've probably spent more time talking about your dad's need to have control over his life than anything else; control over his time; control over his work. You know, don't you, that he never sought a tenured position because he didn't want anyone else deciding his future. He refused to be judged by their criteria. He spent all those years at the university on grant money he raised so he could be his own boss, have his own research funds, be able to make his own decisions and control his time. I'm actually surprised he didn't have the same reaction to Iron John that you're having."

"The person you're analyzing is right here, you know. Are you saying I'm a control freak?"

"I'm saying the cactus flower doesn't fall far from the cactus. Brandon might as well know, since he's now a man, that there have been some influences on how he thinks. One of them is tonight's 'Iron John' narrator."

"So, Dad, what about the control thing? Did you get it from your father?"

"I'm not sure what IT is, or that IT's a control thing, but, maybe, in a roundabout way, I got something like that from my father—from watching how little control he had over his life. The crowning incident occurred about fifteen years ago, just a few years before he retired. I got a consulting gig in Hawaii and thought I'd take him along. He had passed through there in World War II, loved *South Pacific,* and mentioned he'd like to get that way again some day. We'd never traveled anywhere together. Never. As I thought about the possibilities, it got to be a big deal to me. His health was already failing. The years of battle were behind us. It was something I really wanted to do with him . . . for him. I called him, sprang the offer, and he became almost excited—"

"Almost?"

"He wasn't much given to expressions of emotion, but I could tell he wanted to do it. He had two weeks vacation coming, so that didn't look like a problem. I called him back the next night to confirm the details. His boss had told him they couldn't spare him. The other clerks—he was a forms expediter at a factory in Dayton, Ohio—offered to cover while he was gone. No way. His boss said it would set a bad precedent. Dad knew that was bullshit. It sounded like his boss—I hate that word—was just mean, or maybe jealous, or, who knows, but the bottom line was, he had power over my father. I remember the catch in my father's voice when he told me he couldn't go. He sounded broken. I think he was ashamed, too. I vowed then that no one would ever have that kind of control over me." I paused, recalling my decision not to press my father so as not to increase his hurt. "I reacted by downplaying the whole thing, telling him it was no big deal. There would be another time. But it was a big deal. And there wasn't another time. So, yeah, I guess you could say I picked up an obsession about control from my dad."

We sat quietly for a moment, then Brandon said, "That's pretty sad, Dad. I've heard you say you never wanted to work for anyone, but I never knew what was behind it."

"I suspect there's more than that, Brandon," Malcolm suggested. "Critical incidents grow out of . . . Let me, umm . . . When the first big rain falls after the dry winter, the desert blooms overnight. Those plants aren't dropped suddenly from the sky. They come from seeds that have been waiting a long time, part of a system that includes long periods of dormancy. When I heard your reaction against Iron John's control, I heard your dad in there with you, two blooms in the same system. Which doesn't mean you don't have your own take on these issues." He paused to let us take in his mischievous expression. "And when you're fifty I think you should still meet your father and tell him again to get off your back."

"No, I think I'll invite him to Hawaii."

"I accept," I said. We sat silently awhile, then I continued. "I want to respond to Malcolm's surprise that I didn't react as you did to Iron John's authoritarianism. It's probably because I've been focusing on the story as an initiation myth. It seemed like a good way to get us all reflecting on what tests have to be passed in today's world."

"Why should any tests have to be passed?" Brandon countered.

"There are always tests," I replied. "In traditional cultures the tests were built into initiations. They were clear. You passed or didn't. Now—"

"I hate tests," Brandon interrupted. "You hate bosses. I hate tests."

"Sounds like the same thing to me," Malcolm grinned.

"I'm not so sure," I said. "What would Greenway say was the function of tests?"

"Who's Greenway?" Brandon asked.

"My major anthro professor at the University of Colorado, one John Greenway, who did fieldwork among the Australian Pitjandjara people for about fifteen years with Norman Tindale, probably *the* world's expert on Australian Native rituals at that time. The Pitjandjara conduct the most severe initiation in the world, what they call the 'ceremony of man making.' It opens with dancing and singing, then moves to testing the boy's endurance. He's circumcised with a stone knife. When the elder cuts off the foreskin, the boy must make no sound. Though no anesthetic is used, he can't even grimace. He sits bleeding while the men continue dancing and his male relatives cut up and eat the foreskin."

"I'd be out of there," Brandon said.

"Then you'd disgrace your father. You'd never become a man. You'd never get a wife. You'd never become part of the tribe. For all intents and purposes your life would be over."

"Iron John's test suddenly looks pretty good," Brandon joked. "I'll guard the water."

"The circumcision is just the beginning," Malcolm warned.

"I'm not sure I want to hear the rest," Brandon said, "or are you making this up, like campfire ghost stories?"

"You can read it for yourself in Greenway's book, *Down Among the*

Wild Men. He was talking about *real* men, not mythical ones. After being circumcised, the Pitjandjara boy goes into the desert with one or two male mentors. I forget all the details. But he hears the sacred bull-roarer, the voice of the spirits. I don't remember which comes next, the tooth evulsion or the subincision. Take your choice."

"I can guess what a tooth evulsion is. What's a subincision?"

"The boy's male relatives get down on their hands and knees. The boy is laid across their backs. He must lie perfectly still. An elder takes a stone knife and cuts from his balls to the head of his penis. Greenway says it's like cutting open a hot dog. If the cut is wrong, the boy bleeds to death. He must make no sound. Tindale recorded the ceremony on film in the 1930s. The boy he filmed apparently screamed. After being severely beaten, he was speared to death for disgracing the sacred ceremony."

Malcolm spoke softly, quietly presenting the facts without embellishment or editorial. Brandon listened attentively, transfixed, our clowning around forgotten.

"For the tooth evulsion, a stick is used to dig a tooth out, one of the upper incisors. Sometimes a rock is used to pound it out. However it's done, an incisor is extracted. As with the circumcision and subincision, the boy must show no pain."

"And then he's a man?" Brandon asked.

"After the initiation ceremony, the boy goes alone into the desert wilderness for several weeks. He must survive completely alone. When he returns, he is a man. He has no doubts about being a man. Little boys throw toy spears at him and he laughs. He takes his place in the tribe as a man."

Malcolm turned to me. "You said that passing tests is important to initiation. I think Greenway and Tindale would say that passing the tests *is* the initiation."

"Go on. Tell Brandon their explanation for why the Pitjandjara ritual is so harsh."

"Difficulty of an initiation is directly proportional to the harshness of the tribe's environment. The Pitjandjara inhabit a desert even more harsh than here—the world's hardest initiation for the world's harshest environment. For the tribe to survive, the individual had to learn to survive. Once a boy passed the initiation tests, he could face any fear, endure any pain, suffer any deprivation. Tindale and Greenway felt great respect for native peoples and their rituals. They opposed the missionaries who advocated outlawing initiation practices."

"Did Greenway ever comment about initiation in modern society?" I asked.

"He expressed nothing but disdain for the coddling nature of Western civilization. I think he saw the loss of initiation rites as directly related to a loss of manhood in modern times."

"He has lots of company," I added. "Bly and many others argue that in the transition from agricultural to industrial societies the father was removed from the farm to the factory so the son lost any consistent or intensive contact with a male model. The responsibility for socialization was taken from elders and assigned to schools. The hunter and warrior who had assured the survival of the tribe became an emasculated factory laborer or managerial bureaucrat."

"So if you don't hunt or fight, you're a wimp. That's completely bogus," Brandon contended.

"Being considered wimps is just the start of the list of modern male afflictions. As a man, you, we, risk a long list of dysfunctions. We have a duty to warn you that men have been diagnosed as sexually insecure, socially alienated, psychologically battered, parentally inept, politically impotent, materially greedy, spiritually empty, physically violent, mentally void, and morally decadent—all this confirmed daily on television sitcoms. And we can't get together to help each other out because we're homophobic."

"Take me out of the 'we,' " Brandon insisted.

"I'm not putting you in the 'we,' or Malcolm, or myself. But, as men, as a father, these allegations are the context within which we have to define for ourselves what masculinity is about, if it's about anything."

"I don't see how initiations would solve any problems," Brandon speculated. "Boys would come out of the initiation and still have to work for bosses. The whole thing sucks. To me, it just seems like tribal initiations were a way for the elders to control the young, order them around, punish them, brainwash them, and kill off any signs of individuality."

"I'm not arguing that tribal initiations should be reintroduced to solve modern identity problems," Malcolm responded, "but it's important to understand how they were viewed from within. Your concern about maintaining your freedom and individuality is a very Western notion. Boys brought up in a tribe want more than anything else to become contributing members of the tribe. That's what it meant to be a man."

"They put the tribe above themselves?" Brandon asked.

"They wouldn't make the distinction. Native American boys who undertake a vision quest do so for themselves *and* the tribe. If they receive a vision, they return and share it with the tribal elders. The whole community benefits from the individual's vision."

"But the elders tell them to undertake the vision quest, don't they?" Brandon asked.

"No. Boys learn that it's an option, but not every boy undertakes the quest. The boy and the shaman must both decide that he's ready. It's a shared decision."

"So you're saying that Native American elders aren't as authoritarian as the Pitjandjara?"

"Elders conducting initiations only appear authoritarian from outside their system, judged by our cultural values. My sense is that the initiates experienced their initiators as trustworthy authorities who were passing on knowledge and wisdom. Being a trusted authority differs from being authoritarian as much as being a mentor differs from being a boss. Initiations didn't disappear from Western society for lack of authoritarians," Malcolm grinned, "but trustworthy authorities became extinct somewhere along the way. I'd say that Iron John appears authoritarian to you because his authority hasn't been established and made credible."

"I can relate to there not being trusted authorities today," Brandon said, "but," he continued grinning, "it doesn't sound all that attractive if having them around means they get to whack away at your penis and order you to do whatever they think is best for the tribe."

"You may be onto something," I affirmed, feeling the importance of the point, not just for Brandon, but to understand my own intense reaction to the issue. "Most anthropology is written from the perspective of what functions for tribal survival, but the detailed record shows that life in the tribe was not exactly idyllic. The African boys I knew in the Peace Corps were scared to death of being initiated. Of course, making them scared was part of the process. Still, the elders used real knives; boys bled real blood; cuts were deep; penises rotted from infection; pus filled the wounds; fasting led to dehydration; boys were crippled; some died. I knew Gourma boys who never returned. Some who did return were disabled. That may have helped them survive in a very harsh environment, but tribal survival came at high individual cost."

"Admittedly, individuals suffered, but they also benefited," Malcolm countered. "You have to look at it in terms of their system. The initiation is conducted by the tribal elders to symbolize the death of the child and the rebirth of a new member of the tribe—a full adult. That's why the father can't initiate his own son, because the son's actually being separated from his parents and brought into the tribe. Sometimes that involves literally tearing a terrified child from his mother's skirt or kidnaping him while he sleeps. When the boy returns to the village from the initiation camp, he doesn't return to his parents' hearth. My sense is that this separation serves a crucial psychological function. Because parents and children will live their entire lives within the same territory and interact within the prescribed roles of the extended family, some mechanism for psychological independence must be provided for the children to become fully functioning adults. Initiation is that mechanism."

"You're saying that passing the initiation means freedom from parental domination. I can see that," Brandon confirmed, "but isn't it just substituting tribal domination for parental domination?"

"The word 'domination' carries a judgment. Try to analyze it without valuing individual freedom above all else. In subsistence societies the future of the tribe is always uncertain so control is essential for survival. With small numbers of genetically related people, the tribe must carefully control who marries whom. Subject to periodic famines, the tribe must control the sharing of scarce food. In the face of threats from other tribes, slave traders and colonizing armies, the tribe must guarantee the commitment of warriors to die in defense of the tribe. Given the unpredictability of the gods, the shaman must control the willingness of tribal members to sacrifice in order to appease and cajole temperamental deities. The benefit of all this control was tribal survival. The individual gained a place of security and defined status in the tribe. The cost to the tribe was loss of flexibility in the face of changed conditions. Sure, from our perspective the individual lost freedom, but personal choice was a luxury subsistence societies could not afford and a pain individuals did not seek."

"I'm not arguing against traditional ways," Brandon insisted. "I just don't think they're relevant today. I don't get people trying to reintroduce initiations to give men a male identity. It's just an excuse to indoctrinate."

"Good word," I agreed. "And the 'tribe' can take a variety of forms: a distinct cultural group in Africa, a religious order, or a fraternity. Indoctrination certainly captures how my own fraternity initiation felt."

"Yours?!" Brandon's exclamation drilled home that I'd never shared my own traumatic initiation. I hadn't thought of it for years, but that night at the confluence of White and Shinumo, stimulated by Brandon's reaction to Iron John, I relived it, transported back as I told the story.

Note

1. I had heard this criticism by word of mouth before our canyon conversations. I found the following in print later:

> [Bly] used fallacious interpretations of myth and folklore and a faulty translation of a Grimms' fairy tale to support his argument that contemporary American men were suffering from a traumatic wound and needed a wise mentor to help contact their essential wildness and become wholesome warriors, confident of their prowess to provide for and defend their communities. . . . Yet, in many versions of Iron Hans, the wild man as so-called mentor was the devil, and there was never a wound of significance. The focus in the tale of Iron Hans was a boy fleeing and overcoming the devil!

Jack Zipes (Professor of German, University of Minnesota), " 'Genuine Masculine' Reinforces Male Elitism," *Minneapolis Star Tribune,* August 7, 1993, p. A15.

16. Moon Shadow

I had pledged a fraternity my freshman year at the University of Cincinnati. Someone from the fraternity had visited me at home in Dayton shortly after I was admitted to college as an engineering major. He made being part of a fraternity sound at least as important as getting a college education, so I pledged.

We had to wait on upperclassmen, responding to their every whim. Displeasing one resulted in demerits and punishment. Hazing included long hours standing at attention, bowing on our knees before seniors, and wearing stupid-looking beanies all quarter wherever we went. They sent us to serve at a sorority dinner wearing dresses, bras, and panty hose. We had to go downtown to Fountain Square dressed like prostitutes. Once we had to play football in the middle of the night with a large, raw fish. On another night they lined us up naked and poured wintergreen on our genitals. The sting, extremely painful, wouldn't wash away. They found out I didn't drink so one night they made me get drunk—and sick.

I quit before the quarter and the pledging ended, escaping to a small apartment and a high school acquaintance who needed a roommate. The other pledges tracked me down and the fra-

143

ternity's president, vice president, and chairman of the alumni group were waiting for me one day when I returned from classes. I especially remember the president, a sophisticated and self-confident senior whom I had admired from the moment I met him. He had never participated in the hazing.

He explained the bonding that was taking place among the pledges. These would be my brothers for life, but I had to show I was a worthy. He praised my intelligence. (I later learned they really needed my good grades because several pledges were failing school.) He appealed to my sense of manhood. All three went back and forth, alternatively flattering and shaming me.

On the verge of tears and feeling embarrassed, guilty, and confused, I chose silence rather than rebuttal. They went at me for a couple of hours, refusing, they said, to let me ruin my life. Finally, when they saw I would not relent, the vice president turned mean. He warned that they would pass my name through the Greek system and no fraternity would ever accept me. I was washed up, a failure, not worthy of them. Someday I'd look back on this as the worst decision I'd ever made, he promised, and I'd have to live forever knowing I wasn't tough enough to stick it out. He sounded disgusted. They turned to go and the alumni chair spit out a final condemnation: "You only get one chance like this to be with the best. You've blown it, Patton. You've blown it for all time. You are screwed."

The president hung back and put his arm on my shoulder: "If you change your mind, call me. It's not too late—yet. But I agree you'll live with regret the rest of your life if you drop out. It's a terribly lonely world out there. We all need brothers we can count on. I'd be honored to have you as a brother. Think about it and call me."

I called two days later and said I'd complete the pledge period if I didn't have to move back into the fraternity. During the final weeks of hazing, I became the favored target of abuse. The other pledges shunned me to avoid putting themselves at risk. On the final night before induction, the vice president made me stand in the entrance hallway nude all night holding a stick so that each entering brother-to-be could swat me.

We were led blindfolded into the induction ceremony to the sound of chanting. After incantations and oaths, we were allowed to open our eyes to behold a candlelit room with robed figures holding swords. We signed a large book amidst a chorus of voices extolling the virtues of brotherhood. A raucous and drunken celebration ensued through the night. The president made a special point of telling me how proud he felt. The vice president ignored me.

The next day I resigned. My letter stated no reasons. I never returned, refused phone calls, and evaded attempts to meet. I don't remember that it felt good to quit. By the end, I found no satisfaction in passing their test because I didn't respect either them or their test. To the contrary, I felt angry and ashamed that I had fallen for the ruse that I needed to prove my manhood, for when I had returned, I had already determined to quit after induction—after I'd shown I could make it. I didn't tell anyone about quitting, certainly not my father. He had never gone to college and my being part of one didn't matter to him one way or the other.

When I finished relating my story, the shadow of Brandon's form shrugged, then spoke. "It's like, not real. I mean, I get that it happened, that it still happens, but I can't imagine actually going through that kind of initiation."

"I don't recommend it," I said, feeling emptied out.

We lapsed into shared silence, individually pondering the star-filled sky. I liked telling Brandon stories—both ancient stories and my own, the two flowing together. I liked the way he listened: absorbed, questioning, wanting more, then challenging what he heard. One moment quiet, the next animated, he reminded me of his six-year-old self reacting to Dr. Seuss. Yertle the Turtle should have been forced to apologize for climbing on top of all the little turtles. The Sneetches should have gotten smarter, faster, before all their money was spent. He, Brandon with a Stick, would have put a quick stop to the mischief of the Cat in a Hat. I wanted to ask him if he still thought he could run a zoo better than young Gerald McGrew, or hear a Who better than Horton. And now, no longer a child, was he willing to try green eggs and ham? And what had it been like that afternoon for him to again *Hop on Pop*?

"I'm really anxious to see the river tomorrow," Brandon announced, breaking me out of my reverie. "I feel ready."

"Nothing to be ready for," Malcolm said. "It's not a test."

"Right," I quickly agreed. "In fact, you don't even have to come. Let's just say that Malcolm and I are hiking on to the river. We'd welcome your company if you'd care to join us."

"I'll let you know in the morning. It depends on what other offers turn up overnight. I'm not particularly interested in going if Malcolm's going to croak on the way."

"If you avoid going places where people might croak, you'll have nowhere to go," Malcolm replied.

"And you'll never find the Lorax," I added.

"Lorax?! Weird, Dad. What made you think of the Lorax?"

"You remember?"

Brandon pretended to look hurt. "Of course, I remember. The Lorax ran away to find a place where human beings couldn't destroy the environment, or so said the Once-ler. Maybe he escaped to the Grand Canyon."

"You remember!" I exclaimed, jumping up and tapping his head. "He remembers, Malcolm! He actually remembers!"

"Easy, Dad. It's not that big a deal."

"Could be, Brandon. Could be very big," Malcolm said. "I hate to break it to you, but I'm afraid you may just have passed a test."

"No, no test," I protested. "Absolutely not a test. A memory, not a test."

"Malcolm is being a Grinch," Brandon added.

"Okay, not a test," Malcolm agreed. "But I have a test. My body wants to test this sandy beach as a bed. I'll give you the results in the morning."

"And I'll give you mine," Brandon replied. "Good night, Malcolm. Night, Dad. And," he added, speaking into the surrounding darkness, "good night, Lorax."

A few minutes later, collapsed on my sleeping bag, listening to Brandon's breathing, I remembered reading to him at bedtime. Often, stretched out beside him, I'd doze off. He'd poke me and insist I read on. Some nights he just took the book and finished himself. I'd awake much later, disoriented, lights out, finding myself still in bed with him. Tonight, he'd gone to sleep first. My body felt drained, but my mind was not ready to shut down.

Something about his Iron John reaction wouldn't let me alone, like a pesky mosquito that refuses to be waved away. He had listened to the story eagerly, like a boy, but had responded as a thoughtful adult. I found myself savoring what he had to say, hungry to hear his thoughts, to find out how his mind worked. This need was as clear to me as the cloudless night sky, but not really a surprise. What I had not anticipated was how Brandon's reactions would evoke emotional responses in me. Long-buried critical incidents in my own coming of age were bursting forth from their hidden sepulchers.

I got up and pursued the buzzing mosquito in my head back and forth along the stream. It was then that contemplation of the Great Unconformity led me to ponder the gap in coming-of-age rituals between modern society and ancient times. I realized we could not close the gap between former and present times by simply reintroducing traditional initiation rites. I had been attracted by that possibility, but Brandon's reaction said it wouldn't work for modern young men who have tasted choice and soaked in the stream of individuality. And it would not work for me because I wanted to play a part.

In reacting against Iron John, Brandon had rejected the control, manipulation, and domination of traditional initiations. How might a new coming-of-age paradigm differ? It would begin by honoring and affirming the initiate's perspective—and right to have a perspective. Ancient truths would be offered in that spirit, as choices and understandings to be adapted. In traditional initiations the elders instruct the initiates in the meaning of the story. There is *one* interpretation, theirs. Bly's book was written in that mode. As a senior guru of the men's movement, a substitute elder for men who feel tribeless, Bly declares the definitive interpretation of what the ancient story means. He plays the poet-priest who has special knowledge of what all the colors mean, what the hair represents, why the ashes are important—even knowledge of how myth is carried in the genes of men. I understood more deeply the significance of bringing the story but not the book.

If initiations became a dialogue about perspectives rather than the imposition of the tribe's truth, would this threaten the survival of society? *Au contraire.* In other times diverse truths might have undermined the tribe's future, but in today's rapidly changing world, multiple perspectives and new ways of looking at things are our hope for adaptation and survival. Ancient times may have required that the young bend to the will of the group. Modern times demand young people who can move society in new directions by applying their intellects and creativity.

The Great Unconformity became for me that night a metaphor for the chasm between ancient and modern times. Modern youth deserve a coming-of-age journey for *this* age, one that recognizes ancient foundations of human experience, but is separate and distinct in accordance with modern discontinuities and the great unconformity of human potential in our times; a process individually designed for each young person instead of standardized by tradition; rituals of affirmation and confirmation rather than categorization and control; and a process grounded in and honoring rational, scientific thought rather than mysticism and otherworldly spirituality. All in all, a participatory and celebratory process, not a dictatorial, fear-inducing, and authoritarian one. And, of special import to me, a process of intergenerational bonding rather than separation.

I returned to my bag ready to will myself to sleep. I stopped instead where Brandon slept. My moon shadow fell across his bag, as if part of the fabric that enveloped him. Wanting our connection to be more lasting than a shadow was why I had become so taken with the story of Lancelot and Galahad. Lancelot's knighting of his own son had opened the door for them to spend time together as adults. When Galahad fulfilled the quest, his father's quest was also filled, not because Lancelot was living his life through Galahad, but because they recognized and reveled in an inextricable connection. Half asleep, I fantasized an invitation to Lancelot and Galahad, inviting them to accompany us to the river. And beyond.

The last thing I remember was wondering which hallucination was more damning: that, drunk on the virulent elixir of sociological abstractions to which I am especially vulnerable, I had wandered upon a paradigm shift; or that, afflicted with quixotic fantasies from a cactus prick, I was conversing with the dehorsed Lancelot. Or were they but two manifestations of the same affliction, what Malcolm called canyon fever.

Day Three

17. River

Below the confluence of White and Shinumo Creeks, pushing through tall grasses, thick bushes, and large ferns felt strange after the Tonto desert and the starkness of the rocky inner gorge. About a mile below our campsite we came to an open area on the east bank that had once been Bass Camp. About the size of a large yard, the camp lies beneath a vertical rock wall of pink and brown streaked black from seasonal runoffs.

William Wallace Bass lived in the Grand Canyon for forty years with his wife, Ada Diefendorf Bass, and their four children. In the winter they lived and farmed in this subtropical area while it was freezing on the rim. In spring the family moved to a house on the rim and the winter home became a summer tourist camp. A 1906 tourist guide from the Santa Fe Railroad described Bass Camp as a rustic alternative for those who found the Grand View Hotel's $3 a night too steep: "Present accommodations at Bass' Camp. . . are fairly good, consisting of a frame cabin, several tents, and good trail stock; wholesome meals are served . . . ; reached by team from El Tovar, twenty-three miles."

Some of the most famous names associated with the West, Zane Grey and John Muir, stayed

151

at Bass Camp, and Thomas Moran used it as a base when he was doing sketches that would later become some of the canyon's most famous paintings. Just a few artifacts remain from that time, when Bass Trail was a private tourist route. An old washtub had been stuck under a rock slab positioned on stones like a garden bench. A weathered wooden plank had become a display stand for tools, cooking utensils, and mining gear. We inventoried four picks, two axes, a rake, a saw blade, harness parts, a spade, shears, a prospector's pan, a stone sharpening wheel, and a variety of cook pots. A thick metal spike had been driven into the stone wall within an alcove at the base of the cliff; suspended from its circular end was a heavy black iron pot, virtually rust-free. Porcelain chips and broken brown glass were strewn about the area. Two large prickly pears guarded the ruins of a stove, its heavy rusted doors having fallen amid ashes, bits of charcoal, and sand as if concealing an opening into the molten center of the earth. On a small rock table, next to a battered steel coffeepot, remnants of tools in a circle seemed like veterans congregated to share old stories. Near the creek, an open-hearth fireplace of large stones stood strong, though constructed without mortar. A single old cowboy boot, propped up against the wall, cast a lonely shadow. Though it had been proposed that Holy Grail Temple be renamed after his ashes were dropped there, this ghost camp preserved the remains of his life and work—a more fitting place to be known as Bass Tomb.

We lingered at this open-air museum, free to the public and unguarded, speculating on the uses of tools we'd never before seen, marveling at tough leather straps that were still strong and serviceable, and thinking about what we carried that had not been part of that world: sunscreen, insect repellent, plastic bags, and freeze-dried food. Though famous as a tourist destination, it had also been a place of hard work: farming, prospecting, building shelter, and cooking for guests—work done by a few that many might enjoy their leisure. In the inner recesses of the Grand Canyon, a place abundant with natural monuments, those who worked left behind a memorial to human toil. As monuments go in the Grand Canyon, it's a trifling thing. But as symbols go, it struck me as huge.

As we left, I said to Malcolm, "We should probably prepare Brandon for possible porcine danger at the river."

"What kind of danger?" Brandon asked.

"*Pig* boats," Malcolm replied. "Huge motorized pontoon boats belching fumes and noise, loaded with people, food, beer, wine, and tape players. It's not like carrying everything on your back. You're being initiated as a hiker, so your first loyalty will always be to the trails."

"They don't sound dangerous," Brandon remarked.

"Tell him, Malcolm. He'd best know the truth."

Malcolm nodded. "You may come across sweet young things sunning themselves in the rafts or on the beaches. Nothing they like better than a young, rugged, trail-hard stud. But they'll use you and dump you overboard. What's your favorite drink?"

"Root beer."

"They'll have it. They'll invite you aboard for an ice cold root beer and the next thing you know—wham!—you're whisked away, entrapped by sirens of civilization."

Brandon dismissed this with a wave of his hand. I picked up Malcolm's theme, talking to Brandon's back. "On our Apache Point trip, after eight days in the canyon without human contact, a boat pulled onto the small beach at Copper Canyon where we had set up camp. It felt like a mob. They were playing music and drinking beer. We must have looked pretty haggard. Two women approached, very friendly, asking questions about the trail. We were reserved, answered their questions politely, but didn't invite further interaction. They stayed a few minutes, then threw each of us a beer as they left.

"Over dinner we did some serious soul-searching about whether drinking the beers would corrupt our spartan odyssey. After days of nothing but chlorinated water, those beers looked awfully good. We vacillated all evening. In the end, purity and sanctity were preserved. We poured them into the river."

"Well, if you two resisted, I guess I can," Brandon assured me over his shoulder, not quite certain if I was serious.

"That's not the end of the tale. After the trip, driving back to Prescott, we debriefed the episode with the beers. We decided that pouring out those beers was the stupidest damn thing we had done on the trip. We resolved that we'd never tell anyone how stupid we'd been and if we ever again had a chance to get free beers from a boat, we'd drink 'em on the spot, while they were cold, and be glad of it. And if they offered a second round, we'd drink those, too.

"I'm revealing our secret to you now in the spirit of male bonding. I mean, we don't have that many secrets to share, so we have to make do with what few we have, wretched as they may be."

"I'm honored," Brandon jeered. "And I promise never to reveal the secret, until I do."

Just five minutes below Bass Camp the trail left Shinumo Creek, which meandered on toward the river until it cascaded over a cliff, blocking access to the river below. We headed up a rocky, barren hill on a distinct, well-worn path that Bass had built for his tour business. It covered the final mile to the river, going up some five hundred vertical feet, then dropping down gradually below a long, high wall set back from the river. Building it with pick and shovel must have been arduous work.

At the crest of the ascent, the path crossed a substantial promontory that offered our first view of the river—a line of dark olive green dwarfed by the surrounding landscape of steep cliffs and rising terraces. After two-and-a-half days moving toward it, I had expected to reach the crest of the steep path, pause for breath, catch sight of the river, and be awestruck by its magnificence. I was prepared for a rush of emotion. Instead, I had a rush of cognition. I walked out on the precipice, saw the river, and said to myself matter-of-factly: "There it is."

It felt like verifying a research finding. From Swamp Point we had hiked through layer after layer of geologic evidence that a river flowed somewhere below. We covered millions of years of testimony, though the data were not complete what with unconformities and discontinuities along the way. Still, the pattern of evidence led toward one conclusion. Somewhere Muav Canyon would end at a river. Now we had reached the end of the evidentiary trail. I experienced a deep sense of cognitive certainty, always sought after in research, but rarely found.

I tried explaining this to Brandon. He was singularly unimpressed: "I'm sure the river feels better knowing we've confirmed its existence."

"We see something that looks like a river," Malcolm said, "but you boys had better climb down and touch it to make sure."

"You're not coming with us?" Brandon asked surprised.

"I've been there before."

"You haven't been there with Brandon," I reminded him.

"I don't get it," Brandon said. "Why come all this way and stop just short of the river?"

"The river's not my destination," Malcolm replied.

"I know, I know. The canyon is. But the river *is* part of the canyon."

"It just passes through," Malcolm said.

"Like us," I added. "My guess is," I continued, speaking directly to Brandon, "he resents the fact that the canyon has a bottom. Given his druthers, he'd prefer to keep hiking down and down and down."

"Truth be told," Malcolm replied, "I'd just as soon sit here in the shade and watch you two sweat your way down and back."

"I may need your help to save Brandon from pig boaters."

"We've warned him. The rest is up to him."

"Look!" Brandon shouted. A raft appeared upriver, then another and another. Four altogether, distant specks seven hundred feet below us and at least a quarter mile upstream. We watched silently as they took turns negotiating Bass Rapids.

"Malcolm," I said when they had passed out of sight, "we'll need your ceremonial touch at the river." He nodded assent.

We left the crested precipice, circled around below it, and traversed beneath a great cliff. The descent led down a shallow wash strewn with jagged boulders that felt sharp and appeared porous, almost spongelike, a distinct contrast to those in White Creek worn smooth from millennia of flooding. The gully emptied out on an undulating shelf below which, 175 feet straight down, the Colorado flowed through a gorge of black Vishnu Schist.

Brandon quickly outdistanced us, reaching the edge of the river cliff just as another group of rafts came by, this time genuine motorized boats. My view of him was cut off as I hiked behind a small mound and dropped into a gully. When I emerged he was nowhere in sight.

I looked back and couldn't see Malcolm either. I continued down to the shelf and headed upriver toward Bass Rapids. The undulations of the platform, like dunes of solid lava, made it impossible to see very far ahead. Crevices and drainages broke up what had appeared from above to be a relatively flat and continuous surface, completely hiding a person while hiking down and through them. I made my way along the uneven terrain trying to find a high point from which I might spot Brandon or Malcolm, not knowing whether either or both had gone upriver or down.

I felt anxious and annoyed that we'd gotten separated. We had never talked about where we were going at the river. We were just going *to* the river. From above that seemed destination enough. Strange how destinations can seem quite specific when you're far from them and quite vague when you're up close. Like having ten days in the canyon with Brandon.

I walked along the shelf to a beach below Bass Rapids. The silver glow of sun glaring off the black Vishnu hurt my eyes. Though not quite midday, the rock already radiated enough heat to make the air oppressive. Sweating heavily, I felt sluggish, dehydrated, and light-headed. I climbed down a slot in the cliff. The beach offered a sliver of shadow beneath a slight overhang.

The river narrowed and surged as it rushed past the protruding column of cliff that had created and now protected the beach. A series of powerful waves shot forth like an arrowhead suspended in eternal motion, thrusting and pointing downriver, but going nowhere. Unlike ocean waves, these scarcely fluctuated. So much water poured forth that I would not have been surprised to see it suddenly run dry. The wonder was that it just kept surging. And roaring. The most noise we had heard in three days, it seemed that such a sound must eventually crescendo, but like the waves, it gave no hint of its history or future, that it ever had, or ever would, ebb or swell.

Brandon found me, and finally Malcolm. As he joined us, he said to Brandon, "I saw a boat stop near you."

"Yeah, the guy controlling the boat—Do you call him a captain?—he kind of guided the boat near the bank and slowed down so people could see me."

"What did you do?" Malcolm asked.

"I just looked at them pretty blank-like. Don't worry, I didn't wave or do anything to embarrass hikers."

"Good. What then?"

"The second boat actually pulled up on a beach just below me. That's where I thought we were headed."

"They throw you any root beer or goodies?"

"No. Somebody yelled, 'Are you hiking?'"

"Brilliant question. What'd you answer?"

"I just kind of grunted, 'Uh huh.' Then I headed this way."

"You probably got away just in time."

"Is it the motors?" Brandon asked.

"Is what the motors?" Malcolm asked back.

"What makes you so down on the boats."

A large, motorized craft carrying what looked like a horde of people in orange-and-yellow life vests appeared suddenly from behind the wall, disappeared below a wave, then reappeared at the crest of the last wave and bobbed on downriver, screaming voices just barely audible above the roar, arms thrust skyward in happy triumph after the rapids. We watched in silence, barely breathing, as if exhaling loudly would have alerted them to our presence.

"I'm convinced," Brandon remarked.

Malcolm shrugged. "We're all defined by the tribes we belong to—the one we're born to, those we join, and the ones imposed on us."

"I prefer just being part of humankind," Brandon declared.

"Then you're a unitarian, universalist humanist," I laughed, "subtribe secular, considered very dangerous by other tribes."

"I want to be part of the no-name tribe," Brandon said.

"Humanism. No-namism. They're abstractions," Malcolm mused. He scooped up sand in his hands and nodded for Brandon to do likewise. "This is a reality you can hold on to." He opened his hands and let the sand flow out. "Feel the wall of schist against your back. Solid. Concrete. Real. Canyon."

I squeezed the sand so hard it hurt, the coarse grains abrasive and cutting, using the pain to get out of my head, using the feel of the wall to be present.

"So what do you call yourself?" Brandon asked Malcolm.

"I'm content being a Canyon Man." After a moment he added, "But, in the end, we all get defined by the tribes we belong to or get stuck into by others, humans being a tribe-based species."

"Amen. And that being so, while we're at the bottom of the canyon, Malcolm, I thought you might induct Brandon officially into the canyoneer tribe."

"I'd be honored. Take off your boots," he directed, beginning to untie his long red laces. He placed his boots on the sand in front of him. We did likewise, three pairs of dark leather boots on the white sand, facing the river and looking singularly incongruent, as out of place as if arranged by a modern performance artist in the corner of a museum, their meaning suggestive of some implicit possibility, yet ultimately open to whatever the viewers brought to the scene.

"These symbolize your tribe," Malcolm began, "and what's an initiation without a little tribalism. Boots won't take you down or across the river. They're for traversing solid ground. Your dad and I are both hikers. We might some day become river runners—they're mostly good folks—but right now we're hikers and you're being inducted into the canyon hiker tribe. That means avoiding pig boats. Which you mostly did. In recognition of your achievement and in celebration of your new canyon tribe status, I present you the last of the cheese." He handed Brandon a plastic bag containing a slimy mass of molten swiss and cheddar.

"I, um, don't feel worthy," Brandon said, dropping the yellow goo on the sand.

Malcolm stared at the cheese, eyes wide, as if shocked. Brandon picked the bag up carefully by one corner. "Let me see if the river will turn it back into something we can cut." He rolled up his pant legs, tiptoed and danced across the hot sand, and took two steps in. "It's ice-cold," he mouthed back at us, his shout drowned out by the rapids. He took a couple more steps and dipped the cheese below the surface.

"He's a hard case," Malcolm laughed. "We induct him into the land tribe and he immediately heads for the water."

"Do you remember ever being young enough to feel all options open to you—uphill and down, land and water . . ." My thoughts turned into a shrug as Brandon took another step, bringing the water up to his knees. It wasn't really the hiking tribe I cared about. I had followed with interest and amusement a long-standing debate, provoked by the religious right, about whether humanism was a religion. Now I pondered the pros and cons of considering humanism a tribe. A strange analogy came to mind: trying to decide, when Brandon was young, whether using his finger as a gun should be discouraged.

I grabbed Malcolm's water filter from the daypack and joined Brandon wading in the river. I held the filter while Brandon pumped, but our effort produced no water. I remembered Powell's oft-cited observation that the Colorado was "too thick to drink and too thin to plow." But that was not our problem. Little silt now gets past Glen Canyon Dam, but the rapids churned up enough sand and particulates to overwhelm the filter.

Brandon retreated from the icy water holding the slightly hardened cheese up for Malcolm to see. It didn't smell too bad and tasted fine mixed with peanut butter and apple slices on crackers, but we needed lots of water to wash it down. "How risky would it be to drink untreated river water?" I asked.

"Very," Malcolm answered. "There's a lot more than piss in the river. We should take back a canteen full in case of emergency on the trail, but drinking it would be a last resort until we can chlorinate it back at camp."

"What all's in it?" Brandon asked.

Before he could answer, a six-person raft shot out from behind the wall. Not being able to see upriver made each such appearance startling. Two more small rafts followed in quick succession.

"Mostly sadness," Malcolm said as the boats disappeared down river. "Greed, immediate gratification, shortsightedness, anger . . . but mostly sadness." Then he told of the building of Glen Canyon Dam and the ultimately futile fight to stop burying hundreds of miles of pristine canyon lands under water to create Lake Powell, now a recreation mecca. He recalled myriad proposals, debates, compromises, deals, and schemes to feed the West's insatiable needs for water and energy; politicians, developers and officials come and gone; and promises made and broken. The great Colorado now barely dribbles into the Pacific, its waters siphoned off along the way for irrigation and air conditioning. Sitting as we were under the noonday sun, sweating without moving, we could feel water being drawn out of the Earth and evaporating in unrelenting human use. Bass put cables across the river to transport people, animals, and goods in the spring when the river was too high and too filled with fast-moving debris to cross in a boat. The engineering gods now control seasonal flooding and, in so doing, have completely altered the ecology of the river. Beaches are eroding as the dam acts as a giant sieve, markedly reducing the replenishing flow of sand. Species of fish have disappeared from the ever-icy water released from the bottom of the dam. Vegetative zones have been altered and native plants have been overwhelmed by the prolific, imported tamarisk and forced out by hardy exotics.

Malcolm described proposals to add one or two dams in the Grand Canyon. Thus far defeated, such proposals seem likely to be resurrected and are believed by some to be ultimately inevitable to fulfill political agreements negotiated between the Western states and the federal government promising water and power from the river. Meanwhile, the pressure on the entire canyon ecosystem mounts from rapidly escalating human visitation and use, a crisis common to all the national parks faced with reduced funding and increased demand, but especially severe in fragile desert areas and along rivers. In the eighty-five years following Powell's initial 1869 river trip through the canyon, fewer than three hundred people emulated his voyage. Following construction of Glen Canyon Dam in 1963 and the filling of Lake Powell in 1964, river traffic surged like the waves over Lava Falls. In 1972 alone more than sixteen thousand ran the river. The inner-gorge environment was deteriorating so dramatically that the Park Service imposed a fourteen thousand per year limit and proposed banning motors. The concessionaires who operate the lucrative river runs mounted an intensive lobbying campaign with Congress and sued in federal court to save the motors under the guise of protecting the public's right of access and freedom of choice. The oars versus motors debate—row against roar—was resolved in favor of motors, which constitute about 80 percent of river traffic. Not normally given to pessimism, Malcolm, as much by his manner as what he said, enveloped us in gloom about the long term prospects for enlightened preservation. He spoke as a lover watching helplessly as his beloved lay dying of inoperable cancer.

While Malcolm talked, Brandon sat quietly, listening and staring at the river. When Malcolm finished, he asked about the influence of *The Man Who Walked Through Time*. He had just read it and was taken with Fletcher's argument that humans have to learn to leave things alone, to overcome our Western addiction to constantly build and improve. Fletcher had worried that his book would become a requiem for the Grand Canyon. Brandon wondered whether his call for protection had had an effect since so many people had read it.

Malcolm shook his head sadly, but said nothing.

"More people have read—and misread—Genesis," I responded, "and believe that having dominion over the earth means using it up. And, I'm afraid, we've used up our time here."

"You mean we don't have enough water to hang out by the river," Brandon chuckled, appreciating the irony. He got up and went back down to the river's edge, stepped in up to his knees, then slowly bent over, reaching his arms in above the elbows. He stood like that for several seconds, looking intently into the river, then withdrew his cupped hands full of water. Unlike the sand, he couldn't hold it. He flung open his empty hands, plunged them again into the water, and held them there. He may just have been cooling off, but from where I sat, the sun glaring off the white sand so that the air shimmered, it looked like he was embracing the river, trying to hold it in his arms, protect it. The slow embrace erupted into passionate, frantic splashing.

Then he became very still, his expression stony, as if seeing into the Vishnu and beyond. The inscrutable depth of his countenance portrayed what I imagined complete detox might look like. Several seconds or eons later, his disoriented expression impelled me to hug him as I had the four year old who came crying with a bleeding knee. Then, with a slight bow and broad sweep of my arm, as if politely deferring to a medieval dignitary, I gestured for him to lead the way back up.

18. Water Knowledge

Thirst grounded me firmly in the present moment. By the time I reached the trailhead up, I was sweating heavily and mentally dehydrated. I climbed above the path to the edge of a wash and climbed on a boulder. Malcolm, still on the shelf below, was ambling along using a driftwood branch he'd found as a walking stick. Though his gray felt hat stood out distinctly against the black schist, he seemed a natural part of the landscape. In contrast, Brandon's rapidly ascending figure radiated an energy that disturbed the stillness of the afternoon desert. It was clear I wouldn't catch him with more than my eyes. His faded blue T-shirt and khaki pants moved with a sense of urgency against the reddish-brown slope. As he pursued a turn in the barren, moonscapelike terrain, a ridge hid all but his blue-and-white baseball cap, a blue bandana draped from it to protect the back of his neck. It looked from a distance like a French Foreign Legion cap, complete with neck flap, floating surrealistically up the rocky wash.

I lost sight of him, then saw him emerge at the base of the cliff and negotiate the ledge along the concave wall that eventually circled below the precipice before coming out on top of it. He never took a break, looked back, or stopped to drink what little water he carried. I

161

paused to catch my breath at a switchback where two lines of erosion met to form the main drainage I was ascending. One, the primary source for the deeply rutted wash, extended as far as I could see along the main curvature of the hill. The other, a shallow tributary, originated off a saddle between drainages. I could see now that Brandon had left Bass's trail to follow a vertical line of shallow erosion that offered a steep shortcut to the precipice.

I chose to stay on the trail Bass had used, trusting that he had determined the best way up. I stopped to examine how he had reinforced the trail to traverse the steeply sloping terrain and soon found myself pondering the hundreds of times he had passed this way as he hiked back and forth to the river. Had he wondered about himself as a father? Did he worry about the effects on his four children of living in the isolation of the wilderness? Had he contemplated how to stay connected with his adult son?

These questions accompanied me up the drainage and served to distract me from obsessing on the last few gulps in my canteen. While many tributaries contribute to our life flows, I thought, two especially important sources flood our youth. One challenges us to achieve, perform, and accomplish. The other accepts and nurtures who we are, as we are, without regard to accomplishments. We differ in how much of each source we get, want, need, can handle, have imposed on us, and ultimately receive. And here, it seemed to me, was the fundamental tension in all parenting: How much to push? How much to accept? Conditional respect versus unconditional love. We want our children to attain their maximum potential and we want them to know we'll love them regardless of what they attain. These messages inherently conflict. In childhood and throughout life each of us receives and sends more of one than the other. At least I could not recall having ever seen a major drainage formed by tributaries of exactly the same size, length, and strength.

I thought back over the critical incidents of Brandon's life, revisiting moments of parental doubt when I had felt torn between pushing Brandon to do better versus accepting what he said he wanted. I felt that tension as an impediment to the new adult-to-adult relationship we were hiking toward. How could I discard it to be swept into the river with next spring's snow melt? Had Bass struggled with how best to nurture versus how hard to push? Had he found in the canyon the wisdom to transcend such parental paradoxes?

To support my final ascent to the precipice, I took a drink, sloshed the water around my mouth, savored the wetness, and swallowed. I inhaled deeply and exhaled slowly, feeling dryness return instantly, the swallow an instant memory. I resolved not to drink again until I reached the crest. I stopped to admire the endurance of a particularly precarious section of trail Bass had laboriously reinforced, wondering again what kind of father he was. The rocks along the trail offered no answer that day, but I came across answers of a sort, much later and quite unexpectedly.

In 1981 Stephen G. Maurer interviewed William G. Bass, born in 1900 as the second child and only son of William Wallace Bass. The resulting book, *Solitude and Sunshine,* is subtitled "Images of a Grand Canyon Childhood" and contains canyon pictures and remembrances. Reflection after reflection begins, "My Dad. . . ."

> My Dad gave me a beautiful little horse with a white blaze. . . . I loaned a man my little horse to go down to the river. And that was the last I ever saw my horse. . . .
>
> He tied him up . . . while he went across the river and over to Shinumo. He'd left the rope too long and the horse got tangled up in it and fell over the cliff, killing himself.
>
> I was sick about it.

From where we were hiking that day we could look across the river to the cliff from which the little horse had fallen and died. Bill Bass does not recount his father's reaction to the horse's death. How a man handled such a childhood crisis would tell a lot about him as a father.

Bill remembered his father as a storyteller; a fiddler who, with his wife at the piano, led the family in singing most every evening; a man with many friends, including Indians; and a teacher: "It would have been nice if we could have gone to school, but then, we might have learned the wrong things." He loved and bred horses, and when his favorite horse was killed "I remember my Dad bringing home his bloody collar with the bell on it and he was crying."

Bill Bass saw his father up close and shared his work as a gardener, prospector, carpenter, inventer, explorer, and guide. Bass was not absent from his family because he had to go off to a factory twelve hours a day, six days a week, as his urban contemporaries did. Still . . .

> My Mother and we kids were left alone on the rim, for weeks on and more. Not knowing when Dad would come in, sometimes running low on food and water. How night after night we would lie in bed and listen for the sound of the stage wheels, wondering when he

would come home. Or waiting by the window, in the bright sunshine of the day, always waiting . . .

And the excitement when we would hear him in the night, hear the stage tires strike rock up by the hill. . . .

At about Brandon's age, Bill and his father had a falling out. Bill left to work for his father's major competitor, Fred Harvey, driving a Pierce Arrow. In 1920 Fred Harvey won the government contract to run concessions in the new Grand Canyon National Park. In 1923, at age seventy-five, Bass closed his tourist business, the business his son had already left.

It strikes me as unlikely that Bass ever worried about how being raised in the canyon was affecting the self-esteem of little Bill. That was not a question of his time. That it is a question of this time may help explain why the idea of male initiation has been revived, why grown men spend weekends trying to get in touch with the male mode of feeling, and why I was walking in Bass's footsteps pondering questions that he would probably have dismissed as afflictions of too much city life and too little work with one's hands.

Bill Bass learned the value of water from his father and the canyon:

We were always concerned about water. . . . Sometimes we would go to bed at night seeing a little thunderhead come up. Why, we'd sit there all night praying to cause the wind to blow the cloud over us.

No cloud showed anywhere in the sky as I neared the precipice. I reached the crest expecting to see Brandon descending below. I studied the empty trail down the side of the steep hill all the way to Shinumo Creek and back up. He could not have covered that entire distance already. I looked behind me. Malcolm had paused for a rest, leaning on his walking stick, looking out at the river. A raven circled overhead.

To reward myself for the climb up, I slowly lifted the canteen to my mouth. Sunlight reflected brightly off the aluminum, blinding me. I took a mouthful of the hot water, savored it, and swallowed. Then I drained the canteen, took a last look at the river and headed down to find out what had happened to Brandon.

I found him under a huge rock column that had broken away from a distant cliff and fallen until it lodged where the drainage narrowed just above the trail. The resulting cavelike space, just large enough to crawl under, offered the only shade on the hillside. Brandon was lying in straw that looked like it was left over from the burro days of the canyon. His right arm was draped over his eyes.

I squeezed in beside him and drifted into rock-lizard oblivion. The sound of Malcolm's walking stick scraping against the rocky trail startled me awake. I tried to sit up, but hit my head on the overhanging rock. Malcolm plopped down at the opening and gulped some water from his half-full bottle, then passed it to Brandon. After just one swallow, Brandon handed it to me. I took a swallow and passed it on. Malcolm drank again and left a couple of swallows in the bottom, which he offered to Brandon. He then took off his hat, wiped his arm across his sweaty forehead, and observed: "You two are sitting in pack rat shit."

"It's softer than rock," Brandon smiled. He sniffed. "Why doesn't it smell?"

"It's so hot and dry out here, by the time a rat's shit hits the ground it's already dung-dry. Doesn't smell and doesn't even taste much. Try a few pellets."

"I would, but they'd probably just make me more thirsty."

"When did you become expert in rat shit?" I asked. "Before or after you took up shoveling human shit."

"Everybody's got to do something. Shoveling shit's as good as anything, but I don't do the actual shoveling. We therapists facilitate people doing their own shoveling."

"I expect you still get some on you," I replied, then turned to Brandon: "Notice any programs in scatology when you were looking at college catalogues?"

"You don't learn about it in courses," Malcolm answered first. "You study shit up close living in the dorm."

Brandon urged us back on the trail. Just above Bass Camp, he stopped at a pool in Shinumo Creek that drained down a five-foot stone slide into a rock basin. He undressed on the pink rock plateau that bordered the pool and, without hesitation, slid into the cold water yelling: "Since we can't drink it, I'll absorb it." Malcolm and I followed his example, though we entered more gingerly and quietly. Brandon romped and played. We laid back and soaked. We each tried the water slide once, at Brandon's insistence. He, in contrast, slid exuberantly from pool to pool, over and over again.

Watching him, I realized we had seen no toys among the artifacts at Bass Camp. A haunting scene from the book *Encounters with the Archdruid* came to mind. On Lake Powell prior to their trip together down the Colorado, Floyd Dominy, Commissioner of Land Reclamation and advocate of Colorado River dams, had bragged to author John McPhee and preservationist David Brower about putting up 960 feet of fence with his son in one day on his Virginia farm. "I told my son, 'I'll teach you how to work. You teach yourself how to play.' " When I first read that, I aspired to do better. I wondered if I had.

One thing didn't fit, like a scene from a "What's wrong with this picture?" book. Brandon wore a plastic shower cap.

"Why?" I asked, pointing to his head.

"Because," he answered.

"I'm amazed you'd even bring such a thing along." My observation was a question. His answer was a splash, soaking my hair as he slid away down a water chute.

19. The Erosion of Manners

T he fourth night felt pivotal. The trip to the
river dutifully completed, we had five
open days until the final day out. We could
explore the inner gorge or return to the heights.
Between bites of ramen noodles with canned beef
we discussed options, eventually deciding that
Brandon and I would hike up Shinumo toward
Merlin and Modred Abysses while Malcolm
stayed at base camp to enjoy a restful day alone.

We settled back with after-dinner hot drinks
to enjoy the changes that accompanied the twilight. Croaking frogs and clicking crickets foretold nightfall as surely as roosters announce the
day. The cascading whistles of a canyon wren
drifted down from somewhere above us. Slate-
colored dippers fluttered in and out of the brush
along the creek. A striking blue grosbeak landed
on a branch close enough for Malcolm to point
out its thick bill and tan wingbars. Brandon
entertained us with horrible expressions after
each gulp of chlorine-treated water, the hot
chocolate inadequate to disguise either taste or
smell. After he feigned gagging and spewed out
a particularly wretched mouthful, I proposed
that we catch up with the boy in "Iron John" and
find out what kind of water he was encountering
after his banishment from the forest. I gave
Brandon the story to read.

167

The King's son wandered for some time until he came to a great city. He sought work everywhere and finally found a job in the kitchen of the palace carrying wood, water, and ashes. One evening the boy was sent by the cook to serve the royal dinner. He covered his head to hide his golden hair. The King was angered by this unwitting act of disrespect. The boy resisted the King's command to uncover his head by claiming he was protecting a sore. Enraged at the boy's insult, the King ordered the cook to send the boy away.

"It's clear the boy didn't get control of his life by leaving the forest and going to the city," Brandon commented at once. "Now he's got both the cook and King on his case. Major bummer for the boy, I'd say."

"No argument from me," I agreed. "Anything else?"

"He carried three things. That's always a significant number, I'm told."

"Part of your cultural literacy learning?"

"No, my deep religious training. Let's see, wood, water, and ashes. I suppose wood could be nature. Water might be life. Ashes, I would guess, symbolize death."

"You look surprised," Malcolm remarked to me.

"I admit I was expecting a reaction to something else and," turning to Brandon, "you haven't even mentioned it. I would've bet it was the first thing you'd go after."

Brandon grinned knowingly. "I can't imagine what you're referring to," he insisted. So saying, he reached over to his pack, retrieved his logoless hat, and placed it firmly on his head, taking care to achieve just the right position, as if it were to remain permanently attached.

"I gather you're not really into taking your hat off in the presence of kings," Malcolm speculated.

"Or in the presence of his parents and siblings at dinner," I added. "Manners is a long-standing family issue, discussion of which has dominated many a meal."

"I know what to do should the proper occasion ever arise," Brandon asserted.

"What constitutes a proper occasion is the heart of the issue," I replied.

"My manners are fine," Brandon said. "It's another false dichotomy, having manners and not having them. I do both."

"Actually, I'm glad this has come up," Malcolm said. "I've been looking for a chance to tell you two that your manners are not up to Grand Canyon form. You shouldn't use the same Swiss Army knife for the peanut butter and the cheese."

"If you have no other mannerly wisdom to impart, Dr. Gray, we can return to 'Iron John.' "

"I was thinking that Brandon would probably like Claude."

"Who's he?" Brandon asked.

"Claude Lévi-Strauss, anthropologist. He wrote several books analyzing American Indian myths, including one entitled *The Origin of Table Manners.*"

"Why would I like him?"

"He was very critical of contemporary manners. He argued that the original purpose of manners among prehistoric peoples was to mediate their relations with nature so that humans did not upset the natural order of things. Modern civilization, being humancentric, uses manners to emphasize status differences between people instead of providing guidance for acting respectfully toward the natural world."

"Right on! You mean he thought manners had gotten worse with civilization?"

"He had a very specific definition of worse. Humans today fail to exhibit even elementary courtesy toward the environment."

"You mean like ill-mannered people pissing in creeks."

"Joining human water with nature's water is a time-honored display of interconnection, I'm sure," Malcolm rejoined.

"Give an example of a manners myth," I suggested.

"What comes to mind is one about the discovery of fire and not making noise while eating. A boy was left in the forest on his own, probably as part of an initiation. Near death from hunger and thirst, and terribly frightened, he happened on a friendly jaguar. The jaguar took him to a creek, gave him water, washed him up, and then took him to his lair. Since he had no children of his own, he adopted the boy as his son.

"The jaguar's wife cooked for them that night, and that was the first time a human ever saw fire. The boy was so astounded, he stayed by the warm fire all night, hardly getting any sleep.

"The next morning, the jaguar departed to hunt. The boy stayed by the fire and asked the wife for food. She was pregnant and so irritable that she couldn't stand *any* noise. The boy made noise eating the grilled meat. She became enraged. Scared to death, he ran into the jungle in search of the jaguar, but stumbled onto his village instead. He told the villagers about fire. The men were fascinated and, following the boy, snuck up and stole the jaguar's fire. The boy became a hero."

"How is that a story about manners?" Brandon asked.

"Lévi-Strauss says that the boy's a hero to kids whose parents insist they eat quietly. If the boy hadn't made noise, we wouldn't have fire."

"But he was impolite to the jaguar who gave him food," Brandon protested.

"Lévi-Strauss would argue that it was unnatural to chew cooked meat, which is crisp, without making noise. Raw food can be chewed quietly."

"I still don't get it," Brandon said. "How does making noise while eating show respect for nature?"

"Lévi-Strauss, like your dad, was into categories of things and their meanings. Cooked meat, being different from raw meat, requires different etiquette. Cooked meat has had a different interaction with nature in the form of fire. Modern etiquette, on the other hand, requires standard behavior for all occasions: at all times you must eat with your mouth closed. The bottom line is, Lévi-Strauss would have supported your rebellion against bowing thoughtlessly to conventional manners." With that, Malcolm rolled slightly to one side and let loose a round of cannonlike flatulence.

As the night sounds returned, I said, "You've reminded me of a scene from *The Once and Future King*. Lancelot had just returned to Camelot and was describing to Arthur and Guinevere his having seen Galahad with the Grail. The king said that he didn't know Galahad well, but it seemed the other knights didn't like him. Guinevere said that she had found him rude, impolite, and lacking in courtly graces. Lancelot looked right at the queen and replied: 'Galahad and I sailed together six months and never had need of manners. We wasted no time commenting on the charming weather or offering each other tea. Manners are only needed between shallow people to give their empty affairs the appearance of importance. I spent a long time with him and discovered he was a lovely person, lovely inside, not because he always offered me the best seat in the boat.'"

"So we're agreed," Brandon said. "I can ignore the rules of etiquette for society as long as I show respect for nature. And if anyone complains, I'll just tell them that I've simply been above bothering with manners since I gazed on Holy Grail Temple."

"You can do whatever you choose and tell people whatever you want and *you'll* bear the consequences."

"I'll keep that in mind next time I'm asked to serve dinner to a king and have to decide whether to wear a hat."

"Right. Back to where we got sidetracked by manners. The boy in 'Iron John' had to take a job as cook's assistant. He worked hard. I've been thinking some about work myself. When we were at Bass Camp today, looking at his tools, it seemed to me that his whole campsite was a monument to work, as was the trail he built to the river. I got to thinking about passing on to you my thoughts about work and asking Malcolm to do the same."

"Like what?"

"People ask kids what they want to be when they grow up as if they can be only one thing. My dad got locked into a single job. Bass avoided that. He worked as a tourist guide, prospector, farmer, rancher, breeder, engineer, builder, inventer, explorer, entrepreneur, and I don't know what else. Malcolm's doctorate's in anthropology, but now he does family therapy. He's been a professor, wilderness guide, and home builder. I've done several different kinds of things myself. I figure the topic of work might be worth five minutes while we've got the boy working in the kitchen and pissing off the King."

"You think I ought to have a job in college, right? I don't have a problem with that."

"No. No. Whole other discussion. Let me finish. Bass Camp got me thinking about work, but this afternoon, with you sliding and splashing around in Shinumo Creek, I got to thinking about play. In the story, the boy first encounters the Wild Man while playing. His golden ball rolled into the Wild Man's cage. From that time to the end of the story—I can tell you this much without spoiling the ending—the boy never plays again."

"So you want me to play while I'm in college. Great. Consider your advice followed."

"Hold on. Remember, you're not an either-or person. I don't want you to do anything. I'm just letting you know that entering the world of work without losing the capacity to play is one of my struggles. There. End of sermon."

"I certainly haven't succeeded in keeping them together," Malcolm said. "Hiking this big hole is my play. The tightness in my back at the end of a typical day tells me the rest is work."

"It's a weird topic for me to try to think about right now, Dad. I'm just focused on college and doing music. I don't think about music as work or play."

"Sounds like we ought to have you teach us," Malcolm remarked.

"No, no. I'd like to hear you two talk about work. I just don't know how much I can really use right now, you know, really absorb. I hear you about having options. I'm more worried that I have too many interests, that I'll never narrow down and actually be good at anything. But whatever you want to say, I'm open."

"I've got an idea," I said. "I don't want to turn this into two old men preaching at you. Suppose Malcolm and I just have a conversation with each other about our work. Whenever we play here in the big hole, our work is a lot of what we talk about. We've been known to give each other advice. Not follow it—just give it. You'll be witness to two old friends catching up with each other and someday something you hear tonight may come back to you at an important moment."

"Go for it," Brandon said.

So we did.

20. The Great Rift

It started with what seemed like a casual reference. After discussing work and play, Malcolm and I drifted into talking about people Brandon didn't know. He got up to go sit by Shinumo Creek and write in his journal.

"Hold on, Tchombiano," I said, "Help me clean up the cooking stuff first. Don't move, Malcolm. We'll do it."

Malcolm leaned back on his pack and extended his legs out on his worn insulite pad. When I returned from the creek, he observed: "You called him Tchombiano."

"It pops out every now and again. I like to use it often enough to remind him—and me—of our Africa connection."

"It sounded like an expression of affection."

"It is. Did you notice if he reacted in any way?" I asked.

"I'd say he was aware. He doesn't miss much, you know? I remember you told me the name's from Upper Volta, but I don't remember the tribe."

"The Gourma people, about a half million strong in eastern Upper Volta. Now, of course, its Burkina Faso, Land of the Upright People, but to me it will always be *La Haute Volta*. To development economists it's the world's armpit,

173

but I remember the Peace Corps as a happy, fulfilling time. I came to love the people and the Gourmanché language."

"What about Gourmanché?" Brandon called. I was startled, not expecting he could hear us above the creek and night sounds.

"Malcolm was just asking where Tchombiano comes from," I called back. "You want to come explain it to him?"

"In a minute. I'm working on a song about the river."

"I'll be interested in what he tells you," I said.

"He knows why you named him that, doesn't he?"

"Sure. But I've never heard him explain it to someone. I assume his friends or teachers have asked about it. He always signs both middle initials, Q and T, so I imagine people ask about them. I don't know how he explains Quinn much less Tchombiano."

"How do you explain Quinn?"

"All Brandon's names have either people or place significance. All the firstborn Patton men for four generations have had the middle name Quinn, a tradition started by my great-grandfather about whom I know nothing else, not even his first name. In fact, I know virtually nothing about either the Patton or Quinn clans other than what one can learn on the certificates they sell in shopping malls that purport to give the history of family names.

"Brandon's named for Brandon, Manitoba. While she was pregnant, his mother supervised student teachers there for the University of North Dakota. We liked the Gourma tradition of often having names mean something significant related to a child's birth. We considered Dakota, but settled on Brandon. What's your middle name?"

"It's Clyde now," Malcolm mused.

"Now?"

"It used to be Calvin."

"You changed from Calvin to Clyde?!"

"I didn't so much change it as it got changed. I mean, I didn't set out to change it."

"You're not making this easy. Let's start at the beginning. Why did your parents name you Malcolm?"

He laughed. "Malcolm's not my name."

"You're putting me on, right? Is Gray your name? Who the hell am I down here with?"

"I was born Clyde Calvin Gray. In college a friend said: 'You're not a Clyde. You're a Malcolm.' The name stuck. Before I married Dee, she knew me only as Malcolm. So I changed my name to Malcolm Clyde and dropped Calvin."

"Great story," I said as Brandon joined us.

"What's a great story?" he asked. Malcolm repeated his nomenclature odyssey, then Brandon asked: "What brought up the name Tchombiano?"

"Malcolm noticed I called you that earlier."

"Do you ever use it yourself?" Malcolm asked.

"My friends know that's my name. At first it sounds *Italiano,* so they want to know if I'm part Italian. I tell them it's an African name my parents gave me to connect me to the ruling clan among the Gourma where they lived just before I was born. If I ever go there, Dad says I'll be welcomed as a son of the Chief. I don't know if I believe that, but it makes a good story. I don't really use the name or flaunt it or anything, especially at school. It could cause trouble."

"What kind of trouble?" Malcolm asked.

"Almost half the school is African American. If I made a big deal out of it, somebody could take it wrong, like the time Dad almost got killed for telling a black man he was African."

"That's an exaggeration," I protested, pleased that he remembered the story, but disconcerted at what he remembered.

"That's what you told me," he countered with a grin.

"I bet he told you he almost got killed on our first canyon trip too," Malcolm said.

"In at least a couple different ways," Brandon confirmed.

"Don't believe him. What's a little fall off a Redwall cliff? Now then, what's the melodramatic story of this brush with death over Brandon's African name?"

"It wasn't over Brandon's name," I corrected. "It was over claiming Africa as my homeland. It's kind of a long story. You sure you're up for it yet tonight?"

"No place I have to be in the morning. You boys have the abysses ahead of you. I'm sleeping in. The question is whether *you* have the energy to tell the story."

"I suspect I'll sleep better with the story told."

Brandon imitated a drumroll ending in a cymbal crash.

"Thank you for that introduction," I began. "Now then, during graduate school I got a fellowship to do research in Tanzania. I'd only been back from the Peace Corps a year. I jumped at the chance to get back to Africa and especially Tanzania. It was a time of great optimism there. President Julius

Nyerre had a vision of creating a uniquely African socialism, his Ujaama villages. Socialist intellectuals from all over the world congregated in Tanzania to help him create a multiracial society. The Vietnam War was killing peasants in Asia. We had a chance to help peasants in Africa. For a young person interested in experimenting with grassroots peasant socialism in the early 1970s, Tanzania was the place.

"All that would have been enough, I suppose, but the chance to get to Olduvai Gorge was the real magnet. For years that had been the place on earth I most wanted to visit. I had already been to the second place on my list—Timbuktu—on a trek through Mali the last year of the Peace Corps."

"What's in Timbuktu?" Brandon asked.

"The oldest Islamic university in the world, a small adobe structure now turning into sand. But that's not why I went. It's just a small desert oasis town, but it always loomed large in my mind because in my father's fits of rage he'd yell: 'You don't like it here, go to Timbuktu.' I wasn't sure it was a real place, then I came across it on a Michelin road map of West Africa while planning our Peace Corps vacation. I had to get there, which is a whole story in itself. Suffice it to say that I sent my father a postcard: 'Dad, I'm in Timbuktu. Now you can't say I never did anything you told me to.' "

"What'd he write back?" Brandon asked.

"Nothing. He rarely wrote. When I returned from Africa I asked him about it. He treated it as no big deal. The actual place had no meaning to him. He hadn't known where it was or if it existed. It was just a saying he'd picked up. 'Go to Timbuktu' instead of 'Go to hell.' The fact I'd actually been there seemed to diminish its significance for him. I never again mentioned it to him or heard him refer to it."

"It sounds like you were trying, in a way, to please him," Malcolm remarked. "His nonresponse must have felt pretty bad."

"It happened a long time ago," I replied quickly, feeling but not wanting to deal with the sadness that my relationship with my father evoked in me. I hastened on. "My point was that while Timbuktu was second on my list— and the Grand Canyon wasn't on it at all until I met Malcolm—my interest in Timbuktu was nothing compared to my desire to get to Olduvai Gorge. Timbuktu was a shot at my father. Olduvai was *my* passion."

"You must have been a Leakey admirer," Malcolm guessed.

"Were you into Africa too?" Brandon asked.

"No, my interests focused on the Southwest and Native American culture, but you didn't have to be into African to know about Leakey."

"My physical anthro professor was his personal friend," I continued, "and brought him to class one day. I was riveted. White-haired, British accent, tall, confident, wise—if he had asked for volunteers to follow him back to Olduvai that night, I wouldn't have hesitated."

"What'd he say?" Brandon asked.

"He told the story of discovering *Zinjanthropus boisei* in 1959. Leakey and his wife, Mary, had been exploring Olduvai for thirty years. They had found lots of primitive tools, but not the toolmakers. Leakey was sick in bed when Mary came running in yelling, 'I've got him!' She had been exploring a gully that drains into the gorge and found two large teeth and a piece of skull. They excavated the site, sifting through the equivalent of a room of dirt and rock using brushes, sieves and dental tools, and ended up with something like four hundred fragments that they put together like a jigsaw puzzle to form the skull. They nicknamed him "Dear Boy" as a code name to protect the discovery until they were sure what they had and were ready to tell the world.

"His account was spellbinding, like a good detective story. He made us experience what it would be like to finally solve a mystery after thirty years. Then, there was a sudden change of plot. *Zinjanthropus* was not the maker of those tools. He announced that they had just discovered the earliest-known direct link to our own species, *Homo habilis*, meaning 'handy man.' *Habilis* had made the Oldowan tools and had more brainpower than *Zinjanthropus*. What's more—and I remember him being very excited, then pausing as if deciding whether to take us into his confidence—*Habilis* and *Zinjanthropus* lived at the same time, proof that evolution wasn't a straight line."

"Did he talk about Olduvai Gorge a lot? I mean, is it an African Grand Canyon?" Brandon sounded afraid I was going to get sidetracked into the whole history of evolution.

"At the time, I had an image of Olduvai as being like the Grand Canyon. I don't remember him describing it much. It was the name and what it represented that made an impression on me."

"So what did it represent?"

"The Garden of Eden. At least I was left with that impression. It was as likely a spot as any on earth. To this day scientists believe that human beings evolved in East Africa. In a symbolic sense, and maybe even a real sense, we all come from Olduvai. That's why I wanted to go there. It was a pilgrimage, scientific rather than religious, but a pilgrimage none the less."

"What was it like?"

"It's only twenty-five miles long and about one hundred yards deep, but it has exposed rocks almost as old as the Vishnu Schist we were on today at the river. The dry riverbed resembled the terrain here: sparse yuccalike bushes and a few scattered acacia trees, thorny and jagged, not very big. No real shade. Foothills rose gradually beyond the gorge and a mountain called Lemagrut loomed like a rising shadow on the horizon some miles away. The gorge had held the last reservoirs of water during great droughts, so bones and fossils were everywhere."

"Sounds awesome without being awesome," Brandon commented.

"You want awesome? Let me expand the picture. Olduvai is part of the Great Rift Valley—and I mean GREAT, as in cousin to GRAND—the most striking feature of the African continent. It runs about four thousand miles from the Red Sea and the Gulf of Aden through Ethiopia, Kenya, and Tanzania into Mozambique, a continent-long area of earthquakes, volcanoes, lakes, gorges, escarpments, valleys, tar pits, and places with Grand Canyon–like dimensions, more than a mile deep and fifty miles across. While our ancestors may not have evolved precisely in Olduvai, they definitely emerged somewhere along there.

"Okay, all that is context. Here's the story. The experience in Olduvai was very emotional for me. I felt connected, like Olduvai was my ancient ancestral homeland. When I returned to the University of Wisconsin that fall, I registered for a seminar on African Development. Waiting for the first class to begin, I told a black female student about Olduvai. I explained that I knew nothing about my more recent European origins, that my Scotch-Irish name meant nothing to me, and I knew nothing about ancestors beyond my grandfather. Nor was I interested in exploring any European ancestry. My African ancestry gave me all the roots I needed. Being Oldowan African, I said, connected me to all of humanity, not just to one narrow subspecies in a corner of Europe.

"A black man joined the conversation. He already knew her. We exchanged introductions and she said to him, 'Michael was just explaining to me that he's African.' He grew immediately tense and glared at me coldly: 'You're from South Africa?'

" 'No! No! And I hate apartheid,' I insisted, trying to assure him of my goodwill. I then repeated my story, enthusiastically talking about our shared African roots. He went berserk. He was a big man, over six feet tall and very muscular. He screamed curses, accused me of trying to steal his homeland, called me all kinds of names, honkey being the kindest, and threatened to beat this African bullshit out of me."

"And did he do the deed?" Malcolm asked.

"The woman saved me. She grabbed his arm and started cooling him out. Through a kind of daze I could hear her say, 'He's not worth it. Be cool, man. He's just some dumb white boy. Don't pay him no heed. Be cool, man. Be cool. Don't let him get to you. Nobody's taking Africa away from you or anyone.'

"I was horrified. Everyone was watching. I was frozen. Then I started trying to apologize, to explain, but she pulled him away. He left and I never saw him again. She stayed in the class, but refused to speak to me. I've never again claimed African origins, but my attachment to Africa endured and surfaced again when it came time to name my son."

"That's quite a handle you carry, Tchombiano," Malcolm said.

"I'd like to go to Olduvai someday, and to Gourmanché country, but . . ."

"But what?" Malcolm asked.

"The black man was right. We're not African. My having an African name doesn't make me African. I understand how important Africa was to my mom and dad, but the name's about them, not me."

"You're an adult now," I reminded him. "You can change the name if you don't like it."

"I don't want to change it," he replied. "I just don't . . . don't want to flaunt it."

"Did you ever consider adding Tchombiano to your name?" Malcolm asked me.

"I thought about it," I replied. "I even came close."

"Why didn't you?"

"My father. It would have been a slap in his face. He would never have understood."

We sat in awkward silence. At length Malcolm remarked: "I can remember once hating being an Okie, then later feeling pride in my Oklahoma origins. What Tchombiano means to you may change over time, Brandon."

"I just remembered," I added, "that the Gourma people didn't think of themselves as Africans. They thought of themselves as the Gourma, the people. They had no sense of being part of a continent."

"That may have changed by now too," Malcolm speculated.

"I like the idea of common human roots, of being part of humanity instead of some subgroup," Brandon said. "Saying our roots are in Africa would still be limiting. I'd rather just say I'm from—Earth."

"You know, Brandon, your dad and I grew up without pictures from space of an Earth without national boundaries. Every globe we saw in school gave a very divided impression of the world. Your identity's been shaped by a different set of images."

"After discovering the dangers of claiming Africa as my homeland— and I agree, it was stupid and insensitive—I found out that the continents were originally one super landmass called Pangaea. So I contemplated saying I was Pangaean. But that required too much explanation and sounded arrogant and academic."

"You mean it was too revealing," Malcolm quipped.

"Maybe. Mainly, it wasn't accurate since Pangaea predated humans by many millions of years."

"So where do you say you're from now, Dad?"

"I've changed where to what. I'm a humanist, a Unitarian-Universalist, from everywhere and nowhere. Being a Patton doesn't mean anything to me, so I've got no heritage to pass on to you, Brandon. No tribe. No clan. No ancestral territory. We can never say 'my people.' You'll have to settle for being a universalist."

"No problem. I'm quite content just being an Earthling, Dad."

"Hold on a minute, Brandon," Malcolm said slapping him on the leg. "You got inducted into the canyoneer tribe today."

"Right. I'm an Earthling and an inner Earthling."

Afterward, I laid awake a long time, creation stories dancing through my mind. They all accounted for two things: creation of the earth and the earth's inhabitants. Without a place, there can be no people. Without people, place has no significance.

I looked up at the star-filled night and recognized the universe as a place, my place, an omnipresent place. I savored the oxymoronic irony— universalism as a tribal identity.

The temperature just hinted of the coolness that would set in during the middle of the night. I breathed deeply of the still air, recalling something I had read about air molecules diffusing through time and around the globe. I took a drink of water, conscious of its origin from a spring deep within the earth. It felt comforting to be back amidst two-billion-year-old rocks, to be an inner Earthling.

I looked at Brandon lying close enough to hear the slow, deep inhalation of sleep. I put my hand gently on his bag, to feel his breathing, and became deeply conscious of how few extended and uninterrupted conversations we had had in his whole life. Times when TV didn't force us to fit whatever dialogue we could into the space of commercials. Times when the telephone didn't interrupt. Times without competition for airtime from family or friends. Times when we had shared stories and talked about things that mattered.

My Africa story had taken a long time to tell. Stories of connection are like that. Six more days in the canyon suddenly felt very short.

Day Four

21. <u>Abyssus Abyssum Invocat</u>

The Abyss plunges below the Great Mohave Wall into Monument Creek as an isolated chasm. Gawain Abyss drops precipitously below Excalibur, isolated against the North Rim by Guinevere Castle. The only convergence of abysses, the juncture of Merlin Abyss and Modred Abyss, defines the heart of Shinumo Amphitheater between Holy Grail Temple and King Arthur Castle. This convergence called us, not like mythical sirens, but rather like scientists wanting to test theoretical constructs. We wanted to find out what physical realities inspired the nomenclature.

The intermittent calls of dippers and wrens above the steady, even rush of Shinumo Rapids gave sound to the rose glow of early morning as Brandon and I started up Shinumo Creek, the spires of Dox Castle visible high above us on the right, the foundation of Holy Grail Temple on our left. Malcolm chose a day of rest at base camp.

Making our way up Shinumo gorge took us up and down rock walls and back and forth across the creek. We figured we could save some time if we could get up to and cut across the more open Tonto Platform. We searched for a break through the vertical Tapeats, layered like stacked pancakes, though each layer was thicker than the average person is tall. We had to find a way up through some twenty or more such layers with the added complication that the top of the stack overhung the lower, more recently eroded layers. The trick would be to ascend without being exposed to a hundred-foot drop.

I taught him how to read the rock walls as we strategized together. The first place we tried proved unassailable. And the next. The fifth or sixth attempt yielded a place with distinct footholds for leverage, good handholds to pull ourselves up, and no more exposure than falling off the roof of a one-story house. I climbed while Brandon spotted for me under the theory that he would be able to break my fall without both of us tumbling down the jagged slope below. It was not a theory I wanted to test.

The sandstone rock abraded our hands, but we made the climb with only minor scrapes. The last, most strenuous section required a chimney ascent in which we wedged into a crevice and gradually wiggled up. At the top of the chimney I poked my head out and was struck by the dramatic differences between niches. Below, the creek supported a strip of dense tropical vegetation—trees, ferns, reeds, bushes—higher than our heads. Above lay the expansive desert Tonto, sparsely populated with isolated succulents and scrawny bushes, none more than shin high. For a moment, hanging on the top layer of the Tapeats, we were suspended between worlds.

As we reoriented ourselves, morning sunlight reached the Tonto, noticeably warming the dry air. We hiked along the gravelly shale terrain among clumps of dry blackbush, passing fragile toothpicklike stems of Mormon tea and stepping over prickly pears or the occasional barrel cactus. I propelled Brandon forward with a discourse on the difference between hiking down through the Tonto, as we had done descending North Bass Trail two days earlier, and hiking *along* the Tonto, the inner canyon's major highway shelf, as Malcolm and I had done for days during our Apache Point to Mount Huethawali venture. Brandon knew about this difference from reading Colin Fletcher. As we experienced it directly, I pointed out that we were attending "the school of hard knocks," my father's alma mater. He had taken pride in the common sense he had acquired, something he asserted I lacked and would never acquire through the printed word I spent so much time with. Brandon asked what my father meant by common sense and why he valued it so much. My halting effort to explain that which I was alleged to lack may have, ironically, confirmed my father's allegation.

I happily abandoned pursuing this realization for deeper insight as we turned north and took in the dramatic panorama ahead. In the distance a massive wall of red rock rose straight up what looked to be as high as a fifty-story building and an equal distance wide. Above the foundation, four terraced layers of Supai gave the impression of a Japanese emperor's palace. Somewhere below the sharp corner of Elaine Castle's fortress island, the abysses converged.

The going quickly became more difficult along the severely eroded eastern shelf. At first the drainages were shallow enough to cut directly through. Then they became deeper, more like minor side canyons. We stopped to calculate whether we would make better time following the deeper drainages in and around or whether we should cut directly across by bushwhacking down and back up through thorny thickets. Discussion yielding no definitive answer, and Brandon and I disagreeing, I suggested that we test empirically the difference. I followed a burro path around the next drainage. He cut through. His route was a little shorter and quicker, but took more energy and markedly increased his thirst. The next drainage was eroded deeper and scarred with crevices, so he decided to join me in taking the long way round. Traversing each successive drainage became more difficult and time-consuming. We had to begin rationing our water as the ascending sun reflected with increased intensity off the desert floor. After an hour of hiking, traversing five or six drainages, the great wall of Elaine Castle seemed no closer.

We talked on and off as we hiked, less as the heat and our thirst increased, eventually hiking in silence. I wanted to say something about how special it was to be alone with him in the canyon, but I hesitated. Was it the right time and place? I peered ahead to Elaine Castle, studied the rocky ground, looked left and right, mechanically checking out the terrain, gazed up at the perfectly cloudless sky, considered the sun as keeper of time, and wondered what "right" place could ever mean.

I focused on the small clouds of Tonto dust Brandon kicked up with each step. What was to keep me from stopping right there, embracing him, and telling him that this time with him was as special as any I have had on this earth? I was on the verge. Just needed one more bit of analysis, think it through a little more. Would he feel called on to respond? Would the expression of perfection make this moment any more perfect? Quite the contrary. It might replace perfection with awkwardness.

My logic and emotions were at war—and not evenly matched. Waging the war undercut the spontaneity of the moment. I had moved from raw expression to processed calculation. Since calculated expression was not what I sought, but was now inevitable, I had moved into a different time and place. Being now on the other side of the drainage from where this internal dialogue began, I could not turn back to the point of origin.

I recognized the pattern, an old friend. There would be other moments, I told myself. And there always were. Sometimes I even took advantage of them.

My father often expressed his love—whenever he lost his temper. I could remember many belt-lashings in the basement when he'd repeat with each lash: "I'm only doing this because I love you." Slap. "This hurts me more than it does you." Slap. Later, when I was too old to whip, he lashed with guilt: "When I think of all the things I could be doing if I didn't have you kids around my neck. . . . If I didn't love you as a Christian father, do you think for a moment I'd put up with all this?"

The right time and place for my father to express love was when he was in a rage. He raged often, so he told me he loved me a lot. And I never doubted that, in his way (the inevitable conditional clause accompanying these kinds of ruminations), my father loved as much as he was capable.

Lost in this reverie, I almost bumped into Brandon before realizing he had stopped. Another deep side canyon lay ahead. He was squatting, waiting for me to discuss the route. I put my hand on his shoulder, squeezed through to the bone, and, when he looked up, smiled. Slowly I turned toward the great wall that was our destination, broadened my smile, squeezed again, then moved past him to survey the side canyon, removing any necessity for him to respond.

He came alongside me and offered his canteen. After a swallow, I gave it back. We agreed on the route and I motioned for him to take the lead. As I followed, I said, "An image of my father's funeral popped into my head back aways. I was watching the little clouds of dust your feet kicked up and the phrase 'dust to dust' came to mind. Then I flashed on my father's funeral and what you wrote about it."

"Weird," he remarked. "*Yebeday* weird."

"It *was* weird. Maybe even *yebeday*. I've never quite found the right time to tell you before, but I want you to know that, well, I was very moved by what you wrote. It's powerful writing. I mean, I'm not sure that's exactly the right word, but—"

"You can say '*like* powerful.' "

"Huh?"

" 'Like' is what you say if you can't find the right word. My generation knows there's no perfect word for anything, so we say 'like' a lot. You know, *'like wonderful.'* "

"I was trying to be, like, serious, you know."

He stopped to face me. "Sorry. It's strange to think about Grandad's funeral out here, though not as strange as writing about it on a college application, I suppose."

"I'm curious. Why'd you pick that as your topic?"

"I don't know. The instructions said to pick a topic that would reveal something about myself. You said I should make my application stand out. But, basically, it was on my mind, so I just wrote about it. I was actually kind of worried that it would be blasphemy or something to write about it to get into college. I'm glad you weren't offended. I mean, what I wrote was real, but it's unreal to write it on an application form."

Here is what Brandon had written.

We sat in our chairs with bowed heads as the Shriners read their honorary statements, but I seemed oblivious to the sadness. It was a time of remembrance and respect for a lost loved one, yet I was most struck by the illiteracy of the Shriners as they fumbled over their scripts. Ashamed for being distracted, I concentrated my thoughts on the true subject of the ceremony. I had a front-row view of the dead body. I peeked at the pale face and wondered how cold his skin was under all the makeup. Grandpa never played a very important role in my childhood. He coughed and spat and cursed and smoked. I always wondered why he didn't play games with me, or read stories, or tell me exaggerated anecdotes from his childhood. He wasn't very healthy. He wasn't any fun. So I stared at his corpse, unmoved, as the rest of the room whimpered and sniffled.

It was a common funeral, I suppose, not really knowing since it was my first, but I was surprised because I had always thought the stereotypical funeral was an exaggeration. The parlor was a wonderfully neutral mauve with just enough pink to lighten the atmosphere but not mock it. The soothing, yet barely audible muzak floated in the air, tacky as muzak always is. It must soothe some folks, but my musical dogma puts it beyond my appreciation. It grates.

The open casket was surrounded by a botanical assortment that could've been a Rousseau painting if one switched the casket for a voluptuous nude. The entire atmosphere of the room was straining to be subtly uplifting, yet at the front lay a corpse that exuded an overbearing dreariness.

I pondered this paradox, realizing that the conflict in ambience seemed to echo the guests' struggle for emotional control. Their emotions seemed real. My emotional neutrality felt out of sync.

After the Shriners finished stumbling over their scripts, my father took the podium and gave the eulogy. He reviewed his father's life without praise or criticism, but I knew my father well and could sense the love and hate behind the words. He read some of Grandpa's favorite quotes from the Bible. They were appropriate, optimistic quotes. I think it was the first time in a long time that my father had read from the Book. He also talked of those who were important in Grandpa's life: Grandma, his fellow Shriners, and his fellow war veterans. Each party nodded in remembrance as they heard themselves mentioned. I thought of the unmentioned first wife, my father's true mother, and the agonizing story of her death which turned Grandpa into a sorrowful picture of resentment. I thought of the unmentioned children: my father and his three younger siblings who struggled to take care of themselves while Grandpa turned away in self-pity and remorse. I knew that my uncle and two aunts were also thinking of all that was not mentioned in the capsule of Grandpa's life. But for the rest of the audience, the speech was a soothing closure. My father had given them a portrait of Grandpa that sympathized with their sadness and helped resolve their feelings. He nurtured the audience. I felt proud that such a caring man was my father.

The end of the eulogy marked the end of the funeral. My aunts and uncle sobbed in each others' arms. I studied my father's stoic face and saw emotion throbbing beneath his skin. He embraced his brother and sisters with the strength of an oldest child. He looked into their eyes in a knowing exchange. Shared memories passed between them and he exploded into an outpouring of tears that I had never seen from him before. His entire body shook as he wailed in a despair of grief and relief.

I flashed on stories I had heard about my father's childhood: belt-whippings, a lost mother, and the rejected youngest child who my father took in as a teenager. I thought of the anger, bitterness, abandonment, and hardship that my father survived. Then I thought of my own childhood and his devotion to my happiness—his patience, tolerance, and nurturing. He gave me freedom and taught me about boundaries. He didn't hurt me as punishment; he accepted my mistakes and helped me learn from them. He shared his wisdom, but didn't tell me how to live. He didn't leave arguments unresolved or cries unrecognized. He was ever-present, supporting and encouraging my music, writing, creativity, and sense of self. He never missed an important event or rite of passage. He came to my soccer games, school activities, and performances. Most of all, despite a divorce, he was always there for me with unconditional love.

I rose from my chair and made my way to my sobbing father. We stood before each other and I held out my arms, finally feeling some sense of place, some reason for being at this funeral. I held him tightly in my arms in a secure, supportive, loving embrace. A warm, wet cheek pressed against mine. I held him up as he released an anguish of years. I felt that I was finally repaying him in a small way for all the love I had received.

22. In Context

"I'm not sure how to say this or even quite what I want to say," I began as we sat under a lone pinyon tree, taking a brief break. "I guess I want you to know that *I* don't think of my childhood as unhappy or my father as unloving. It's true that he had a bad temper and whipped me some, but it's also true that he kept the family together after my mother died. We were never hungry. We always had shelter. It's true he never saw me perform in the marching band, but he came up with the money to send me to band camp every summer. I don't remember ever being denied anything I needed."

"But how do you justify the beatings?" Brandon asked.

"*Spankings.* I was never battered or bloodied. He left marks, but I don't think he ever broke skin. He did break his hand once when I moved and he hit my hipbone instead of my butt. It was the only time I ever believed him when he said it hurt him more than me." I laughed. Brandon didn't. "After that he used a belt. But you've got to understand, he believed that sparing the rod would spoil the child."

"That's from the Bible, isn't it?"

"That's a common misconception my

father delighted in correcting. He would say: 'Poor Richard may have worried about spoiling a child, but the Bible says it's a matter of love. Proverbs 13, verse 24: *He that spareth his rod hateth his son: but he that loveth him chasteneth him betimes.*' Then he'd grin and proclaim: 'I love my children a lot.' "

"That's crap. Words like 'spanking' and 'chastising' water it down. He beat you, plain and simple."

"Little in life is plain and simple. There are beatings and there are beatings. Have you forgotten that I spanked you?"

"Once."

"Once that would qualify as a good, old fashioned spanking. It was my duty to pass on something from my father."

"You told me not to throw a board or something off the balcony and I threw it anyway and hit you on the head."

"That incident scared me. Afterward, I realized I had been out of control. I felt my father in me. That probably did hurt me more than you. On the other hand, you never threw a board from the balcony again."

"At least you didn't say you acted out of love."

"True enough. My father religiously said he loved me when he whipped me, but even as a child, I think I understood that love was not the primary motivator in his life. Doing his duty was primary. What he expected of us, *quid pro quo,* was obedience."

Brandon spit the words back at me. "Duty?! I can't even relate to the word. What does 'duty' have to do with whippings? And obedience?! Submitting to brute force is a weak idea of obedience."

I couldn't help laughing at his intensity. "Ease up. It's not as bad as it sounds. I realize you don't have a lot of experience with obedience, but the idea has had a pretty long run in Western civilization. I once challenged my father using your argument. He was whipping me for being late for dinner because I was helping a friend with homework. I said something like, 'Would you rather I do what I think is right or just whatever you say?' Big mistake on my part. That just fed his rage. Later, when he'd calmed down, he came to my room to make sure I had gotten the message: 'Twenty times in the first eight chapters of Proverbs the Bible says a son must heed his father. *My son, hear the instruction of thy father* (Proverbs 1:8). *My son, forget not my law* (Proverbs 3:1). *Hear ye children, the instruction of a father, and attend to know understanding* (Proverbs 4:1). *Hear, O my son, and receive my sayings that the years of thy life shall be many* (Proverbs

4:10). *My son, keep my commandments and live; and my law as the apple of thine eye. Bind them upon thy fingers, write them upon the table of thine heart* (Proverbs 7:1–3). *Harken unto me—*"

"Enough already. You don't have to quote all twenty verses. I get the point."

I laughed. "That's *exactly* what I said to *my* father. So he made me memorize all twenty verses and when people from church visited, he'd make me recite them, which," I added, laughing again, "is why I can recite them all to this day. Want to hear more?"

"I don't see how you can defend him and laugh about it," he said, ignoring my playful tone.

"He was my father," I offered softly. "You're judging him by today's standards."

He considered this a moment, then said: "I hear what you're saying. I just have a hard time with any attempt to justify beatings." He regarded me with an intense awkwardness that belied both determination and sensitivity. I liked the care with which he calculated how far to push his point.

"I realize that your judgment comes from things I've said over the years, but when I hear it back from you, it sounds . . . distorted. There was a lot about my father I didn't like. He was extremely demanding and we fought intensely, but he had clear values. He was true to what he believed. That's how he'd want to be remembered. That's how I remember him at this moment. That's what I'd like to pass on to you. He lived in a time when doing duty to family, country, and God was paramount."

I heard what I was saying as if from a distance, like the words themselves, sociologically accurate, analytically safe, and ultimately cold as a midwinter night. Brandon's response was equally devoid of blood connection.

"Just because something happened in its time doesn't make it acceptable. Hitler was a product of his time, too."

"Maybe I've tried to build myself up in your eyes by portraying him negatively. I'm not sure. But I'm afraid I've given you a one-sided, out-of-context, jaundiced view of my childhood. I want to correct that, balance it, if I can."

"It doesn't matter. Why not just leave it alone?"

"It may matter a great deal. Many cultures believe that the spirit of the grandfather is reborn in the grandson."

"Do you believe that?"

"I believe you should know more of him than you do."

"Did you really know him?" he asked.

His question hit me as a challenge, then I saw a softness in his face. He was asking if I wanted to dredge up memories that he knew were painful for me.

"I don't know how well I knew him, but I have memories. Images. I want you to know those. Imagine a man who works hard at a job he doesn't like and doesn't pay much, but supports his family. He takes that family, a pregnant wife and three young children, to church regularly. His wife dies unexpectedly in childbirth. Throughout the three days of the wake and funeral he weeps inconsolably. After the funeral, with the premature baby still in the hospital, he gathers the three children in their living room and says, 'We don't have your mother with us here on earth anymore because she's gone to heaven to watch over us. She's told me she wants us to stay together and I've promised her we will. It will be hard but we'll make it. I promised your mother and I promised God.' Tears flowing, he got on his knees and held us tightly.

"All I would ask is that you include that image in whatever others you have. Even now I can feel how hard he held us, so hard it hurt. He kept the only oath I ever heard him swear."

Brandon started to respond, but I held my hand up. "Let that image linger a bit."

I wanted to let that image linger, not just for Brandon, but for me. I had begun by talking to Brandon and ended talking to myself. It was my own image of my father I was reshaping. Brandon's questions and reactions were like a mirror faithfully reflecting back to me the portrait I had created. Experiencing the stark reality of it through Brandon's portrayal, I knew the image to be a self-serving caricature, distorted because my own memory was distorted. In reframing Brandon's image I was reconstructing my own memories.

In youth I had convinced myself I hated my father. As an adult I adopted an air of superiority, convinced I pitied him. For the first time in my life, as I worked to give Brandon what I thought was a fairer image, I found out I respected him.

I loved him, too, in my way, as he loved me, in his. I had told him that many times in his later years, but those expressions of love had never seemed quite satisfying, not quite enough. Now I knew why. I had never told him I respected him. I had never affirmed that he kept his promise and did his duty.

I think my respect would have meant more than my love. Unknowingly, I had withheld from him that which he most sought. In trying to tell Brandon about him, I understood him in a new way. And my relationship to him. And the conundrum that is fathers and sons.

23. Skeptical Inquiry

The last swallow of water changed our plan. We could no longer risk staying on the Tonto until Shinumo Creek rose to meet it. The great wall of Elaine Castle remained frustratingly distant, far beyond a seemingly endless series of terraces and drainages. I began to despair of reaching the abysses.

We found an eroded break in the Tapeats through which we could scramble back down to the creek. A rock gave way and the root I was holding broke off. I fell and slid the last fifteen feet, landing in an undignified sprawl, scraped and gasping for air, amid dense vegetation and thorns. "I see now why you don't like hiking downhill," Brandon said when he reached me.

"Thanks for the sympathy. I could have been killed."

"Hmmmm. I hadn't thought of that. Maybe you'd better tell me what you want done with your body."

"Ah, to feel young and invulnerable, again. Let's go."

Shinumo Creek, five to eight yards wide and a couple of feet deep, had more water than I had expected so far upstream. We had dropped into a wild garden, at places even junglelike, with dense vegetation, trees, clusters of reeds,

199

tall grasses, and flowering plants. The creek was spotted with rounded boulders, fallen trees, occasional rapids, small waterfalls, and deep pools. We danced across rocks and fallen limbs, moving at a fast pace.

The change of worlds was energizing. I composed poetry in my head about water and gardens versus desert and cactus. Then, chastising myself for setting these worlds in opposition, I started anew, this time portraying their connection—a systems approach in honor of Malcolm. My poetic impulses were interrupted by our arrival. Though we had long anticipated getting there, the actual moment of arrival felt like a surprise. We broke out of some vegetation, ducked under an overhang, jumped across the stream, worked past a rock wall, and found ourselves under a canopy of trees where two streams met—the confluence of Merlin and Modred Abysses.

The first thing that struck me was the perfect right angle of the convergence. Standing at the point of convergence, looking upstream at each, they were indistinguishable. Comparing flow, width, depth, and vegetation, they appeared so much the same that the lack of distinctiveness was striking—the only exception I ever encountered to prove the rule that no two tributaries or side canyons are ever the same. Nothing stood out to beckon the adventurer in one direction or the other.

Yet choose we must. It was late morning. We had to keep within the confines of a day trip, not only because we weren't equipped to stay overnight but because it wouldn't be fair to worry Malcolm. That we could not explore both abysses had become clear at our last rest stop, when we had checked our progress on the map. I had begun thinking about how to make the choice. What emerged was an idea for a ritual test of Brandon's vulnerability to superstition and New Age mysticism.

The moment we broke through to the convergence I said, slowly and authoritatively: "Brandon, I'm going to ask you to do something that may seem strange, but please indulge me. Don't think about it. Just do it."

"What?"

"Malcolm has been telling us to stay open to the canyon, to let the canyon speak to us. I have an idea of what Malcolm would do if he were here. Will you try it?"

He shrugged.

"I'll take that as a yes. Go up each stream until you're just out of sight. Don't cross either stream yet. That's very important, but it doesn't matter which one you go up first."

"Is that all?"

"Select a pebble from each. Keep the one from Merlin in your right hand and the one from Modred in your left. Take care to keep them separate. After you have them, come back here and cross to that spot"—I pointed—"so you're right inside the convergence. Position yourself so that you can reach your hands out over each stream, holding the stone from Merlin over Merlin and the one from Modred over Modred. Then focus all your attention on the stones. Concentrate. If Malcolm is right, if you're open to the canyon, you'll then know which abyss we're supposed to enter. Go now."

Brandon started to say something. I raised my hand to silence him, smiled imploringly, then made a single marked movement with my head, nodding him on. He looked sheepish and awkward, like a teenager being embarrassed by a parent in front of friends at some public event, but he did as I asked.

I was updating an old game I had played with Brandon, wondering if he'd remember. As a new parent, I had become intrigued with the child-rearing implications of Carlos Castaneda's *Separate Reality* and Joseph C. Pearce's *Crack in the Cosmic Egg,* two of many books propagating mystic powers of mind and nonordinary realms of psychic experience. One popular premise of those predisposed to parapsychology is that belief is a prerequisite to psychic power. So, when Brandon was learning to talk, I played a game in which he guessed at objects I held behind my back. I rigged the game, however. I was not testing his psychic power, but trying to instill in him the belief that he had paranormal capabilities so that he might, on his own, come to employ whatever powers of mind he might possess. As he grew older and learned to distinguish numbers, we spent hours playing a game in which he guessed what cards I was holding. Again, I fixed the game so that he would think he guessed correctly. From the time he was tall enough to see out the car window, I asked him to turn traffic lights green so we wouldn't have to stop. I then manipulated the car's speed for the desired result, much to his delight.

I treated the power to control the changing of traffic lights as no more unusual than reading the word STOP on a street sign. I reacted to his seeming "ability" to intuit my thoughts no differently than his learning to dial the telephone. Alas, Brandon tired of these games, or I gave up reinforcing such powers in the face of evidence that nothing was coming of my efforts. By the time he started school we no longer indulged in such games, but while I waited at the convergence, I wondered what, if anything, he remembered of them.

To add drama to the moment, I assumed a lotus posture, my eyes closed, breathing meditatively. I heard him return from Merlin, pass me, and proceed up Modred. He returned quickly. "Okay, I've got the two stones. Now what am I supposed to do now?"

I opened my eyes and looked into his. "Do you have the stone from Merlin in your right hand and Modred in the left?"

He checked the stones. "Yes."

"Cross to where the two streams meet. Hold your right hand out over Merlin and your left over Modred. Close your eyes, relax your body, and focus on the stones. For Malcolm's sake, be open."

"What if nothing happens?"

"Where do you get this need to analyze things before they happen?" I chided. "Just go see what happens. Stay open."

He shrugged. I started counting in my head because I wanted to know how long it took. One, one thousand. Two, one thousand. Three, one thousand. I had a momentary image of the crowds waiting around the Vatican for the smoke announcing that a new pope had been selected. Annoyed by this Roman Catholic intrusion, I counted on.

Four, one thousand . . . seven, one thousand. Eight, one thousand. Brandon squatted down. He positioned his left knee slightly lower than the right, shook his arms loose and extended them over the two streams. These movements took four seconds. I couldn't tell if he closed his eyes. Thirteen, one thousand. Fourteen, one thousand. Fifteen . . .

"Merlin," he announced and stood up, dropping the pebbles in the stream as he crossed swiftly back to me.

"What?" I asked, surprised by his sudden movement and distracted wondering if I could retrieve the "magic" pebbles as mementos for Malcolm. But they were lost, carried by the current to rest amid countless ordinary rocks in two feet of water. Damn, I thought, I should have told him to bring them to me.

He stood beside me, repeating the choice, but offering no explanation. We put on our hip packs and he led the way, moving determinedly into Merlin Abyss. He pushed through tall grasses, leaped on and off boulders, and brushed aside branches with energy and agility, unimpeded by the absence of a clear path. I struggled to keep up as he crossed back and forth over the creek, ducked under rock overhangs, and jumped over logs.

My struggle was more mental than physical. I became obsessed with finding out what happened, wondering if he actually thought he had received a message from the canyon. What would I say to that? Whatever happened had certainly lit a fire under him. As he charged upstream, I took a resigned breath and resolved to be patient. Just follow along and go with the flow, I told myself. And that I did—right into the creek.

Just ahead of me Brandon had jumped from a midstream boulder to the bank. His thrust had dislodged the boulder. He lost his footing and fell sideways onto a small cactus with not-so-small needles. I stretched for the midstream boulder he had vacated, misjudged the step, and slipped into the creek, shin deep but still standing. In an instant my boots filled with water and I emerged cursing alongside where Brandon was extracting cactus stickers from his arm. "You okay?" I asked.

"Damn," he said under his breath as he submerged the afflicted arm in the cold water to ease the pain and itching. Then he noticed I was wet. "*You* okay?" I nodded.

He withdrew his arm from the water and busied himself brushing small stickers from his fingers, one of which was bloodied. I noticed an especially long cactus needle in his thigh, pulled it out and showed it to him. "You landed a big one. Pierce you or just stick in your pants?"

"Got me, but not bad." He rubbed the pierced spot on his leg before examining the needle more closely. "Big sucker, huh?"

"Big succulent," I corrected.

"Huh? Oh yeah. Weak, Dad. Whatever, it had my name on it."

"Not getting mystical in your old age I trust."

"No. I wasn't paying close enough attention." He threw the needle down and started to move on.

"Hold up a minute," I said. "We've been trucking hard since the convergence. I need a break to squeeze the water out of my socks."

He looked at my wet feet and I sensed an opening. "There's no particular hurry, is there?" I focused studiously on untying the double knot in my bootstring. "You have some appointment to keep that I don't know about?"

No sooner did the words escape than I regretted the transparency of my ploy. He sat down nearby, got out his canteen, and took a long, slow drink. He worked over his hand and arm, removing the last of the cactus stubble. I got my socks off and wrung them out. An awkwardness hung between us like an invisible chain of iron that bound us together even as it weighed us down. He seemed distracted, even burdened, as if he wanted to say something, but couldn't. Then out it came: "I just chose Merlin to see the waterfall. That's all," he said sheepishly, looking down, his voice so low I had to strain to hear him above the sound of the creek.

"I take it you didn't get a signal from the canyon?"

He nodded.

"You're telling me nothing happened back there, right? No message. No movement of a pebble in your hand. No signals from Merlin." This last I said mockingly, making light of the ritual assignment now that I knew how it had turned out.

"Right. I had already decided I wanted to come up Merlin if we couldn't do both. Why'd you want me to do that thing with the pebbles?"

"I'm not disappointed, if that's what you're wondering. And I certainly wasn't asking you to fake a mystical orgasm for me or for Malcolm. It was an experiment. Not much of one, to be sure. Malcolm would probably say that fifteen seconds to get a message from the canyon is not exactly bending over backward to mystery but, hey, we took a shot. You reported your experience honestly. That's all I would ever ask. I hope you know that."

"So what was that all about? It was pretty weird."

"Think of it as your skeptical-inquirer test. You passed."

He wrinkled his face. "Huh?"

"Skeptical inquiring is the very unholy quest for scientific explanations of seemingly nonordinary phenomena. You've just qualified for induction. Congratulations."

"I have no idea what you're talking about."

"There is an organization of Skeptical Inquirers, officially The Committee for the Scientific Investigation of Claims of the Paranormal. I'm an associate member. They debunk things like fire walking, telepathy, astrology, UFO abductions, circles in English cornfields, and messages from pebbles in the Grand Canyon. There are always explanations, at least so far. James Randi is probably the best-known skeptical inquirer. He'd be worthy of consideration as a hero if you were into heroes which, I know, you're not. He was awarded a MacArthur Foundation Fellowship, popularly dubbed a 'Genius Award,' for his devotion to exposing charlatans like the not-at-all-amazing Kreskin. Years ago he offered to pay ten thousand dollars to anyone who could conclusively demonstrate psychic powers. Then he formed an educational foundation which will award a million dollars for any psychic demonstration. See what was at stake with those pebbles! Alas, you're in good company. In a quarter century, no one has come close. He's also a magician, 'The Great Randi.' I suspect he would feel very much at home in Merlin's Abyss. I'll tell you more later, unless you've changed your mind about lunching here."

"No. I want to make it to the waterfall. It shouldn't be too much farther by the look of the Tapeats." He rose, his demeanor again jovial and energetic. "I'm glad that's over. It was getting strange there for awhile."

I smiled. "I've got bad news for you. It may not be over."

"Huh? What d'ya mean?"

I put my hand out. He pulled and in one motion I rose and moved past him. Upstream a few yards I stopped and waited, looking back with what I hoped resembled the sly grin of the conjurer. "Something as yet unexplained did happen."

"What?" he asked, doubt obvious in his tone.

"All in good time."

"Sure," he hissed, sounding tired of the game.

"Okay," I said. "Hear me out. I'm a skeptic, not a cynic. I remain open to possibilities. You've shown you're a skeptical inquirer too, so let's go inquiring. I enjoy a good mystery, and we now have a mystery to solve. Or maybe Merlin really has performed some magic with you. Let's find out."

"What are you talking about?" he asked, interested now, my seriousness evident. "I don't get it."

"I can't tell you yet, while the test is still underway. But believe me, I'm not pulling your strings. We may have stumbled onto a mystery. Let's go find out."

I took the lead, hiking as fast as I could, not worrying about wet feet or occasional thorns. Now Brandon had to scurry to keep up with me as I trucked upstream to explore the mystery of Merlin Abyss.

24. Merlin Pool

Knocking aside tall stalks and wide blades of tropical vegetation, sometimes hugging the cliff walls, other times following the creek bank, we bushwhacked deeper into Merlin Abyss. The Tapeats cliffs diminished as we ascended, though we could only gauge how much at rare openings in the dense greenery created by plateaus of shale, smooth from centuries of winter runoff and spring floods. Between two mounds of rocky rubble where the Tapeats had cracked, we encountered a series of stepping stones through what seemed like a groomed Japanese garden. At another spot a crevice had allowed the stark Tonto environment to spill through and creep below the Tapeats, creating a cactus oasis within a few yards of Shinumo. Then the angle of ascent increased markedly and the creek became rapids.

Brandon had resumed the lead so he saw it first. The sides of the creek had narrowed into steep cliffs and our boots lapped the water as we moved along the edge looking for rocks or logs to step on, ducking under overhanging branches and stepping foot over foot in a balancing act along the muddy bank, pretending that it mattered whether or not our feet got wet. At the sound of the falls we abandoned that pretense

207

and charged forward, bouldering straight up the center of the creek. Brandon craned his neck above a tall boulder and exclaimed, "Wow! Phenomenal!"

I climbed up behind him and stared dumbfounded that such a place could exist in the desert.

Water being so precious in the canyon, a waterfall becomes the liquid equivalent of the Hope Diamond. The tumbling wall of water, twice as tall as Brandon and equally wide, engulfed me, leaving me searching for the conversational equivalent of a reality-pinch. "If this be Merlin's illusion," I said, "I'll take it."

The translucent falls poured into a calm pool, almost a perfect circle bounded on three sides by two-story-high walls of moss-covered rock. The clear water flowed into Shinumo Creek past two boulders, each as large as the chalkstone we had found wedged in the Tapeats narrows on our descent. Viewed from below, these massive boulders seemed to guard the pool from intrusion. Viewed from above the boulders took the form of a sculptured exit, directing the flow of water from the tranquil pool to the rushing creek below.

The foliage along the perimeter formed both a border and canopy, the branches of cottonwoods extending in places out over the pool to shade it, making the water below dark and opaque. On one side a massive log fell diagonally from the top, spanning the entire face of the falls, caught halfway into a somersault as floodwaters dropped away and left it without enough thrust to complete its acrobatic turn in midair. Far behind the falls, looking like a curtain backdrop, rose great vertical heights of redwall that formed the base of Elaine Castle.

We took all this in from a large rock slab that was half immersed in the pool—a stone counterbalance to the great diagonal log across the falls. The portion above water was just large enough to invite stretching out for rock-lizard time after lunch. Scattered rays of sun found their way through the canopy of leaves to skitter across the still surface beyond the bubbling base of the falls. Once our eyes adjusted to the alternating shade and shimmering, we spotted several large brook trout, their leisurely circling accentuated by darting minnows in the shallows. I reminded Brandon that, in White's version of the Grail myth, Merlin once turned young Arthur into a fish to give him perspective, "so he would not have neglected to add a piscine touch to this pool to make it seem real."

I settled on a poolside slab while Brandon set out to explore. He climbed up and around to get above the falls, then down the mossy wall to stand beside, then disappeared behind the white curtain of water. I looked through, instead of at, the falls and could just follow his progress, like a grainy shadow across a flittering movie screen when the film has run out. He crept along what I presumed to be a ledge, then the shadow vanished. I sat up, watching intently, waiting and imagining calamities. Shortly, he reappeared on the same side he had entered, carrying a mass of something in his hands. He rejoined me on the slab as I finished removing my boots, still carrying the vines he had grasped trying to cross behind the falls but which, in pulling loose, had forced his exit.

"So, Dad, do we eat or swim first?" he asked, placing the vines in the sun to dry.

"That's a weighty decision," I replied. "I'd better hold some food in one hand and water in the other and—"

"You do that. I'm starved." And he reached for lunch.

"Ah, Merlin," I meditated aloud, "tis a bittersweet moment when youth asks for the counsel of an elder and then rushes on without waiting for a response. How can the impetuosity of youth be restrained to higher purpose and deeper contemplation?"

He ignored me, hungrily devouring peanut butter and crackers. We ate the last two apples and nearly finished the gorp we had, saving enough for one break during the descent.

I felt exhausted. We had hiked fairly steadily for at least six hours. The swim would have to wait. Even Brandon allowed as how he might indulge in a few winks before testing the water. We agreed that we could spare another half hour, then we would have to depart. Before napping, however, there was the unfinished agenda of Merlin's mystery.

I pulled out the map, compared it to the surrounding terrain, and said: "I put us about here." He looked where my finger pointed, made his own analysis, and agreed. I put the map back in its plastic wrap and repacked the remnants of lunch. "How did you know the waterfall was here?" I asked.

"The map," he replied without hesitation.

"We just looked at the map. The waterfall isn't marked. It's too small to show up. There is no indication of a spot like this. *Nothing.*"

"Then Malcolm probably mentioned it," he suggested, but his voice lacked conviction.

"Malcolm has never been up here."

"Then I must have read it in Annerino or in Harvey or Colin Fletcher. Whatever. Somewhere I had to have read it." From his insistent tone I sensed he had begrudgingly grasped my point.

"Fletcher did not come this way. Harvey and Annerino only describe North Bass Trail. None of them describe Merlin Abyss. The first I knew of this waterfall was when you told me you chose Merlin because of it."

"So what are you saying?"

"We have a mystery to solve. How did you know a waterfall was here?"

"I just figured that wherever the Tapeats begins would have a waterfall of some kind."

"Wouldn't that presumably be true for Modred as well? Why, then, choose Merlin to see the falls?"

He didn't respond. He just looked at me quizzically, as if waiting for my explanation.

"The Tapeats coming down North Bass Trail dripped a little," I offered, "but in no way hinted of this. What struck me when we took our last break was the way you said you wanted to see *the* waterfall, matter-of-factly, like it was something you *knew*."

"I was just hoping or guessing. You're making it into some big mystery. It's just a waterfall."

"Perhaps. But this is how superstitions, mystical beliefs, and psychic assertions are born. Some serendipity occurs. A random coincidence grabs the imagination and—Presto!—before you know it, a New Age sect is born. Add a dash of holographic metaphors, stir in some selective, out-of-context references to quantum physics, and boil it under Heisenberg's Uncertainty Principle and you've got a concoction you take on the road and sell to P. T. Barnum's beloved masses. Easier than breaking into the spotlight as a musician, I assure you. Musical success actually requires some talent.

"So, sure, it's just a waterfall. The question is how you knew with such conviction it would be here. Maybe you have psychic powers. Sure you don't want to turn in your musical aspirations for mystic stardom? I can see it now: The canyon seer with bighorn totem. Could be a huge attraction. There's not much money in skeptical inquiry. Just truth. Hardly even a contest in our times."

"I'll stick to music."

"Fine. But that doesn't mean you can avoid explaining how you knew about the waterfall. I know you don't like tests, initiation or otherwise, but this one's been thrust upon us."

"What's your explanation?" Brandon asked.

"It's not my test," I replied. "But maybe I can help. Malcolm has said initiations are mainly old men telling stories. Have I ever told you about losing my horse in Africa?"

"Under a waterfall?" Brandon asked, grinning.

"A waterfall in the flat savannah of Upper Volta! That would be a challenge even for Merlin. You up for the story now or after swimming?"

"You decide. It's your story."

"Only until I tell it. Then, it's yours, too."

"Now, then," he said, laying his head back on his hip pack.

"Once upon a time—actually, twenty-three years ago—your mother and I lived in a two-room adobe house in Fada N'Gourma. Shortly after our arrival I bought a horse from the chief of Bogui, a small village ten kilometers east of Fada toward the Niger border. Buying this horse seemed like a good way to establish a relationship with the chief since Bogui was to be the main site of my agricultural extension work.

"The horse turned out to be a fairly worthless nag. His hooves were so overgrown that he couldn't trot without stumbling. I knew little about caring for horses or riding, so he was mainly a pet, though I rode him once a week or so."

"I'm trying to get a picture of you riding a horse in the African bush," Brandon interrupted. "Did you have a saddle?"

"I rode bareback with a halter. Your namesake, Tchombiano Lamourdia—the family name, being most important, was always used first—had helped me negotiate the purchase, trying to counsel me how to bargain. All the people from the village assembled to observe the transaction. I knew I'd pay too much, so trying to save face, I told the chief in halting Gourmanché that I expected to pay a little more than the horse was worth because of my respect for him. Lamourdia told me in French that this made no sense, but I thought the chief looked pleased. Of course, I had no way of knowing whether he was pleased at this honor or, as Lamourdia insisted, pleased at having fleeced the *bompieno*—the white thing. The Gourma, like most peoples of the world, reserved for themselves the honor of being the only real *human* beings."

"*Bompieno,*" Brandon repeated.

"A few months after purchasing the horse I awoke to find him missing from the stall I had built in our small compound. We checked in Bogui, but no one had seen him. Lamourdia made inquiries around Fada. Nothing.

"I went to the extension office to seek advice from Monsieur Lompo Bernard, the director I worked for. It was Friday. He told me if the horse didn't turn up over the weekend he would take me to someone who could locate anything that was missing. With that bit of intrigue to console me, I left.

"On Monday I returned and reported the horse still missing. He told me to return at noon and he'd take care of it. Offices were open from 7 A.M. to noon, then 2:30 P.M. to 5:30 P.M., because it was too hot to work in early afternoon and the Gourma are rock-lizard-time connoisseurs. Africa's where I learned to nap. When I returned he said something had come up and we'd have to go after work, so I should come prepared to spend the night and bring five hundred West African francs."

"How much is that in dollars?" Brandon asked.

"About ten dollars. So I got the money and that evening he drove me in his gray Citroen pickup some thirty kilometers north. The dirt road was extremely rutted, so it took well over an hour to get there. On the way, he told me about growing up in the village we were going to. When we arrived everyone came out and there was a lengthy round of greetings after which we were served some millet beer in gourds. Dinner was *sabu,* a puddinglike bread made of millet that we dipped in okra sauce with, in his honor, some chicken innards.

"At length, near dark, we went to the hut of what Westerners would call a medicine man or witch doctor. I no longer remember the proper Gourma term, but it was a word connoting respect and spiritual powers. Literally, his Gourma name meant, *One-Who-Speaks-with-the-Earth.* We went into his hut. He wore no special clothes, and was bare-chested with baggy pants of handwoven cloth—typical farmer garb. However, he wore several unusual straps around his neck from which hung brass figures, small cloth bags, and leather pouches.

"I was seated across from him on the smooth dirt floor next to Monsieur Lompo. We went through the extensive Gourmanché greetings, then he asked me what question I had for the earth. I looked at Monsieur Lompo. He nodded that I should go ahead.

"Monsieur Lompo's demeanor was more respectful than I had ever before witnessed. We called him *Le Chef*—like calling someone Chief or Boss—not just because of his position, but more, I think, because of his commanding presence. He was about fifty-five years old, a large man, rotund, distinguished looking; a man of some wealth with three town wives, several more village wives, and a large number of children. Everyone I had ever encountered in Monsieur Lompo's presence deferred to him, even the regional commandant, who had been sent out from Ouagadougou and, technically, was Lompo's superior; but, being a Mossi, and younger than Lompo, he was always deferent. So Lompo's deference to *One-Who-*

Speaks-with-the-Earth made a big impression on me. I asked in halting Gourmanché, 'Where is my horse?'

"He nodded, smiled, and drew a large circle in the dirt on the floor, a circle that encompassed the entire space of perhaps four feet between us. Within this circle he formed several mounds of dirt. The dirt was very, very fine, as if it had been sifted. The surface was completely smooth except for the mounds he made and circle he drew. Having made two or three mounds, he bent his right ear to the earth like he was listening. Suddenly he pounded the floor and spoke very fast, almost chanting, using a language I didn't recognize. Then he took pinches of earth from the mounds and sprinkled them about in the circle. Next, he moved his fingers across the earth rapidly, making marks, quickly smoothing them out, then making more marks. His arms and fingers moved very quickly, like he was typing messages to the earth, hesitating briefly to read what was written, erasing, and then making more messages. This went on for some time."

"How long?"

"I really can't say. I was totally absorbed in watching. I didn't wear a watch since knowing the precise time was seldom of value. Over and over he pounded on the earth, talked, bent over to listen, then pounded again. I found out later that Monsieur Lompo couldn't understand any of it either.

"At length he stopped, sat up straight, and looked at me so intently that I felt he was penetrating my mind. In the dim light his eyes glowed like unblinking fireflies. Monsieur Lompo nodded to me and made a movement with his right hand. I took this to mean I should pay him. That brought me back to everyday reality. He accepted the fee and wished me good health— *Laafia, bompieno, laafia.* He extended the same wish to my wife and children, a blessing that hardly inspired confidence since Peace Corps volunteers in those days could not have children. Another fleecing of a *bompieno,* I thought. As we rose to go, he announced: 'Your horse is at your compound.' "

I stopped at this point in the story and looked at Brandon as blankly as I could manage. After a long, silent pause, he grinned and said: "All right, I'm game. Was it there?"

"Was the waterfall there?" I grinned back.

"You're saying the horse was there."

"No," I laughed. "When we arrived back at my house next morning, Monsieur Lompo took the unprecedented step of getting out of his car and engaging me in conversation about Bogui and my work there. He didn't comment on or seem surprised by the horse's obvious absence—obvious because the place I kept the horse was between the house and the compound wall, clearly visible from the street. I thought it impolite to point out that *One-Who-Talks-with-the-Earth* had chalked up a big goose egg with his prediction—though not with his fee."

"Bogus!" Brandon exclaimed, sitting up. "Did you ever get it back?"

"While we stood there in the street talking, within ten minutes I'm sure, a man came walking down the road leading my horse. He went through lengthy salutations, first with Monsieur Lompo and then with me. He explained that he would have been there sooner, but he did not know the town well, being from a village some twenty kilometers to the south. He had first gone all the way to Bogui where the horse was known to have been sold to the chief, the man being from the village where the horse had been born. At Bogui they directed him to the *bompieno* in town."

Brandon laid back down without saying anything. I did the same, gazing up at small patches of blue through the green canopy above. At length he asked: "So how do you explain it?"

"I don't."

"Come on. You must have an opinion or a guess."

"What I *know* is what I told you."

"That's it?"

"That's it. Filed under 'UNEXPLAINED.' You want an opinion, I'll give you an opinion. Life would be a bore if that file were ever empty."

"But the way you told the story leads to the obvious conclusion that the earth told him where your horse was."

"I didn't say the earth told him anything. I told you he spoke to the earth, wrote in the dirt, pounded on the ground, and listened. Then he told me I'd find my horse at home and I did. End of story."

"Come on. You must have an opinion."

I thought a moment before replying. "Without data, my opinion means no more than the next person's. Science has a rule: *Extraordinary claims require extraordinary evidence.* Claiming that the earth revealed the whereabouts of my horse would be an extraordinary claim. The evidence, however, isn't extraordinary. First, in a literal sense, the horse was not at my compound when he said it was. But, let's say we allow for ten minutes of error in the prediction, not to mention likely distortions in my memory of events after all these years. How would a skeptical inquirer proceed? We might ask the man who found my horse who else knew that he was bringing it to me. The Gourma villages have constant movement among them of people who are kin, and traders going to and from the market. A lot more data would be needed to fill in gaps in the evidence and eliminate alternative hypotheses. Monsieur Lompo may have known the horse had already been found and decided to put on a show for me. I don't even know for sure what the medicine man said. So there are huge gaps in the data. Agreed?" He nodded. "Can you think of anything else to study?"

Brandon looked thoughtful. "If he was willing, I suppose you could track other predictions the medicine man made and see if they came true."

"Good. You might systematically follow up a random sample. And skeptical inquirers have done a lot of that. The results are far from extraordinary. In fact, most predictions made by supposed seers are too vague to validate, you know, like fortune cookies. 'You'll overcome a great obstacle.' Depending on how you think about it, driving home from the Chinese restaurant in traffic could be interpreted as overcoming a great obstacle."

"So you don't think the medicine man talked to the earth?"

"No, I saw him talk to the earth. I can even believe that he believed he got an answer. I simply don't have enough other data to draw any further conclusion. Given what I do know about the world, however, the burden of proof falls to those who make extraordinary claims because . . . ," I waited.

"Because extraordinary claims require extraordinary evidence," Brandon repeated.

"Which means, as a skeptical inquirer, you begin exploration of a seeming mystery by looking for an ordinary-reality, scientifically based explanation. Mark Twain showed how a skeptical inquirer solves a mystery in his story of *A Connecticut Yankee in King Arthur's Court*. The well of a fabled monastery had mysteriously dried up. The friars, having prayed and fasted to no avail, became frantic for a fix. They challenged Merlin and the time-traveling Yankee, dubbed Sir Boss, to a competition to see who could remove the enchantment that was supposedly causing the calamity. Merlin went first, appearing in full-length magician's gown embroidered with cabalistic signs, pointed purple hat, flowing white beard, and lignum vitae wand in hand. He uttered strange incantations, waved his wand over the well, and burned colored powders that sparked and created great clouds of smoke. For a week he worked until, exhausted, he pronounced that a spirit of the East, the most potent of all enchanters, had cast a spell on the well that could not be broken by mortals. Twain, as the narrator, credited it as a great performance, observing that it takes a lot of stamina and stage savvy to keep people's attention riveted as long as Merlin did with absolutely no result.

"Meanwhile, Twain's hero had entered the well chamber and determined that it merely had a leak causing water to be diverted underground. Once Merlin had given up, our skeptical inquirer repaired the well with cement, thereby making his reputation in King Arthur's Court as the greatest magician of the times. And he was a true magician, in the original sense—a *magi*—one who knows how nature works and how to work nature."

Throughout this account, Brandon had been lying back, gazing at the sky. When I ended, he sat up and looked at me earnestly. "So you really do agree that I probably read about the waterfall somewhere or just guessed it was here?"

"I don't know how you knew it was here," I replied simply.

"But you believe there's a normal explanation of some kind."

I thought for a moment and offered a response I conjectured would have meant the most to me at eighteen when I looked back at it thirty years later, the reply I never got to the question I was never allowed to ask.

"Let me answer like this. Last night Malcolm told us that in Australia, before and during the Aboriginal circumcision ceremony, the air is filled with the terrifying whirring of bull-roarers, which the initiates are told means dangerous spirits surround them. In many parts of Africa, the spirits appear as roaring lions or leopards; in South America they may come as jaguars; and in Oceania they may appear as crocodiles or sea monsters. These are not pretend spirits, not even to those playing them. They experience them as real. What's common to these initiations is that the young men are told what's real. No questioning. No doubt. The bull-roarer *is* the voice of a spirit. The elder dancing in a leopard mask *becomes* a leopard spirit. The costumed sea monsters who attack and terrorize initiates are *real* monsters. Explanations come in stories and myths and the initiates are told what the stories mean, how to behave, and what to think. Modern catechisms leave out the drama, but not the thought control and fear of Satan.

"It's the exact opposite of your Unitarian Coming-of-Age ritual. After a half year studying various religions and traditions, you each made a formal declaration of your beliefs and no one questioned your right to believe whatever you chose to believe. Now we're doing that with Iron John, this waterfall, and my lost horse. We, as elders, tell the tales. The canyon provides a setting to have experiences. And *you* decide what they mean. Instead of giving you my explanation, I'm offering a mode of inquiry and some principles for arriving at your own conclusions."

Brandon thought a moment, then looked at me, grinning. "You really don't have an explanation, do you?"

I returned his grin, then stood and pointed to the waterfall. "Science and nature provide more than enough wonder for me. But, as both a sociologist and as Malcolm's friend, I can let myself enter the fantasy world of canyon consciousness, totems, and talismans. It's a fascinating world Malcolm describes. You'll have to decide for yourself whether it's harmless conjuring or outright delusion."

I pulled Brandon up and put my arm around his shoulders. "I'm perfectly prepared to entertain the hypothesis that Merlin led you to this waterfall. For pure entertainment and fantasy, no one beats Merlin. But I'll tell you this for damn sure: I wouldn't look to him to lower my cholesterol."

"*Oyea gengaway,*" Brandon intoned.

"Exactly," I affirmed, and shoved him into the pool.

25. The Real Abyss

Brandon disappeared in a huge splash and came up screaming, "Yowl! Youp! Yow-eeee!" He thrashed about to generate warmth, swam over directly under the waterfall, played under the falls, turned back and swam under water, came up for air, saw me and waved, went back under the water, and started swimming back toward the boulder. I retreated so he couldn't pull me in. From a safe distance I shouted: "I'll swim after rock-lizard time. Enjoy."

I awoke in a midday mind fog, needing a second to remember where I was. I tried opening my eyelids. Even with my hat over my eyes, the brightness hurt. I let them adjust for a few seconds, then removed the hat and sat up. I saw Brandon standing naked on the larger of the two boulders that blocked the water's descent into the creek. From my vantage point, slightly above and to the side, I could study him unde-tected, his shoulder-length hair enveloping his face as he looked out across the pool, his dark pubic hair providing contrast to his wheat-colored body. His arms were folded across his chest and he stood very still, peering into the water. Then, in a burst, he leapt forward into the pool.

Rarely are we permitted, after toddlerhood, such unfettered moments of parental observa-

219

tion. Such an occasion cannot be planned any more than a spontaneous expression of love can be solicited.

I climbed down to join him. He came out gasping. "Ummmm, that feels good. It's deeeppp. I can't touch bottom anywhere." Then, he turned to the pool. "Sorry for disturbing your tranquility, fishies. Can't be selfish, though. Have to learn to share."

I undressed slowly, still groggy from my nap, then slipped into the water and retraced Brandon's invisible path, modestly emulating his shouts, induced involuntarily by the cold. My body reacted against the shock with a thermal charge that gave me a warm tingling throughout of heat in the midst of cold. I noticed with surprise and satisfaction that our swimming had no effect on the sparkling clearness of the water. I looked up from studying how the rock lined the pool just in time to get hit by the full force of a hard splash as Brandon jumped in again. I climbed out, my body feeling numb, drained, and, at last, detoxed.

We repeated this ritual several times. The cold would force us from the water, but the depths drew us back in. I finally yielded to the westerly origin of the sun's rays, alerting Brandon that we weren't leaving any margin for the unexpected during our descent. He insisted on one more cannonball, took a final turn under the waterfall, and climbed out.

Dressed, booted, and ready to take our leave, we stood together for a final look, close enough to touch arm to arm. "This is quite a place you brought us to," I said, "however you decided. My thanks to you and, of course, to Merlin. And let me know if you come up with an explanation." Then we were off.

Late-afternoon shadows engulfed the gorge as we arrived back at the convergence of Merlin and Modred Abysses. We continued on without pause or ceremony. The pace Brandon set matched my outer limit. I ignored messages from my legs screaming for a break, then dropped in relief beside Brandon when I found him stopped in an area thick with brush where a collapse in the Tapeats wall had dumped rocks along the bank. He had been watching for the place where we had descended that morning into Shinumo Creek from the Tonto Platform above. "Up or down?" he asked as I downed a swig of water.

We examined the map, saw we still had a long way to go, and considered our options. "It comes down to how adventurous we feel," I concluded. "We know the Tonto route, but finding a way back down through the Tapeats will be tough, especially in the dark. We've been making good time down this gorge, but ahead lies unknown territory. It's your initiation. You make the call."

"It's probably faster hiking straight on down instead of going in and out around all the drainages on the Tonto. I'd just as soon keep going."

The first hint of trouble came where the creek dropped into a rocky gorge with smooth, slippery walls on both sides. We found just enough terracing on one side that by stepping slowly, foot over foot, and leaning in toward the wall, we made it, relieved not to fall into the cascading, waist-high water. Around the next turn we followed a narrow ledge under an overhang that ended at an impassable, inward-sloping wall. A midstream boulder pointed to an escape route across to the other side. From there we climbed a terraced series of ledges that led some fifteen feet up, over a precipice, down along a rapids, and around a small waterfall.

And so it went: hard, slow, tiring, but doable. We expected Shinumo to be joined by Flint Creek at any time, but instead the gorge just got narrower, the water deeper. We came to another small waterfall and rapids, negotiated a way around, and perched on two large boulders in the middle of the creek, marble smooth walls and overhangs on both sides. In front of us was a reservoir created by a massive boulder that dammed the gorge, leaving no route along either side. The only way forward was through the pool. In the flat, ebbing light we could not tell how deep it was nor how swift the current. The view beyond the boulder was restricted. So were our options.

My primary concern was not the thirty yards of water below us, but how many more such pools might lay ahead. We stripped, wadded our clothes in our T-shirts, tied our boots together, and arranged the clothes, boots, and hip packs so that the whole load could be carried over our heads. "Ready?" Brandon asked.

"It'll probably be slippery," I warned in reply, "so be prepared to swim. And if we're forced to let go of something, let's drop our clothes. Walking naked is easier than barefoot."

His grin told me he understood I was saying the things a parent feels compelled to say. His scream as he entered the frigid water cut off his effort at reassuring me. He dropped immediately into waist-high water, holding his boots and pack in one hand and the wad of clothes overhead in the other. As he pushed slowly forward, the water became chest-high, making it harder to brace against the current. He called back, "The bottom feels solid. The footing is fine."

Suddenly he was under water. He dropped straight down, as if pulled by some submerged monster. I tensed, ready to jump in. A hand reappeared holding the boots. Then his head. He looked back as he gasped a breath. It looked like he wanted to call something back to me, but couldn't. He kicked forward, holding onto the things in his hands and letting me see the boots high overhead. Then, just as quickly as he had gone under, he had his footing again, the water chest-high, then waist-high, then he reached the other side, gasping for breath.

With the noise of the cascading water echoing in the gorge I knew I wouldn't be able to hear him that far away. What could he tell me that I hadn't already seen? I slipped into the water, ready for the drop-off, so I went from walking to treading water without going under.

"Sorry about the boots," he said as I climbed out beside him, admonishing himself for failing to heed my one parental caution.

"Looked to me like you did well just hanging onto them." I stretched on tiptoes to peer around the boulder blocking our path. "We need to hurry. Let's get dressed and move. It can't be far to Flint now," I asserted, wondering if my lack of conviction showed.

Beyond the boulder we negotiated a ledge of sloping rock that ran just above the waterline, then a series of rapids, small waterfalls, drop-offs, and more ledges. The descent had become mountaineering rather than hiking. After a particularly precarious section, we took a breather.

"I'm glad we came this way," Brandon remarked. "It's awesome."

"Beautiful. Spectacular. Stunning," I agreed, a willing participant in ignoring our increasingly dire predicament as dimness foretold nightfall. In wet pants we were too cold to sit long. For a few minutes the going was easier until we came to a ledge just wide enough to support half the width of a foot. At its end loomed another large boulder, larger still than the one that had dammed the gorge above. It blocked our view and our way. Brandon worked his way along a crevice and under an overhang until he reached the boulder, which was higher than he was tall. He peered between the boulder and the side wall for what seemed like a long time while I waited some ten yards back, there not being space for both of us where he crouched. He finally looked back, not at me, but behind me. I followed his eyes as he retraced our route until his gaze returned locked on mine. "We're fucked," he said matter-of-factly.

Adrenalin surged in me. I made my way closer to him, leaning my weight into the rock wall for balance. I groped for an edge or crevice to use as a hand hold, but found only blemish-free, water-polished rock. My feet ached and knees felt like moss as I balanced precariously behind him.

"Is there any good news?" I asked.

"There's a blind drop-off here. I can't see how far down it is." The massive boulder damming the gorge and blocking our descent had created a waterfall. Water poured over the top and around the sides in a way that prevented him from looking over and down without getting swept away in the surging current.

Brandon had been studying the formations around us while I was maneuvering close to him. "There's no way up and around that I can see, at least no safe way. We'd have to climb above the Tapeats, probably have to go all the way back to where we came down this morning."

I confirmed his assessment, adding: "That would make it completely dark long before we got back. Malcolm would be shitting bricks." It would be a tough call for Malcolm having to decide where, or even whether, to search for us in the dark. If he was sure we needed help, he would come for us as I would for him, without hesitation. But such certainty was impossible. Getting himself hurt would put us at greater risk if, ultimately, the real need was for someone to hike out for rescue. Three of us were potentially fucked in the canyon, not just two.

From my vantage point, clinging to the rock wall, unable to see past or get around Brandon, I couldn't add to his assessment. I could only observe that this would be our real descent into the abyss. Once we went over, there was no way back up if we couldn't reach Flint. We'd be trapped.

Though cold, tired, and tense, I felt quite clearheaded. Just to be sure, I undertook a conscientious clearheadedness examination to make certain I was thinking in a way that would not lead to self-recriminations later. Realizing at once that no such guarantee was possible assured me that my mind was still functioning. If Brandon should be seriously hurt, or worse, I would blame myself unmercifully the rest of my life. That awareness, and its accompanying terror, told me I was mentally alert. It was decision time.

Brandon regarded me calmly, waiting to hear what we'd do. "Don't look at me," I said with resolve. "You're in a better position to assess the situation than I am. You've laid out the alternatives clearly. I can't think of anything to add. We can go over or back up. I'm with you either way."

He looked above, around, and below, then back at me. His eyes told me he had no hesitation for himself. He had a look of calculated abandon I had seen earlier at the waterfall just before he jumped into the pool. *I* was the problem.

"I think we should go for it," he said hesitantly, indicating he was prepared for a contrary decision from me.

"Then go for it," I said with finality.

He started taking off his boots. I wanted to advise him to leave his boots on for protection, but it didn't strike me as a great time to say something parental. What, I asked myself, would I say to Malcolm in the same situation? I'd give him my best advice and he'd do whatever he thought best. I should treat Brandon with the same respect, I admonished myself. I have to figure out how we can discuss options without it becoming a father-son hierarchical thing. Brandon would want my best shot. It's all in how I say it.

Just as I resolved to speak, Brandon said, "I think it'll be better if I keep my boots on in case I hit something. They're already wet anyway. You'd probably better keep yours on too, at least until I yell back to you what I find. Let me give you my stuff and you can throw it over with yours once I'm down."

Before I could tell him how impressed I was with his judgment, he had turned, slipped into the current and was gone. I heard his splash. I willed myself to breathe, but couldn't. I strained to see over the falls. The top of his head came into view, then disappeared, then came back into view, bobbing up and down. Then he got far enough beyond the drop-off that I could see his whole head. He turned and looked back but I couldn't read his expression in the dim light. He started to swim on, then turned, treading water with difficulty because of the boots. "Throw me the stuff," he yelled at the top of his voice.

He retrieved what I threw and, treading water, waved me in. The current sucked me over, then under. I came up quickly, disoriented. I followed Brandon's shouts to the end of the pool, using all my energy to move the heavy weights on my feet. He reached out and helped me up on the rocky beach. I looked anxiously ahead to see if we had trapped ourselves between drop-offs. The dense vegetation and flat terrain told me we were down before I actually spotted the line of Flint Creek.

Brandon gazed back at the dammed gorge. "If we had come this way this morning, we wouldn't have made it to my waterfall."

I noticed with pleasure how he referred to it, but, still catching my breath, my heart still pounding out disaster scenarios in my head, I could only manage to nod my agreement. I wanted to say something meaningful or symbolic or at least memorable, but I couldn't speak. I just sat there drained. Brandon, meanwhile, matter-of-factly analyzed the consequences for our whole day if we hadn't decided in the morning to hike the Tonto instead of following Shinumo into Merlin. Nor did he give me much time to ponder what thoughts I might render appropriate to the moment. He had been monitoring my breathing, noted it had returned to easy panting, reached for his hip pack, and commanded, "We'd better get going. It's almost dark. We've still got at least an hour ahead of us and we don't know what it will be like from here. You ready to truck?"

He was in charge and that was fine with me. "Lead on," I said. I had started to say, "Lead on, son." But it came out just, "Lead on."

26. Original Sin

Though we had been in the canyon four days, the hike along Shinumo Creek was the first time we had experienced the lingering dusk without being busy at camp. We had the rare chance to experience the natural rhythm of time unfolding—slow, steady, inevitable. No clouds or light show distracted from the impending certainty of night in the deepening hues of the darkening sky.

After what seemed a long time of hard hiking up and down ledges, back and forth across the creek, Brandon moved as if we'd just started out. Or so it seemed as I struggled to keep up. "Hold up, Tchombiano," I finally called to his ever-retreating back. "I'm dragging ass. We'll make better time if I stop a minute to recharge."

"No prob. There's a flat spot on an outcropping up ahead."

"I don't dare close my eyes," I said as I spread out, "so I'd better talk to stay awake. Besides, something's rattling around in my head like a tune that won't go away. As you've undoubtedly noticed, Malcolm and I curse like pig-boaters down here. It's part of the freedom of the canyon. You've joined in with an occasional 'shit,' 'damn,' or 'goddammit,' but I realized back there I'd never before heard you say 'fuck.' Given the circumstances, it made a big impression and reminded me of a—"

"You have a story about fucking?!" Brandon interrupted, laughing.

"I have a question. Do you remember the very first time you said 'fuck'?"

"You're kidding."

"Just checking. I didn't think you'd remember. But my first time came back to me in a flash when I heard you say it.'"

"You mean your life started passing in front of your eyes just before you jumped?"

"Not my whole life. Just one incident. It's a good illustration of how our coming-of-age experiences have been different."

"Like how?"

"Cursing was absolutely forbidden to me. Mouth washed out with soap for 'crap.' Sent to my room without dinner for 'darn.' Grounded a week for 'dang.' And a full-scale belt-whipping when 'goldarn' once slipped out. Major sin. Risking hell kind of sin. Given all that, as you might imagine, the forbidden language took on gargantuan significance."

"Actually, I can't imagine," he said.

"Satan's lurking presence, trying to tempt me, felt very real. He exposed me daily to the kind of gross, mean, taunting, and hurtful profanity that male seventh- and eighth-graders specialize in. I knew Jesus had put me in that school on purpose to test me. I prayed that it would be said of me as Saint Paul wished it said of him, 'I have fought a good fight, I have finished my course, I have kept the faith: Henceforth there is laid up for me a crown of righteousness.'"

Brandon whispered something under his breath, as if uttering an incantation against evil.

"Amen," I smiled. "I believed everything I experienced was for some reason, that God had a purpose for my life, and I had to set an example for others, witnessing for Jesus through my behavior. That's why I remember as one of the vivid memories of childhood the day I fell into Satan's grasp. I skipped 'damn,' 'bitch,' and 'shit' and plunged right to the bottom of the abyss."

"You scored an F," Brandon laughed.

"Big time," I confirmed. "It happened on one of the first spring afternoons too warm for jackets, so I had tied mine around my waist. All the way down the long hill from school three eighth-grade 'colored' girls—that's how we referred to African Americans in those days—followed teasing about my 'skirt.' I was a mere sixth grader. In addition to being older and bolder, their sexual taunting played on my vulnerability as a proudly non-sexual Christian, meaning I was ignorant about sex and easily embarrassed as only a shy, pure, school-smart, street-dumb, and evangelical white boy could be at the advanced age of eleven.

"The ring leader, Felicia, was already quite buxom, a fact that had not escaped my Christian notice. 'That boy sure nuf is dressed like a girl,' she taunted. 'I wonder what's under his skirt. I wonder if any little ole white thing is under there.'

"The other two giggled. 'Felicia, you too mean, girl. You gonna plum embarrass that pore white boy to death,' they warned, urging her on.

"She didn't need encouragement. 'I seen you watching my titties,' she said to my horror. 'Hey white boy, take off that skirt and we'll see what you got, then you can feel my titties.'

"I prayed: 'Jesus, I know you are testing me. Forgive them their impure thoughts. Let my body be the temple of God and my mind worthy of your purpose.' The more they taunted and the louder they giggled, the faster I walked and the harder I prayed.

I never looked back, never gave them the pleasure of knowing how my flesh was mortified. At the bottom of the hill, as I turned to cross the rail-road tracks, Felicia snuck up and grabbed me in the crotch. 'He's got a hard on,' she yelled to the whole world. 'My titties done made his little white thing grow up under that there skirt.' And the three of them ran off screaming and laughing.

" 'FUCK YOU!' I screamed.

"It just came out. Had a train been coming down the tracks, I could not have moved. I was planted there listening with fascination and horror at this sound that Satan had emitted through me. My first impulse was to ask God's forgiveness. What stopped me, I suspect, was how good it felt. Having entered the firegates of hell, I stood there trying to imitate the boys who daily, hourly, used this magical oath with deftness and authority. 'FUCK YOU, Felicia! FUCK YOU.'

"It would take many more years and lots of railroad tracks before I could curse with nary a twinge of guilt. But that's how it started, how your father lost his linguistic virginity." So saying, I jumped up exclaiming, "I'm reju-venated. Let's truck."

"I've been trying to remember my first time, but I'm afraid it's lost," Brandon lamented.

"That's the point," I replied, pulling him up. "You'll never have my affection for or overindulgence in profanity because it's never been absolutely forbidden to you. You still have the capacity to reserve your oaths for special occasions, which is as it should be. I say that because I learned anew from you today the awesome effect of discretion and precise timing. It rivets the attention of the listener." With that I pushed Brandon ahead. "We've got places to go and people to see. Move the fuck out!"

After that the trek to base camp is a blur. The horror of impending darkness having been my companion all afternoon, I cursed myself for not bringing along a flashlight. After all we'd been through that day, I thought, it would be an absurd tragic-comedy to get hurt tripping over a stone on the path. I admit to being susceptible to a sense of irrational karmic justice where good and bad ultimately balance each other out. It had been an amazing day—a wonderful four days. My joy was tempered only by the sense that, at some point, we'd have to pay for all that wonderfulness. But as the first stars appeared, I found myself laughing at the absurd notion that I was important enough to be running a karmic balance sheet—the lingering, hard-to-wash-away residues of years of fear-inducing Sunday school. The feeling of cosmic insignificance so often reported in wilderness experiences engulfed and comforted me. Contrary to everything I knew about myself, I found solace in the impending darkness. I can't say why. But the fear I had been expecting, the terror I knew was just under the surface, never materialized.

The dim light heightened my senses and awareness. I found I was noticing more about the terrain in the contrasts of the shadows than I had seen in the light. The distinct outline of a tree or bush against the purple sky highlighted every branch and leaf. I could see the texture of a boulder in such detail that it felt like my eyes suddenly had the capacity to touch. My heightened senses were attuned like radar, giving me detailed information about everything around me, scanning for any possible danger. Being forced by the darkness to really look at the path, I saw each stone, twig, hole, thorn, or exposed root—details that typically escaped my attention in daylight. I experienced what I suspect the mystically inclined would describe as a sixth sense, but I interpreted it not as an added, new, or different sense, but as greater use of, perhaps even the seamless integration of, the ordinary five, making the darkness palpable.

Climbing up and down crags, jumping back and forth across the creek, and bushwhacking through water-side vegetation suddenly felt like walking on a wide, open highway. That morning I had tested the stability of each midstream boulder to avoid slipping into the water or twisting an ankle. Now, returning, I danced across the rocks that marked the intersection with White Creek just above base camp. I turned back, looked at where I had crossed, and was stunned by the contrast with the morning's cautious and calculated crossing. I was jolted out of this reverie by Malcolm's greeting to Brandon: "Decided to stay out late, I see. Any trouble? Where's your dad?"

His words seemed suspended in the air, as did Brandon's reply, each word drawn out, deep, like the sound on a tape recorder when the battery is low. "He's . . . right . . . be . . hind . . . me. . . . No . . . trou . . . ble. . . . Mer . . . lin . . . was . . . awe . . . some. . . . Aannddd . . . I'mmm . . . star-rvveedd."

Brandon went on talking, but I didn't track his words. The reference to hunger brought me crashing back into ordinary consciousness. I presume I had been working off an adrenalin high or infusion of endorphins. Whatever it was left instantly with the awareness that we had made it back. I was drained. My body felt heavy, my legs so dead I had to will myself to take each step in the sand to make it the twenty yards up the beach to Brandon and Malcolm, like a marathoner stumbling across the finish line and disintegrating. I collapsed near the cookstove, aware in seeing the blue flame that it was totally dark. Malcolm was using a flashlight to cook. "The old man looks like shit," he laughed. "What've you boys been up to?"

Day Five

27. Rim-World Intrusion

Malcolm lagged behind right from the beginning as we began our ascent out of the canyon. I was amazed at how refreshed I felt after our arduous adventure in Merlin Abyss the previous day. In contrast, Malcolm's day of rest had left him stiff and brooding, resistant to the uphill challenge, resistant to retox. I considered alerting him that I intended using the next segment of 'Iron John'—the boy's encounter with the King's daughter—as an opening to ask him to share with Brandon his wisdom about the labyrinth of male-female relations, but I was inclined to count on his spontaneity rather than ask him to prepare. Besides, his sour countenance invited no intrusion into his begrudging ascent.

Leaving Malcolm to his thoughts, then, Brandon and I pushed ahead at a steady pace. He asked questions about my childhood and work, and shared his thoughts and hopes about making good music. I probed what he meant by "good," which opened up a leisurely on-and-off philosophical exchange deeper and richer than any we had ever had. I reveled in the extraordinary luxury of walking and talking with my son, absent an agenda—the sheer pleasure of cadence, words thrumming the rocks under our feet.

235

Over dinner of vegetable soup and canned stew we congratulated our-selves on having made it all the way back up the Redwall and onto the Esplanade. Hiking uphill typically takes longer than going down, but being now canyon hard and not lingering at rest breaks, we were making better time coming up than we had on the descent. "We should be able to get back to the saddle between Swamp and Powell before noon tomorrow," Malcolm said, "then I think I'll let you two go on to Powell while I mosey up to Swamp Point."

"Swamp Point? You're not coming to Powell with us?" I asked.

"You two did okay in Merlin, and if you can find a waterfall on Powell's dry plateau, now that will be a showstopper."

"Wait a minute," I said, "something's not right here. Before the trip you were hot to do a recon on Powell so you could take Dee and the kids up there some day. Now you're suggesting Brandon and I go alone. What gives?"

"You won't need me on Powell. It's perfectly flat. There's no trail to find. Just stay along the rim."

"I'm not worried about getting lost. Goddammit, this isn't like you. Be straight with me."

"We've left three days to do Powell. I thought I'd take a day to make sure we can get back to Flag, then I'll join you."

That was it! Suddenly I understood Malcolm's brooding. He had had a full day alone to think, time to remember that we didn't know how we were getting back to Flagstaff. While we were having our adventure in Merlin, he was worrying about the damned car. It all came back to me full force.

Malcolm had insisted on driving his recently purchased 1971 Mercedes, a classic, to get us to Swamp Point. The odometer showed about 40,000 miles; it wasn't clear whether this represented 140,000 or 240,000 miles. He knew that, given the distance and back-country roads, using this trip to get familiar with his "new" car would be risky, but he was still in the infatuation phase, feeling the glow of a good deal on a rare find. The car had glided along the highways to the North Rim like it had just come off the showroom floor, but we hadn't gotten very far on the deeply rutted road to Swamp Point before his infatuation turned to dread. Worn springs and flaccid shocks made the car's underbelly vulnerable to every exposed rock, of which there were many. Brandon and I had hiked alongside, hoping that lightening the load would make a difference. It didn't. The inevitable, frightening thump killed the motor. Our relief at eventually getting it restarted gave way to dejection when Malcolm discovered he couldn't get out of first gear.

We then persevered for two more hours in first, proceeding cautiously lest we lose all forward motion, intermittently stopping to consider our options, including going back, leaving the Mercedes, and hiring someone with four-wheel drive to bring us out. But that would cost a day or more and Malcolm was determined to make it, several times steering off the road and driving though the brush when the road was impassable. Once at Swamp Point, during a hurried dinner under threatening clouds, we had considered whether to deal with the car then or later, played out the worst-case scenarios, and joked about our lack of mechanical prowess. In the end, it was Malcolm's call. "We're here. Let's get on into the big hole," he had decided. So we determined to move ahead, cut our trip a day short to deal with the car, and, in the interim, put it out of our minds. I had succeeded beyond my expectations. Malcolm apparently hadn't.

He was generously offering Brandon and me more canyon time together while he dealt with the hassles. His offer was all the more generous because the problem of getting to Flagstaff on time was mine, not his. I had the flight to catch, the consulting commitment to meet. His timeline was more open. He had undoubtedly spent part of his day of supposed rest and relaxation chastising himself for bringing the Mercedes into the wilderness and a good deal more time thinking about how to get a foreign transmission repaired two hundred miles from Phoenix. In all that thinking he had decided to take the solution on himself. It wasn't a sacrifice I could accept. "And just what would you do to fix the Mercedes while we're on Powell?" I asked.

"I'll hike out to that little store and gas station at the turn-off from the main road and get help. With luck, I might even catch a ride with a logging truck in the forest. If it can't be fixed, I'll rent something or figure out what's available." Before I could protest, he added, "It's not a two-person job."

"Maybe, maybe not, but I'll go out with you just in case and we'll let Brandon do a solo on Powell. With two of us we'll have someone to come back with information in case the other person needs to keep dealing with the car."

Malcolm and I went back and forth about whether two people were needed and who should bear responsibility. Our banter brought us no closer to agreement on a strategy to handle the problem, but it did turn what had been a barely perceptible glimmer on the distant horizon into a harshly glaring sun that blotted out everything else. Brandon's initiation, which was supposed to reach a crescendo on Powell Plateau as we gazed out at distant monuments and the majesty of the Colorado River, now looked like it would end with ignominious smirks from an auto mechanic who would have quite a story to tell about being called by a couple of professor-types to fix a Mercedes, of all things, deep in the wilderness.

Brandon, having been silently observing our inconclusive but increasingly gloomy disputation, finally had heard enough and interrupted. "Hiking down you two were giving me all this stuff about 'Be here now,' and 'We're getting detoxified,' and not bringing the crap of the world into the canyon and it turns out you've carried the Mercedes all the way down North Bass. Chill out. Nobody should go out early. Let's just stay with the original plan. You're missing the canyon worrying."

"That's all very good in theory," I replied, "but this is real-world time. We have a real problem and there's no easy solution. Ignoring it won't make it go away. I won't lie to you. I'm bummed."

"Give the kid a break," Malcolm retorted. "Lie to him. Parents lying to their kids and themselves is what keeps family therapists in business."

"That's Malcolm's way of saying he's bummed too," I explained.

He continued as if he hadn't heard me, with uncharacteristic cynicism. "And don't pretend you've never lied to him. That's why fathers aren't trusted by the tribe to initiate their sons. They can't be trusted not to lie— even to themselves. All fathers are liars. Manhood comes at the price of that knowledge."

"And do you have some equally insightful wisdom to share about what cars to drive into the wilderness?" I asked.

"I'll hike out and get help for the car while you two put the finishing touches on your initiation script," Brandon offered. "Sounds like it needs a little polishing."

Malcolm laughed big and full, an easy, delightful laugh that blew the tension back above Swamp Point. "Your young ram there's a keen observer and he's been observing us all too well. He knows we're not going to let him go out alone. Hell, it took all three of us to guide the damn car in. The only solace at a moment like this, when your kid's got you absolutely by the balls, is to know that his day is coming and some day his kid will have him by the balls. Screw the Mercedes. We'll figure it out tomorrow."

"Wait a minute. Wasn't someone just telling me that ignoring problems won't make them go away?" Brandon chided.

"We've shifted gears," I explained. "We've shifted from an ignoring mode into a don't-make-the-decision-until-you-have-all-the-information-and-have-to-make-the-decision mode. We'll see how long it takes us to get to the saddle, what the weather looks like and how we feel, then we'll decide. Even if we decided now, we'd probably rehash the decision again tomorrow. So I'm with Malcolm. Let's let it go until tomorrow."

Malcolm nodded agreement. Brandon shrugged. I sighed deeply and, after a moment, continued. "We can't let our first full day of uphill end on a downer. There's no easy way to make the transition, but let me try shifting gears again. I've been looking forward to 'Iron John' tonight. The King's daughter is about to make an appearance. The plot thickens. Romance is in the air. Can I interest you two in a little bedtime reading to lighten the mood? And I've got a surprise for you."

They agreed that we'd clean up the cook gear, unroll our sleeping bags, and reassemble in fifteen minutes. I deliberated about how much to read. For better or worse, the Rim World had intruded. Malcolm and I couldn't enjoy climbing Powell with the broken Mercedes in clear view at the tip of Swamp Point. One or both of us would be hiking out early. With that in mind, it seemed appropriate to bring some degree of closure to "Iron John."

28. The King's Daughter

King Arthur and Guinevere Castles lie just west of a plateau that extends eight miles into the canyon from the North Rim, ending in Point Sublime. They emerge from a single massive foundation that looks like two giant, clawed feet, each more than a half mile long. The clawed foot of Arthur and that of Guinevere are joined as one at about 6,000 feet before they separate into two distinct masses of rock, King Arthur Castle rising to 7,026 feet, Guinevere Castle a little less.

Lancelot Point projects out from the North Rim, pointing at the nearby castle of his enchantress, Galahad's mother, Elaine. At over 8,000 feet, Lancelot also looks out over Guinevere and Arthur, though they have much greater mass. Arthur is positioned between Guinevere and Holy Grail Temple.

None of this could we see as we gathered in the fading light, but I felt aware of our symbolic surroundings as we approached the boy-meets-girl climax of the "Iron John" story. Indeed, so much had the contrasting passion play of the Arthurian legend been fermenting in my mind that I was tempted to substitute that tale as a way of reopening with Brandon a discourse on core components of any modern coming-of-age curriculum: sex, love, and romance.

241

While hiking that afternoon and anticipating our evening discussion, my thoughts had drifted back over Brandon's sex education, at least what I knew of it. As recommended in the parenting books we devoured after his birth, we answered his prepubescent questions about sex matter-of-factly whenever one arose. The easy part was providing correct information. The harder part was deciding on advice.

The only sexual advice my father gave me came unexpectedly the day I left home. "You'll meet a lot of women in college, but don't be in a hurry to get married. And never pay for sex. Patton men don't pay. Have you got all your suitcases packed?"

At fourteen Brandon had participated somewhat reluctantly in a weekly sex-education program offered by the Unitarian church, a national curriculum adopted locally. Parents met separately to review the basics their kids were getting downstairs. None of us had had sexual discussions with our own parents. Our discomfort was palpable. Riding home, I'd tell Brandon about the parents' discussion and ask about his class. Much of it, he said, rehashed school "stuff." Having boys and girls together meant some awkwardness and giggling, for example, when handling diaphragms and condoms or analyzing pornography, but the group had jelled and "anything" could be asked.

Once, however, near the end, he asked a question that had somehow escaped coverage. We were talking about menstruation, one of the topics covered that evening. I told him about the differing patterns among women I had known and went on to tell him about research on men's understanding of menstruation done by one of my doctoral students. For her dissertation she had interviewed a sample of men hypothesizing that they'd have a lot of misconceptions. Instead, she found nearly total ignorance. They didn't even know enough to know the wrong things. I assured him that he was already better informed than those men, something I thought he could feel good about, but if there was anything else he wanted to ask . . .

His question burst out like it had been fermenting for a long time: "How many holes do women have?"

I almost replied jokingly, counting ear holes, nostrils. What stopped me was a glimpse of his rigid body as he stared straight out the windshield, holding his breath. I had been thinking of him as a big, take-on-the-world teenager. His little-boy question whisked me back to the toddler I had carried on my shoulders. I told him I could remember being confused about that myself and then answered his question straightforwardly. He exhaled hard and said that's what he'd thought, he just wanted to be sure because one of the boys was insisting otherwise.

I went on to assure him that there was a lot to learn and that when he turned sixteen, I had decided I would tell him what I'd learned about sex— "stuff they can't cover at school or church." I added that there was nothing magic about that age so I hoped he'd feel free to ask anything that came up in the interim. I was only mentioning my intentions, I explained, so it wouldn't come as a surprise.

That was my first open commitment to what I had long thought about doing. The week before his birthday we set the date, without joking or resistance on his part, a fact that pleased me, though I can't say he showed any particular enthusiasm. The talk took all of a Saturday morning. I recount here a bit of what transpired because it hardly seems fair to allude to The Talk as a significant event in my relationship with Brandon and then leave the content a mystery. I don't presume to be offering a script for other parents, but rather backfilling to provide context for our canyon discussion that night and insight into its import for me. For, as a result of the "Iron John" reading and subsequent discussion, I found out what Brandon had taken away from our talk. That knowledge was all the sweeter for being rare, parents seldom getting the chance to find out what morsels of sustenance have been absorbed and retained by our children from the millions of words served up to them.

I began the talk with some family history, explaining that my father had never talked to me about sex, nor had his father before him. That seemed a family tradition worth breaking. I then explained how I intended to proceed in a way I hoped would help put him at ease. I would share as openly as I could what I knew about and had experienced. I promised not to ask what he already knew or didn't know, what he'd done or hadn't done. I hoped he'd feel free to ask questions at any point, and I assured him I didn't intend to pry or offer advice.

The ground rules laid, I reviewed briefly my puritanical upbringing, partly as a way of explaining some of my subsequent sexual experiences, embarrassments, uncertainties, and anxieties. None of these were television talk-show material, to be sure, but they did seem to capture his attention and they came without commercial interruptions. We talked about my younger brother's homosexuality, about which he already knew a great deal, and his adjustment to living with AIDS, about which he knew very little. I gave him the first marriage manual I ever purchased in my quest to learn about the female body, a book with detailed color photographs of sexual anatomy, and told him of my vow to pass it on to my children because of its importance in my sexual pilgrimage—not, I added, to suggest that books are necessarily the only or best way to learn such things.

As I moved from topic to topic, connecting personal disclosures with what I knew of generalizable patterns, Brandon, in contrast to his usual restlessness, appeared calm, focused, and present. He asked a few questions, mainly seeking elaboration of some point or more details about a story. To give the succession of anecdotes some coherence, I remember emphasizing that the central thing I've come to understand was that *sex is about 10 percent physical and 90 percent mental.* This seemed to make an impression as his eyes widened and he sat up straighter.

I explained that this 90/10 split was my own perception, though what I knew of research would support the basic premise, if not the exact statistic. I added that it was undoubtedly somewhat different for different relationships, but I felt confident asserting that sex had more to do with the head than any other body part. And that, I emphasized, was what I wish someone had explained to me in my youth.

This seemed to interest him, so I went on at some length about how touching your lover's mind, and being touched in turn, informs and changes how you experience each other, sexually and otherwise. The purely biological part of sex was easy, I assured him, as evidenced by the world's population explosion. But mutual satisfaction appeared to be rare, a result of head deficiencies and insufficient sensitivity, not inadequate body parts.

He asked what caused head problems about sex. I replied that we all carry voices and videos in our minds, tapes playing over and over telling us what we should think, how to feel, what to see, and how to react. These societal voices are hard to control, hard to erase, hard to record over, and hard to distinguish from what we want as individuals. Our sexual software builds layers and layers of instructions disguised as hormones, so we often aren't aware that what passes for physical attraction is controlled by psychological programs not of our making and replete with societal viruses.

His demeanor had been quite serious up to that point, so his sudden grin disconcerted me. After some back and forth, it turned out he was amused by my mixing audio recording with video and computer software metaphors. So I asked which worked best. He suggested I stay with the idea of mental tapes and asked for examples. I explained that the mind ultimately interprets what the body feels. Two women could be touched in exactly the same place, in the same way. One feels pleasure, the other pain. One might welcome the touch, the other might feel invaded by it. To an external observer, the physical behaviors and stimuli would appear identical. What's different is what's in their heads.

Two men masturbate. One feels wonderful release. The other feels guilt. Two women have orgasm. One feels joy. The other feels shame. Touching another person's body also touches that person's mind and emotions. The body is an important pathway inside to feelings and thoughts, not all of which are freely chosen.

He said he understood the general idea of mental and societally imposed tapes, but he still wasn't sure how it affected him personally. So, I suggested that, like it or not, most women would experience him first as MALE before experiencing him as Brandon. The tapes are screens and stereotypes. The challenge would be to *behave* in a way that created a unique and wonderful category named BRANDON that was different from the societal category MALE. Being MALE could be a barrier. Being BRANDON would be an asset.

He commented that the distinction still seemed pretty abstract, so I tried to make the point concrete by saying that, as a male, he had dues to pay for things men have done to women through the ages—and are still doing. Violence. Rape. Harassment. Discrimination. Domination. I gave examples of how my relationships with women had been affected by their past societal experiences and sense of abusive male history. He understood, he said, but he didn't care for the notion of paying dues. He just preferred to be himself. I suggested he just keep the male-history context in mind and watch for any ways in which old societal patterns might show up in his personal relationships.

We then moved on to talk about how humanist principles can inform sexual relationships. I explained that most people looked to religious rules and commandments for morality—mostly a list of "thou shall nots"—but humanists are guided by principles rather than rules, principles of mutual respect, responsibility, and thoughtful, rational, intentional action based on careful regard for consequences. He agreed *in principle,* he said, suddenly grinning, but it still seemed pretty abstract. So we talked about mutuality. How do you know what another person wants? he asked. A lot of times he wasn't real sure what he wanted.

Knowing you don't know is a pretty good place to be, I suggested. I've observed you observing, I told him. You read people well. It will come.

As The Talk came to an end, I reached into my lower desk drawer and took out a package of condoms. A major dilemma parents face, I said, is how to prepare their kids for sex without appearing to be suggesting that they ought to be having sex. He flashed a sardonic smile that seemed to say, Don't look to me for help. I explained that giving the condoms to him symbolized my recognition that he was now a man, probably already making sexual decisions, that he had the biological capacity to reproduce, and the responsibility to be intentional and exercise judgment.

That's the gist of what I remember. Afterward, I took a long nap, exhausted, wondering what he had heard and what, if anything, would remain with him. Now, more than two years later, camped on Bass Trail just west of King Arthur and Guinevere Castles, below Holy Grail Temple, I was to find out.

As we came back together after cleaning up from dinner, I offered my assessment of the situation. Depending on what we decided to do about the Mercedes the next day when we reached the saddle, it appeared likely we wouldn't be all together the next night. I suggested, therefore, that we read the rest of the story, but limit discussion to the next segment.

They agreed. Brandon then read the remaining pages.

Though the King had been enraged by the insult of the boy's covered head and ordered the cook to send him away, the cook took pity on the boy and got him work gardening. One day, looking into the garden from her palace window, the King's daughter accidentally caught sight of the boy's golden head and became intrigued. There follow a series of three encounters in which, each time, she ordered him to bring her flowers and, when he did, she tried to get his hat off to see his golden hair. Each time he resisted. She then threw coins to him which, disdaining, he gave to the gardener's children.

Meanwhile, the country had come under attack. The boy wanted to help so he returned to the forest and called Iron John, who equipped him with a great horse and warriors. They arrived just in time to save the kingdom. The knight (the boy) then disappeared. The King, mystified, announced a great festival in hopes of attracting the mysterious knight. The highlight would be seeing who could catch the golden apple tossed by the King's daughter. The first day, outfitted by Iron John in magnificent armor, the boy caught the apple and rode quickly away. The second and third days, he repeated the feat. However, while escaping the third time, his helmet fell off, revealing his golden hair.

The King's daughter searched for the boy back in the garden and recognized him as the mysterious and triumphant knight. She told her father, who commanded him to appear before the Court. Confirming that the boy *was the knight who saved the kingdom and, probing further, that he was of royal lineage, the King promised to grant whatever he might wish. The boy requested the daughter's hand in marriage. The boy's father and mother were invited to the wedding, at which Iron John suddenly appeared. It turned out that he, too, was a great King, but had been turned into a Wild Man by a sorcerer's spell. The boy's actions had broken the spell. Iron John promised all his wealth to the boy.**

"So, Brandon, what do you make of the encounters between the golden-haired boy and the King's daughter?" I asked.

"Well, if I was inclined to be critical, which you know I never am, I'd say the point of the story isn't very practical."

"How so?"

"It says boys should aspire to marry princesses, but there aren't that many left. And monarchy isn't exactly politically correct these days."

"So you found nothing relevant to our times?"

"Well . . . I did notice that the story introduced the girl and money at the same time. He gives her wildflowers. She gives him coins. It seems an intentional connection, like," he grinned, "once you start dealing with women you also have to start dealing with money."

"That's certainly practical. Would you agree, Dr. Gray?"

"Sounds like eternal wisdom to me," Malcolm confirmed.

"Perhaps you'd be willing to elaborate, anthropologically as well as personally."

"As you wish. Until recent times, wealth and status were primary criteria for arranging marriages. Dowries and bride prices were paid. From the tribe's or society's perspective, joining a boy and girl involved economic, social, and political alliances between families, clans, and sometimes whole tribes."

"And there were no family therapists," I chimed in, "not until the Western world decided that love should replace economic status as the basis of marriage."

"Are you saying love should not be a consideration?" Brandon asked.

"I'm not saying anything. We're trying to decipher the meaning of a twenty-thousand-year-old story that, having been retold over the centuries, supposedly offers some reservoir of societal wisdom about coming of age.

---

*As noted earlier, this skeletal outline in no way does justice to or is a substitute for the full Grimms' original. Just enough is summarized to provide context for our discussion.

The word 'love' never actually appears in the story as retold by Bly. There's obviously a strong attraction between the two, but there's also a solid economic and status basis for their marriage. I trust you noted that the King asks who his father is, and finds out the boy is really a wealthy prince, *before* offering the boy whatever he wants as a reward."

"I thought you were trying to convince me the story's somehow relevant to me. I'd say you just undermined yourself."

"Let me try a different angle, then. The Arthurian legend makes the point better anyway. The marriage of Arthur and Guinevere epitomizes a functional arrangement—an economic and political alliance between two kingdoms. Arthur grows to love Guinevere, but the real passion is between her and Lancelot. Their obsessive, illicit love undermines societal stability and destroys Camelot. You get the moral, I trust?"

"Sure. You're warning me not to have an affair with a queen. I promise I won't."

"I'm not warning you about anything," I insisted. "I'm talking sociologically, not parentally. I'm not making a case for or against romantic love. I'm just talking about its consequences. Love is a less stable basis for relationships than economics from a societal point of view. The connection of wealth with marriage may be less acknowledged today than at any time in history. Yet, marital status is still a major factor related to poverty. Divorced women and unwed mothers account for . . . Help me out here, Malcolm. I've lost his interest."

"Hold on! I get it," Brandon exclaimed. "Let me check this out. Are you hinting that you brought me down here to tell me you've arranged a marriage for me with a wealthy princess?"

He turned abruptly to Malcolm. "Are you in on this, Malcolm?" He turned back to me. "Well, what's she like? Do you have a picture? Although, I suppose, looks don't matter in arranged marriages. Okay, but I've got to know what music she likes. It will be a real bummer if she has a radically different taste in music. I trust you thought to check, father, sir?"

Brandon was in a groove. "All right, let's get to the bottom line. How much is she worth? Gross? Net? How gross is the net? What are you offering me to give up the ideal of love?"

"Hey, it's not necessarily either-or," I protested. "In 'Iron John' love and economics appeared to work together."

"And in Camelot they didn't," Brandon countered. "As I remember, even Merlin fell victim to romance, letting himself get seduced, which is why he isn't around to help Arthur at the end."

"You've been too influenced by the version written by Cistercian monks," I countered. "They pushed the ideal of the quest for the Holy Grail as a way of countering the growing influence of romantic love in medieval courts—better for knights to be questing for God than for women. We've brought you to the Holy Grail"—I pointed above east toward the Temple—"so you can get that part of the quest out of the way and turn your attention to women. Being a modern man, you get the myth that you can have it all. Right, Malcolm? Malcolm?"

"Huh? Oh, I was thinking that the story of Iron John doesn't deal with the most important part of male-female relationships—what happens after marriage."

"I assume you're talking about more than sex," I interjected.

"It doesn't matter so much what brings a man and woman together, it's how they work at the relationship on a day-to-day basis that ultimately makes the difference. Today, all the focus is on the initial attraction, finding someone, having sex—but there's no guidance about how to do the work that builds a long-term relationship."

"So that's why couples end up in therapy?" Brandon asked.

"Sure, if they're committed to work at the relationship. A lot of people associate going into therapy with a failing marriage. What it really means is that one or both partners recognize a problem. Then, a big determinant of whether therapy can help is whether they're willing to work on the stuff that's important. It's hard work. Therapists don't do the work. We just facilitate it. I don't know if your dad's ever told you, but Dee and I became family therapists as a result of going into therapy to work on our marriage."

"There's this notion that if two people love each other, it shouldn't be work," I commented. "In your practice, have you noticed any difference between men and women in being willing or able to work on relationships?"

"It varies a lot, but I think women are more willing. Men don't seem to know how—and they're less likely to try. Women seem to understand that it takes work and they often lament that they have to do the work alone."

"What do you mean by work?" Brandon asked.

"It's a lot of things. It means working at understanding. It means paying attention. It means negotiating—how you spend time, money issues, children, household tasks, relatives. Dealing with baggage people bring with them, like stuff from childhood, relationships with parents, and previous love relationships. Most of all, dealing with feelings. Talking about them. Staying in touch with feelings. Sharing them."

"What about people married fifty years who say they've never had a fight?" Brandon asked.

"They probably don't talk to each other. Just go through the motions, oblivious, or suffering in silence, because the church says to stay together. Maybe there are good, rich marriages without conflict. I haven't seen one. I'd want to take a close look before celebrating fifty years without an argument. Conflict's as normal as a cold front from the north bumping up against a warm front from the south and causing a thunderstorm. Then it blows over. Honest arguments are part of a couple's work. And, from what I've seen, most couples need to learn to fight. Conflict is important, a way to open things up, get feelings out. A way to get to mutual understanding."

"So the boy and the King's daughter are off to a good start because they've got conflict over whether he's going to take his hat off?" In the dull grayness Brandon's expression was hard to make out, but his tone sounded playful. Malcolm's didn't.

"The Iron John story goes as far as getting a woman into the young man's life, but nothing's happened to prepare him for what comes later."

"You're implying his winning tournaments will cease to impress her after a while," I suggested.

"It may even cease to impress him."

"And the solution to relationship problems will not be for him to go off and catch golden apples for her?" I asked.

"She seems to be into golden apples, it's true, but the odds are that at some point she's going to want to talk with him. So far, when she wants to talk, he runs away. Typical pattern. He goes off to war and plays in tournaments instead of hanging out with her. When he reverts to that behavior later on, the relationship will be in trouble."

"You two are being pretty rough on poor Iron John," Brandon protested, sitting up. "No short story can cover everything."

"I'd just say this, Brandon," Malcolm replied. "I think avoiding talking to a woman about what's under your hat may end up being a relationship issue long-term."

"It seems to me," I offered, "it's open to interpretation. I've come across some Jungian analysis that interprets Galahad's chastity and Perceval's purity as representing the importance of cherishing the inner feminine in males and having nothing to do with sex or male-female relationships. But I'm a simple sociologist. I'll leave those kinds of interpretations to poets and those practitioners of Malcolm's craft who prefer symbols to everyday reality. For my part, the story's meaning seems pretty straightforward. It's part of a man's journey to encounter women. Whether a man is attracted, repulsed, scared, and/or in love with a woman, the point is that part of coming into manhood is encountering women. Can we agree on that much?" I asked Brandon. He nodded. I turned to Malcolm. "Agreed, old man?"

"Agreed, old man," he replied.

"Then, Malcolm, it's time for you to give Brandon your wisdom about encountering women. That's the evening's surprise—for you both. You've started, Malcolm, but I'd like Brandon to get all he can from you. He's already heard my perspective."

Malcolm moved uncomfortably, his back obviously tired. "Just a minute," he asked. "When did you give him your wisdom? Did I miss something?"

"When Brandon turned sixteen we had a father-son talk about women and sex. Then again a couple of months ago, when he turned eighteen, we had a follow-up talk. He's heard from me. Now he should hear from you."

"What did you tell him? I should know that before I say anything more. You know I'd *never* want to contradict anything his father said."

"No! No! No!" I protested. "I'll take that risk. You shouldn't be influenced by what's been said before this very moment. Brandon should get the straight scoop from you, here and now."

"It's okay, Malcolm," Brandon said. "If you haven't figured it out, it's okay. It won't matter much anyway since it seems my marriage is being arranged for me. I'll just count on coming to see you if we run into trouble later on."

Malcolm laughed.

"I did kind of spring this assignment on Malcolm unexpectedly," I said to Brandon. "It's late. Let's let him sleep on it and he can give you some of his wisdom about women after he's applied his wisdom about cars tomorrow. Success with the car will put him in the right mood to share with you his success with women. Of course, failure with the car—"

"I still want to know what you told Brandon when he was sixteen. What'd he tell you, Brandon?"

Malcolm's question riveted me. I became perfectly still, aware in the momentary silence that I was holding my breath.

"I think you'll like what he told me," Brandon said. "It's right down your alley. Even though he claims to be a simple sociologist tonight, back then he told me sex is mostly psychological. The physical part is easy, he said. What makes the difference is what's in the head. It's all a matter of perspective and two people respecting each other and being sensitive. I guess the sociological part is, society has a lot of influence over what's in your head and you have to be aware of that and sometimes worry about it or change it."

I exhaled slowly, trying to be quiet enough that they wouldn't notice, letting myself luxuriate in what I had just heard, being transported back. I did not remember our talk as succinctly as he recounted it. He had boiled it down to essence. A single phrase became a drumbeat in my head, a rhythm beneath the night sounds. I could not remember any other time as a parent when I knew with such certainty that I had been heard. I wanted to stay with that feeling, that sense of harmony.

"Excuse me," I said, interrupting one or the other of them without noticing who. "I've got to take a piss, then I think I'll do a little stargazing. I'll leave you two to talk."

I walked up Muav Canyon far enough to be out of earshot. The stars shone so brightly I found myself listening, expecting to hear them sparkle in rhythm with the words in my head: "He heard me."

Day Six

29. Mercedes

We woke to a cool morning reminding us we had climbed back to the Supai. Over breakfast we took up once again the Mercedes question. I could feel the retoxifying effects of debating the options. There being no consensus we postponed the decision again, agreeing to hike on to Muav Saddle, have lunch, and decide.

We hiked briskly in the cool morning air, traversing the Esplanade easily and reaching the Hermit Shale in what seemed like no time at all. Brandon trucked on ahead and got to the abandoned cabin first. Someone had stashed a water bottle since our brief stop there on the way down, another rim-world intrusion, undercutting our preferred illusion that we had the canyon to ourselves.

From Muav Saddle we could see the Mercedes at Swamp Point, pushed back in along the rim. As Malcolm looked up at the object of our indecision, I announced: "I've been thinking about this damn decision all morning. There's no good solution, so here's what I propose. Malcolm and I will hike out together and check it out. We know that something is dangling down. Maybe we can undangle it. Brandon, you stay here and solo tonight. If we get it fixed we'll be

255

back in the morning. If not . . . who knows? If we're not back by mid-morning, figure that you can do a day hike, but come back here for the night again. Do the same each day. If we're not back in three days, come up at first light. We'll leave a note under a cairn where we camped the first night. If we need you before then, one of us will come down and get you."

They mounted no resistance. Malcolm agreed that a solo would be a good experience for Brandon. He could get water at the dripping springs above the Coconino. The old men, the worriers, would go on to the rim to do both their worrying and, maybe, their problem solving.

The decision made, we were anxious to get going. We had made such good time that the sun was not yet overhead. We sorted through our packs, leaving the stove and first-aid kit, but taking the rope. With extra food in the car, we left most of what remained for Brandon. We shouldered the light packs and I said to Brandon, "We'll see you when we see you."

"Right," he replied.

We found the car key where we'd left it, hidden under some old logs and a rock. The car started right up. First gear still worked, but that was all. Malcolm drove past the clearing at Swamp Point to a spot where the ruts were especially deep. He maneuvered onto the mounds that framed the tire-dug furrows so that I could squeeze under the car. His larger physique wouldn't quite compress between iron and earth so he was left to peer in as a kibitzer. My face was so close to the bottom of the car that my nose touched if I looked straight up. With the oily car bottom, the dirt road, and Malcolm on one side, very little light penetrated, making it cavernously dark.

By the time Malcolm retrieved a flashlight, my eyes had adjusted enough to make out the shapes underneath. Peering over my nose, through my feet, I could see the rear axle with its large round hump—the lowest point under the car. I realized that if the car rolled, the axle would crush my head. Heeding my urgent request, Malcolm lodged large rocks in front of and behind the front wheels. Breathing easier, I maneuvered next to whatever was dangling. Blobs of oily dirt fell in my face as I tried to grasp the hanging rod. "Shit!"

"What's wrong?" Malcolm asked.

"When I get close enough to see, I can't touch it. When I move back to get hold of it, I can't see up where it's attached."

"Come out and we'll drive it up on something to get more room," Malcolm urged. I heard his real message, that I didn't know what I was doing. He was right. As a kid I had hung around a neighborhood Texaco station where the night attendant let me pump gas while he played cards with his buddies, but I had never progressed beyond the gas pumps. It made perfect sense to me that Malcolm should be the one to tinker with his car, so I yelled: "Just give me a goddam minute. This is obviously a job for a sociologist."

"Just don't make it worse," he cautioned.

I managed to position myself so that I could get my right hand on the object in question. Arduously rubbing off the greasy dirt, it began to take some shape. A small ring was connected to a round rod a couple inches long. That attached to a flat arm which was connected to something that went into a housing of some kind. "Move the gear shift around so I can see if this thing has anything to do with the gears."

He got up on his knees, reached inside the open door, and jiggled the gearshift.

"YES!" I shouted. "It's jiggling. Do it again."

I maneuvered my hand up to where the thing would supposedly be attached and found a cylindrical, knoblike protrusion that felt like it was the size of the ring. I tried to fit the ring onto this cylinder to no avail. I settled for holding the ring hard against the cylinder while Malcolm again moved the gearshift. I felt movement in my hand. "That's it! I've found the thing it came off of. Shit!" Another oily glob fell on my mouth. "I need some kind of rag," I sputtered, blowing away the glob as I spit out the words. Feeling suddenly claustrophobic, I slithered to the edge of the car for air.

Malcolm handed me something to use as a rag. "Come out and we can jack up the car to get more clearance."

"There isn't room for both of us to do anything and we need one person on the gearshift. Let me try it again."

I managed to wipe my face. My glasses were filthy, but at least they protected my eyes. I took a deep breath and slithered back under. I had been trying to slide the ring on with the rod hanging down. This time I tried bending the rod up so that it fit in the space above. I forced the ring onto the edge of the cylinder, but that was as far as I could get.

"We've got second gear now," I heard Malcolm call faintly through the car floor. "I'll try third." As he did so, the ring slid off, jerked down, and whacked me on the nose. I emitted a cursing scream, more in annoyance than pain, but it was enough to mask what Malcolm said. He was quickly laying back along the car, trying to peer under.

"What happened?" he asked, his voice alarmed, but not, it became clear, because of my scream. "We just lost all gears. I can't get it back into first. It's just loose. Doesn't even feel like neutral."

"That's fine," I pretended. "That tells us we're messing with the right thing. It's just a matter of making the pieces fit. Get back in and let me try again."

I was really thinking that we needed tools. It seemed fixable, though we probably couldn't repair it with just sticks and stones, the tools available at the Swamp Point Wilderness Garage. I slid my head directly under the dangling rod, trying at the same time to work the flashlight into my mouth so I'd have a free hand, but there wasn't space for my head, hand, and a flashlight. I'd have to do it by feel. I could look or touch, but not both, and I couldn't look with the light. "I'm primarily a visual type," I said more to myself than Malcolm.

"What?" he asked.

"I just think of myself as a visual type and this job is going to require touch—not my strong suit."

"What the hell are you talking about?"

I didn't answer. I was feeling around, focusing first on the cylindrical knob and then moving my hand slowly along the rod until I held the ring in my fingers. I felt it inside and out, translating touch into images, using my tactile sense to see. But that proved a problem. In translation the dirty, greasy parts became clean, sparkling brass and shiny stainless steel. What I "saw" was so different from what I felt that it was distracting. I had to shut off the visual translation and make my fingers my observational tools. I commanded myself to FEEL: "Stop trying to fix it. Focus on knowing it. Slow down. Feel the shapes and connections."

Malcolm asked, "What do you feel?"

"Lots," I said. "I'm starting over, getting familiar with what's here. I was too impatient before. Just give me a minute."

"I'm not going anywhere," he replied sardonically.

I let loose of the ring, shaking my hand and fingertips to void them of past sensations, then began exploring anew, this time more systematically. What else was in that space? Bolts, nuts, metal, and . . .

"There's two more of these goddamn things up here!" I yelled.

"Two more what?"

"Right next to the thing hanging down are two more things that feel the same but are attached. Move the gearshift again and let me see what happens to them."

Malcolm reached into the car and jiggled the gearshift. Nothing. He laid back down by the side of the car.

"Did you feel anything?"

"No, but that probably just means it's all connected. We've got to think like German engineers. There's three things. They feel the same. They're right next to each other. They probably are interconnected and they should fit the same way. It should all be very logical, just a matter of feeling out the logic."

I felt the two connected rods. Their position was different from any I had tried. I used the rag, which I now noticed was the T-shirt I'd left on the backseat for the trip home, to wipe off more grease. This exposed a small bump on the dangling ring. I found the same bumps on the connected rings. Then I felt serrations inside the ring and a slight notch. I found a matching-size bump on the cylinder.

I tried maneuvering the dangling rod into the same position as the connected rods, but it wouldn't fit. I jiggled and jiggled and suddenly the loose rod slipped up at a new angle. I worked my index finger into the ring while using my middle finger to find the little nipple on the cylinder. I paused, holding the ring in position. Breathing heavily and sweating profusely, I felt claustrophobic again and a bit dizzy. Malcolm had been patiently quiet. He must have heard my deep breath. "You okay? If I really squeeze I can get under."

"I think I've about got it. I just can't get it to fit. . . . Goddamn sonofabitchin' engineering!" I screamed.

"What?! What?! What's the matter?!"

"You won't believe it. The sucker just slipped on. I just pressed a little and the ring slipped completely onto the rod clean and smooth as can be. Try it. TRY IT!"

He quickly slipped in the clutch and pushed the gearshift forward. "We've got first back!" he yelled. "Second seems to be there, too. We've got third. And reverse. They're all back!"

I slithered out from under the car grinning through grease, dirt, and oil—a big, broad Cheshire cat grin. "Yes!" I screamed, pumping my left fist in triumph.

Malcolm pulled the car forward. "She feels fine, gearshift tight, like it never happened." His grin easily matched mine. "What kind of sociology was that?"

"Just had to get things lined up right." I looked at those two fingers. "You know what it felt like—Don't laugh now!—the first time I ever found a clitoris."

Malcolm shook his head, laughing. "You've been in the wilderness too long, Patton."

"I'm serious. Same damn fingers too." I studied those two dirty digits, still feeling the nipple, still in touch with the sudden moment of release when the ring slipped on over the receiving cylinder. "Just think, Clyde, these primate appendages evolved in Olduvai so we could massage clitori and repair Mercedes."

I put my hand down but didn't change the position of the fingers. "I don't know if she'll hold all the way back," I said. "There's no way to tighten the ring, but I know how it works now. It would be no problem to fix again."

"I'll have to watch you. You'll be under there diddling with that thing every chance you get."

I thrust my hand into the air, exclaiming, "We did it. Wait till we tell Brandon."

Our shared ecstasy revealed how preoccupied we had been with the car the last couple of days. On the surface we had tried to model rational decision matching and doing what had to be done. Only with the problem behind us could we admit to ourselves how anxious we had been.

The sun shone high above. The repair had taken less than an hour. "So what do we do now?" I asked. "We could still give Brandon his solo and go down in the morning. Or we could truck back down right now and gloat. I vote for gloating."

"You'll get your chance to gloat either way," he replied. "I worked up an appetite pushing the clutch and shifting gears. Let's eat, get you calmed down, and catch some rock-lizard time."

I screamed at the top of my lungs. "WE FIXED A DAMN CAR, BARE-HANDED, WITH NO TOOLS. WE SHALL NOT BE DEFEATED BY TECHNOLOGY. TECHNOLOGY IS OUR SERVANT."

"Brandon knows now. Feel better?"

"I feel great. Now I can eat."

We had a delicious lunch of sardines and crackers after which I settled on my sleeping bag below a large fire-scarred oak to meditate on things technological and human, and fell immediately into a deep, postorgasmic sleep.

30. Diddly-Squat

Lost in the reverie of technological triumph, I did not notice that we were already back to Muav Saddle. On awakening from our naps, we had decided to leave Swamp Point at once and rejoin Brandon so we could get on to Powell Plateau the next morning. Malcolm had stopped at the fork where the trail led down into the canyon or west across the saddle. He was looking back and forth the way one looks before crossing a street. "The bus doesn't stop here," I said as I came up behind him.

Again he looked both ways, ignoring me. "Look at the contrast, the way the trail starts to turn gray to the east as it picks up the Coconino and is brown on the saddle as it leads into the forest. The transition between strata is subtle and gradual here in this fault line. Hey, Patton, no point in being down here if you don't pay attention. Did you see the cactus flower doing a purple solo along the trail? It's soooo good to be back below the rim."

He took off his pack and shook his arms, then his whole body. "As soon as I get back below the Kaibab and into the Toroweap, I can feel the toxins draining." He sat his pack against a small pine, then walked below the path and down a slope to the top of the Hermit Shale where he picked up something.

"Look at this," he called back, holding up what looked like the rusted remains of a tin can. He pointed below us. A casual look showed no more than a steep, eroded slope about fifty yards long before a cliff. The closer inspection Malcolm urged revealed rusted remnants strewn over the hillside among the rocks, brush, small pine shoots, and manzanita.

"This looks like the dump site for the cabin," he continued as I joined him, "probably where the CCC [Civilian Conservation Corps] boys threw their garbage, tin cans, and broken tools. Fifty years later it's still here, blended in some, but still here."

"I don't suppose they were into 'Take only photos, leave only footprints.' "

"I wasn't condemning them. They were who they were, acting with the understandings of their time. Given the way hydrologic engineers keep playing with the river, our generation is doing far more damage to the canyon's ecology than the CCCers did throwing away cans."

"You did retoxify up there. Think we'll contaminate Brandon?"

He shrugged and threw the remains of the can back down the slope. "It belongs here now," he said. As we went back to the trail, he asked, "What are we going to tell the kid?"

"I've been thinking about that."

"I figured you had."

"I think we should be very low key, you know, nonchalantlike. Act like repairing a '71 Mercedes is all in a day's work for us. If we make it a big deal, he'll be tempted to put it down. If we play it down, he'll have the opportunity to build it up to the phenomenally great accomplishment it was."

He looked at me with a devilish grin. "So, you sociologists still think reverse psychology works."

"I don't know that we think any kind of psychology works. We put our faith in the fingers," I proclaimed, holding up my hand in the position of recent triumph.

We approached the cabin quietly. I rounded the corner and saw Brandon sitting on the steps, writing in his journal. He looked up, startled. "What's happenin', dude?" I asked.

Malcolm rounded the cabin behind me. "Hello, Brandon. What's for dinner?"

Brandon's eyes grew big, his mouth opened, his hand still poised with the pencil on his notebook in midsentence. "What's wrong?" he asked. "Can't you get the car started?"

"No, it's fine," I said, removing my pack.

"What do you mean,'fine'?" he asked, genuinely confused.

I took a long drink from my canteen, though not really thirsty. He watched me intently as I pulled it down from my lips and slowly wiped my mouth with the back of my hand. Ignoring his question I asked, "So, what've you been up to?"

He stood, journal in one hand, pencil in the other, stepped down, and positioned himself directly in front of me. "Come on, why are you back so soon? If you need my help to push the car, just say so. You don't have to pretend everything's all right."

"He doesn't seem to believe his old man, Malcolm. Tell him. Isn't everything fine?"

"Everything's fine," Malcolm repeated in a deadpan voice.

"What about the car?" Brandon demanded, not bothering to disguise his annoyance at our coyness.

"It's fixed," I said.

"Really? How? Was somebody up there?"

"Would you listen to that, Malcolm? That hurts. My son, my own flesh and blood, doesn't believe that his father and friend could fix a little problem on an old car without help from some magically appearing mechanic. That really hurts."

He turned and climbed slowly up the three cabin steps and sat in the doorway. "Just let me know when you two are ready to tell me what happened."

Sitting on the lowest step, I stretched my legs out long and straight, bending forward as far as I could, just touching my head to my knees. I then turned and explained what had happened as matter-of-factly as I could. I concluded, "So the car's fixed. We're back on schedule. Tomorrow we do Powell Plateau. Simple as that. End of story."

Malcolm, reclining against a large pine tree in front of the cabin, nodded approval of my account and got up. He made his way past me, squeezed past Brandon, and went into the cabin where our food supplies were in black garbage bags on the old table. Brandon followed Malcolm into the cabin to help pick dinner.

"What have you been up to?" I asked through the doorway.

"First, I wrote lyrics for some songs for our band. I was just starting to catch up in my journal when you appeared. I haven't had a chance to write in it since Saturday when we went up Merlin. Now I'll have to change what I wrote."

"Why?" I asked, wondering how our unexpected return could have affected what he wrote about Merlin.

"I started off by explaining that you two had gone to deal with the car, so I'd have plenty of time to write. Here, I'll read you what I wrote."

There was intrigue in the way he made this offer. Malcolm stopped sorting through the food. Brandon retrieved his journal and settled in the doorway to read.

> *Wednesday. I've been too busy to write so I have a lot of catching up to do. At the moment I'm alone. Dad and Malcolm have gone back to the trailhead to see if they can fix the Mercedes. Neither knows diddly-squat about cars, so I'm here until whenever.*

He looked up with a twinkle in his eye and said grinning, "That's the part I'll have to change—'diddly-squat' to just 'diddly.' "

Malcolm chuckled, gave him a solid squeeze on the shoulder, and pronounced, "Well done, Brandon." Looking through the doorway at me, he said, "You see, Papa, the kid does appreciate what you've done. What finer compliment from a teenage son than to admit that his father actually knows 'squat'—or was it 'diddly.' Whatever. I hope I get as much recognition from Jacob when he's eighteen." He turned back to rummage through the food, enjoying the fantasy of his grown son someday recognizing his squatsome wisdom, perhaps even having that recognition come in the canyon.

Brandon took his pencil and started writing again in his journal, speaking each word out loud as he wrote: "Dad and Malcolm are back now. I stand corrected. They know diddly. They fixed the Mercedes."

It was a modest entry, but you take your victories where you find them. The ramen noodles that night never tasted better.

31. Warrior

As much as any other part of "Iron John," I had been anticipating hearing Brandon's reaction to the boy's transition from gardener's apprentice to warrior. Bly's interpretation of the warrior spirit had inflamed advocates and adversaries in a war of words over what it means to be a man. One part of me was attracted to the warrior ideal. Growing up four-eyes, skinny, and a favorite target of bullies, I had longed for a defender. As I grew older my fantasies turned to intellectual warriorhood: overwhelming physical brutality with superior cunning. Countering this attraction, I found it hard to dissociate warrioring from violence and war. Ruminating thus made me all the more glad that our pattern for discussing "Iron John" began with Brandon's reactions.

We settled after dinner under a large oak looking north toward Fire Point separated from Swamp Point by Castle Canyon. An easy breeze and hint of a splendid sunset contributed to tranquility. Unhurried in the early evening, unburdened by the Mercedes, and untired given our easy hiking day, we could focus on "Iron John" undistracted. I reread the account of the kingdom suddenly threatened by invasion from a large and powerful army.

265

The King's men had ridiculed the boy when he offered to join the combat, offering him an old, lame nag as his war steed. The boy rode the broken-down horse to the edge of the forest where he called for the Wild Man to help him as promised. Iron John not only equipped him with a fire-blooded warhorse, but also put him at the head of a great contingent of warriors. They approached the battlefield with the King on the verge of defeat and likely annihilation, turned the tide of war, and pursued the retreating soldiers until all had been killed. Not staying to accept the King's gratitude, much less any reward, the boy returned his steed and warriors to the forest, retrieved his sorry nag from Iron John, and returned to his place with the gardener, whereupon he was further ridiculed and accused of hiding during the battle. When he asserted that he had contributed to the victory in his own way, the men rolled on the ground in hysterics.

I looked up from the page to find Brandon shaking his head disapprovingly. "What?" I asked.

"I can't get into it."

"Into what?"

"Glorifying a massacre."

"A massacre?"

"Take no prisoners. Kill every last man. Slaughter them in retreat. Yeah, a massacre."

Not being inclined to defend the boy's actions, I looked to Malcolm. He remained silent. It suddenly looked like a very short discussion. At length I said, "Bly says the invading army symbolizes evil trying to infiltrate the soul, that's why it has to be totally destroyed. But he mainly wants to give modern meaning to the ancient ideal of the warrior. He thinks we've lost touch with our internal warrior psyches. He's struck a responsive chord with a lot of men."

"That's a big jump from the massacre in the story," Brandon protested skeptically. "Too big a jump for me."

"Bly advocates a warrior spirit with a compassionate heart. He thinks warriors should learn to dance as well as fight."

"That's all well and good, but it's not in the story. The boy in 'Iron John' doesn't dance or have a compassionate heart. He slaughters the opposing army as it retreats, plain and simple."

"You've hit on one of the major criticisms of 'Iron John.' Bly tries to rework the warrior metaphor to mean strength of spirit, but . . . I heard a radio program where a leader of Women Against Military Madness said, 'The myth isn't the story of Iron John. The myth is that there are gentle, compassionate warriors.' "

We lapsed again into silence. I studied Brandon's athletic frame, trying to imagine him in warrior garb. I couldn't. Not in armor. Not in a marine uniform. Not as an Indian brave. I had never seen him really angry. I'd never witnessed him in a fight, except. . . . I shivered as repressed feelings of fear, anger, and ambivalence washed over me, taking me back to one of my moments of greatest parental doubt, a teachable moment when I didn't know what to teach. At that instant I had felt bound at the waist by a great chain, pulled first in one direction by warrior allies and then in the other by philosophers of nonviolence, ending in a stalemate.

"Do you remember the indoor soccer game last year against that suburban team that pushed and tripped and talked trash whenever the referees weren't looking. Then when you guys retaliated, the refs always seemed to catch you. Your game was thrown totally off. Your team got lots of penalty minutes and you took a swing at one of their players. Remember?"

"I remember an ambulance in the parking lot the next week. The same team had done a high-low on a guy and broken his neck."

"What's a high-low?" Malcolm asked.

"One player slides behind a guy into his legs, while another slams into him high from the front."

"What made you bring it up?" Malcolm asked me.

"I watched that game with three or four other fathers. We lambasted the other coach and referees, which only made things worse. One of the fathers admitted admiration for the opposing team's tactics. They were winning. Watching you get tripped, slammed hard into the sideboard, whiplashed, and knocked down, all in the space of about two minutes, I threatened to pull you out of the game. They warned that I'd embarrass you. At half-time two of us talked to the coach and suggested forfeiting before someone got hurt, but you guys were riled and insisted on playing. Part of me wanted you to stand up for yourself and retaliate. Part of me was scared you'd get hurt. In the end, I just watched."

"We were mad as hell, but we lost anyway."

"Not long after that, I came across a book called *Fire in the Belly* by Sam Keen. He admitted to feeling considerable ambivalence about the warrior psyche, then concluded that 'so long as the world is less than perfect the warrior can never wholly retire. It still takes gentleness *and* fierceness to make a whole man.' I felt to my core the conflict between gentleness and fierceness watching you play soccer. Emotionally I wanted you to fight back, but my head told me it was silly to risk injury over a soccer game. I didn't know what to tell you."

Brandon laughed and winked at Malcolm. "Do you believe that?"

"Sounds pretty un-Michael," Malcolm agreed.

"Wait a minute. I'm sharing a moment of serious ambiguity here. Are you saying I told you what to do?"

"Not during the game, but afterward, on the way home."

"What'd he tell you afterward?" Malcolm asked.

"He asked me what I'd learned."

"And you said?"

"I said they were assholes and the refs were idiots and it wasn't fair and I cursed a lot and banged my fist on the dashboard. When I finally calmed down, Dad looked over at me and said one of those things that sticks with you. 'You have a right to complain,' he said. 'Everything you say is true. As your father I was angry and scared and wanted to stop the game. I'm glad it's over and you weren't hurt.' Or something like that. But here's the part I really remember. He said, 'Now that the game's over, let me put on my professional evaluator's hat and tell you what I'd say as your private consultant. It didn't work to fight back. Your team was more skilled. You were better players than fighters. I suggest you either learn to fight or give it up.' So I gave it up."

I laughed. "I don't remember saying that, but your swing was pretty pathetic, which was more a reflection on me than you. I'd obviously neglected your warrior training."

"Too late now. You'll just have to live with the guilt when I get beat to a pulp."

"You've reminded me of a story told by Admiral Elmo Zumwalt," Malcolm said. "He watched from a window while his little son got beat up by a bully. He said was it was the hardest thing he ever did as a parent, but he knew his son had to learn to defend himself because he wouldn't always have his father around to protect him."

"Admiral Elmo? You can make up a better name than that, Malcolm," Brandon kidded. "Do you have a whole repertoire of Admiral Elmo stories you tell Jacob?"

"Admiral Elmo Zumwalt's a real person. He headed up the Navy during the Vietnam War. He's the one who ordered Agent Orange be used to clear the jungle for Navy patrols. His son, Elmo the Third, the one he watched get beat up, commanded an attack boat along the defoliated waterways. After the war he developed cancer. He went through years of agonizing pain and treatment before he died with his father by his side."

"Heavy," Brandon sighed. "Did the Admiral admit that . . . you know, I mean, what'd he say about Agent Orange killing his son?"

"He saw no point in second-guessing himself. He felt he'd acted on the best information available and then did his duty."

"Duty," Brandon scoffed, spitting out the word.

"Duty's not high on Brandon's list of virtues," I explained.

"It's not even *on* my list," Brandon corrected.

"Fine," I said. "The question Bly raises isn't about doing duty, it's what we do with the primordial warrior that he thinks dwells within us. Does that strike a responsive chord at all, anywhere, deep inside?"

"NO!" Brandon declared vehemently, sitting up straight. "During the Persian Gulf War they kept referring to 'our warriors for freedom.' More like somebody told George Bush his penis wasn't as big as Reagan's so he bombed Iraqi civilians."

"Collateral damage," I corrected.

"Huh?"

"They weren't called civilians. They were designated collateral damage."

"That's not funny, Dad. It's sick."

Malcolm looked intently at Brandon. "You just had to register for the draft, didn't you?"

"Yeah, right while the Persian Gulf War was going on. I thought about not registering, but they've got the system tied in with applying to college. You can't get in without a selective service number. I ended up getting registered twice, once at Dad's and again at my Mom's address. I can do my duty twice!"

"I had forgotten the draft was still going on," Malcolm said softly. I guessed he was thinking of his own young son.

"They're not actually drafting, just registering."

"Has your dad told you about the draft during Vietnam?"

"Some. I know there was a lottery." He turned to me. "You got a low number, I think."

"82."

"Was low good or bad?"

"Unless you wanted to be drafted, it was very bad. Everyone through 195 got drafted, in numerical order. Everyone through 215 had to have a physical and be ready. Above 216 was safe. I remember the first number drawn: September 14. I knew a guy whose birthday made him fourth on the list. Until then, he'd always considered being born on Valentine's Day good luck. A random universe—two fourteeners in the first four numbers."

Brandon asked about my experiences evading the draft. He'd heard bits and pieces, but never made the connection to Olduvai. My draft board bought the argument that doing research in Tanzania would contribute to the battle against Communism. Studying the sociology of rural development became defense research. But Brandon showed more interest in the conflict with my father, his shame as a World War II veteran and American Legion officer at having a long-haired, bearded, and war-resisting son. In the end, as public sentiment turned against the war, we were reconciled. He decided I had been 'too smart to become cannon fodder for a war the politicians weren't committed to winning.' It was an interpretation we could both live with, especially once he convinced himself that I had 'served my country,' even if it was only in the Peace Corps—emphasis on the *Corps*.

Malcolm recounted his Vietnam years, his father not a factor because he had gone his own way while Malcolm was still a boy. About to be drafted, he enlisted and went through naval aviation and preflight training in the Navy.

"That's why you knew who Admiral Zumwalt was!" I exclaimed. "I remember General Westmoreland—he delivered my college commencement address amidst antiwar demonstrations—but I didn't recall Zumwalt. You never told me you were in the navy."

"I wasn't in long. The navy had learned that it wasn't in its best interest to have officers who weren't committed. After six months in the navy, I wasn't, so I turned down my commission. I preferred the risks of two years with the fleet to four years as an officer. It turned out the fleet didn't want me, so I ended up taking my chances with the draft. By then the draft board didn't want me either."

"What was it like in officer training?" Brandon asked.

"I found out I wasn't willing to give up complete control of my life to so-called superior officers. I hated it, and I'd have been a lousy officer. Giving orders isn't my idea of a good time. And I was no better at taking them. I had to get out."

Malcolm shifted the focus back to Brandon, asking how his friends had reacted to the Persian Gulf War. Brandon recounted his antiwar activities: writing letters, participating in demonstrations, representing high school opponents of the war on a radio program, and helping organize a major protest at school.

"Tell him what you did," I urged.

"It wasn't that big a deal. Dad got excited because we made the evening news for like five seconds."

"Just tell him what you did," I repeated.

"We took about twenty black poster boards and wrote in gold the names of all the seniors, over four hundred names. Then we taped them together to make it look like a replica of the Vietnam War Memorial. We paraded through the lunchroom until the principal made us go outside. That's what attracted the TV news."

"How'd the other students react?" Malcolm asked.

"Two girls freaked, screaming that we had put a death curse on them by putting their names on black. Others got upset because they thought we were saying they were against the war when they weren't, so we let people cross out their names if they wanted to. Outside, students started shouting for and against. A lot were supportive. Most didn't care one way or the other, but we got them thinking. Still, it was just one day, not like some great sixties' protest."

"Hey," I said throwing a twig at him, "every generation has to play the hand it's dealt. Our generation just got dealt a longer, more alienating war."

"The lives of men throughout the ages have been defined by war," Malcolm observed. "And the lives of women and children."

"It sucks," Brandon said.

We sat silently for a while, gazing out at the red sky beyond Fire Point. At length Malcolm said softly, "I had really forgotten that draft registration was still happening. Did you register as a pacifist?"

"You don't register as something. You just register so they can find you. But if I am drafted, I will declare myself a pacifist."

"When did you decide that?" I asked, genuinely surprised at the certitude he exuded.

He grinned. "A minute ago."

I considered asking if his conviction applied to all war or just the Persian Gulf variety. Would you have fought Hitler? Would you kill to defend your wife against a rapist or your children against kidnaping? Tired, absolutist questions. I wanted some other tact. "Arthur would have understood and agreed with you, at least, in the end," I offered.

"King Arthur?!" Brandon asked. "He was hardly a pacifist."

"Remember in the beginning of *The Once and Future King* how Merlin taught young Arthur, the Wart, by turning him into animals? He became a fish, an ant, and a bird."

"I remember vaguely."

"During World War II, T. H. White wrote a sequel, *The Book of Merlyn,* to work through his struggle with being a conscientious objector. He came to see the Arthurian legend as a fable about war's futility. The central question in the book is what humans, in the person of Arthur, can learn from animals, given that we are the only species that makes war on our own kind."

"So what does Arthur learn?"

"The book opens with Arthur in despair the night before the final battle against Modred's forces. As he weeps, Merlin appears and says he's returned to complete Arthur's training and that to do so they must return to his tutors: badger, snake, owl, goat, hedgehog, a stuffed pike, and a couple of others. The animals analyze man's warring nature. Merlin turns Arthur into a gander at one point and he falls in love with a goose and finds peace at last. Being turned back into a man depresses him further. He laments his failure to reorder the world from Might Makes Right to Might For Right. He considers a failure his effort to divert knights from killing each other by turning their attention to the quest for the Holy Grail. In the end, he and the animals can find no antidote to war. It's human nature, though there is some slight hope that nature could be tamed through 'education without coercion.' That phrase has stuck in my mind."

"What happened to Arthur?"

"He negotiated a truce giving Modred half his kingdom. He kept half to experiment with noncoercive education. When he met Modred to sign the treaty, one of Modred's officers raised his sword to kill a garter snake, mistaking it for a viper. Arthur's forces thought their king had been betrayed and rushed forward. Arthur was killed just as Lancelot arrived. Lancelot buried Arthur and went to Guinevere's abbey to give her the news. She refused to see him, so he retired to a hermitage where he took up gardening. In contrast to the sequence in 'Iron John,' Lancelot went from warrior to gardener."

"Swords into plowshares," Malcolm remarked.

"It'd be better if there were never swords," Brandon countered.

"Better, but not likely," I suggested, "at least not according to White. So you're left with having to confront man's warrior nature. The options appear to be Modred's evil warrior, where might makes right; Arthur's good warrior, using might for right; Bly's dancing warrior, cultivating strength of spirit; or some kind of antiwarrior, fighting human nature."

"Bogus options," Brandon protested quickly. "I don't fit any of those categories."

"Others will categorize you if you don't categorize yourself," I argued.

"That's their problem. If they need to categorize me, they can put me down as a musician."

"I like that," I said. "I like that a lot. At least if you're drafted it might get you assigned to the drum and bugle corps instead of the infantry."

We fell again into silence as the sky to the west did what Arizona is so deservedly famous for. Suddenly Malcolm declared:

"John Wesley Powell defied categorization."

"Doesn't history categorize him as an explorer?" Brandon asked.

"He was an explorer *extraordinaire,* to be sure. But he was also a soldier, geographer, ethnographer, cartographer, author, politician, geologist, biologist, linguist, administrator, teacher, and philosopher. You'd be hard pressed to name something he didn't do."

"Music?" Brandon asked.

"He sang."

"Did he compose?"

"I believe so."

"Then tell me more."

32. Powell Was Powell

Recounting to Brandon the heroic accomplishments of Powell, a humanist in words and deeds before that distinguished and controversial designation had emerged, struck me as the perfect way to prepare for ascending the plateau that bears his name. I had no way of knowing that the lesson to be extracted from Powell's life that night would be directed at me, and that Brandon would be the teacher. I was caught so off-guard, I didn't even have time to mount serious resistance. My defeat was total.

Malcolm began by recounting how Powell had lost his right arm in the Civil War. During the Battle of Shiloh, he was shot as he raised his arm to signal his troops to fire. Infection led to amputation, but he returned to command troops at Vicksburg and participate in Sherman's march across Georgia. His warrior credentials were impeccable at a time when the cause was black and white.

After the war he became a professor of geology at Illinois Wesleyan University and curator of the Natural History Society. Following scientific expeditions along the Mississippi, Ohio, and Illinois rivers, he turned farther west to the unknown canyon country of the Colorado, becoming the first to run the river

275

through the Grand Canyon. That 1869 expedition took four months and included many life-threatening moments, like the one recorded in his journal on August 27.

> About eleven o'clock we come to a place in the river which seems much worse than any we have yet met in all its course. . . . We clamber up over the granite pinnacles for a mile or two, but can see no way by which to let down, and to run it would be sure destruction. . . . High above the river we can walk along on the top of the granite, which is broken off at the edge and set with crags and pinnacles, so that it is very difficult to get a view of the river at all. In my eagerness to reach a point where I can see the roaring fall below, I go too far on the wall, and can neither advance nor retreat. I stand with one foot on a little projecting rock and cling with my hand fixed in a little crevice. Finding I am caught here, suspended 400 feet above the river, into which I must fall if my footing fails, I call for help. The men come and pass me a line, but I cannot let go of the rock long enough to take hold of it. Then they bring two or three of the largest oars. All this takes time which seems very precious to me; but at last they arrive. The blade of one of the oars is pushed into a little crevice in the rock beyond me in such a manner that they can hold me pressed against the wall. Then another is fixed in such a way that I can step on it; and thus I am extricated.

At one point the national press reported that Powell and his party had been killed. He emerged to disprove those rumors, gained national renown, and led another, more extended expedition in 1871. His book on *The Exploration of the Colorado River and Its Canyons* was followed by scholarly writings on ethnography, geology, social science, natural history, and philosophy. His devotion to science was absolute—he had no use for religion—and was evident in the institutions of knowledge he created and directed: the Bureau of Ethnology and the U.S. Geological Survey. He played a major role in the establishment of the National Geographic Society and the Geological Society of America, and served as president of the American Association for the Advancement of Science.

His wife, Emma Dean, accompanied him on Rocky Mountain expeditions. In the summer of 1867 she became the first recorded woman to climb Pike's Peak. Their only child, Mary, was born during his second Colorado

River expedition. Malcolm knew just enough about Powell's family system to portray him as a devoted family man at the center of an extended family of siblings and in-laws, nieces and nephews, whose wife was his partner and whose prominent suffragette sisters he actively supported.

Having led the mapping of uncharted Western territories, Powell advocated basing the development of the frontier on scientific assessment of its water resources, with decisions made in the public interest. He crusaded against the widespread belief, popular even in Congress and among some scientists, that "rain follows the plow." He fought corruption in land and homestead distribution. He argued for preserving forests for watersheds. He wrote extensively about the limitations of arid farming and irrigation, drafted legislation to map and conserve water sources, and fought special interests trying to purchase and monopolize water rights. He prophesied the cyclic inevitability of catastrophic droughts following years of adequate rainfall and overdevelopment of arid lands. His predictions came true. In short, he was the first scientific conservationist at the beginning of the Western battle over water.

He was no less dedicated to documenting and preserving native cultures. He was the first to recognize the value of indigenous ruins in the Grand Canyon and to work for their preservation. He documented the native cultures he encountered throughout his explorations of the Southwest, recording their kinship practices, agricultural and hunting methods, social organization, and, especially, their mythology. For example, he was first to record the Unikarets story of the Grand Canyon's creation.

> Many years ago when wise and good men lived on the earth, the great Chief of all the Utes lost his beloved wife.
>
> Day and night he grieved, and all his people were sad. Then Rabbit appeared to the chief and tried to comfort him, but his sorrow could not be allayed. So at last Rabbit promised to take him to a country away to the southwest where he said his dead wife had gone and let him see how happy she was if he would agree to grieve no more on his return. So he promised. Then Rabbit took his magical ball and rolled it before him, and as it rolled it rent the earth and mountains, and crushed the rocks and made a way for them to that beautiful land—a trail through the mountains which intervened between that home of the dead and the hunting grounds of the living. And following the ball, which was a rolling globe of fire,

they came at last to the Spirit Land. Then the great Chief saw his wife and the blessed abode of the Spirits where all was plenty and all was joy, and he was glad.

Now when they had returned Rabbit enjoined upon the chief that he should never travel this trail again during life, and that all his people should be warned not to walk therein. Yet still he feared that they would attempt it so he rolled a river into the trail—a mad raging river into the gorge made by the globe of fire, which should overwhelm any who might seek to enter there.

Powell was the first to record the language of indigenous inhabitants around the canyon, but he didn't just study native peoples as scientific curiosities. He became involved in their struggle for survival, pleaded for aid to assist them, and campaigned for justice, as when, while doing fieldwork after his Colorado River explorations, he wrote civilian and military authorities trying to get relief for the destitute Utes, Unkars, Kanigats, Kaibabits, and Shewits. As creator and first director of the Bureau of Ethnology, he worked to preserve the history of native peoples, lamenting as he did so the necessity of such preservation because it foretold their dispossession and demise.

Powell became involved in all the great issues of his day. He took positions on the earth's origins, evolution, military versus civilian control of mapping, private versus public-led development, federal versus state rights, centralized versus decentralized government, basic versus applied research, and school reform.

I learned after our trip that Powell was even involved in the development of sociology. In 1882 he devoted his presidential address before the Anthropological Society to "An Outline of Sociology." When I discovered and shared this with Brandon, he responded with a tribute that added posthumously to Powell's long list of tributes: "Even a sociologist, huh? What a dude!"

Malcolm, when I called him with the news, was more circumspect: "I never said he was perfect."

Powell spent the last years of his life working on a *magnum opus* that was to analyze and integrate every aspect of the universe, human and otherwise, from technology to ethics, truth to error, philosophy to practice, natural law to human consciousness, and earth to immortality. Along the way he considered the ether, stars, earth, plants, animals, and human institutions. His *grand finale* offered an entirely new classification system for the sciences and all of human knowledge.

While I can no longer distinguish what Malcolm related about Powell from what I learned through subsequent reading, the impression left by Malcolm's account remains clear. Like the high plateau that bears his name, Powell altered the flow of everything around him. He towered over the surrounding territory, defined the terrain in all directions, and became the focal point for any who came within his purview.

Brandon asked questions about Powell's motivation, intrigued by his risk taking, determination, and perseverance, and fascinated by his enemies. Having never himself encountered a real enemy, he had no direct experience with the deep, all-consuming hatred that can drive men to do everything in their power to destroy the object of their enmity. Powell's enemies, and they were many, engaged in rumormongering, innuendo, maneuvering in the corridors of power, attacks on his integrity, allegations of personal aggrandizement, and even physical violence. Powell's life gave Brandon a glimpse into the interpersonal battles that can go on over ideological territory. War is not only waged between nation-states; warrioring is not just a call to fight for one's country or tribe. I think Brandon came to understand that Bly's lament for loss of the warrior spirit was about undertaking heroic struggles for personal ideals, not a call to kill another nation's innocents. The important warrior battles are fought day to day throughout life: within, against doubt, ennui, and apathy; without, against opposing ideals, interests, and antagonistic personalities. The moment of insight came when Brandon observed with both conviction and some distress, "I can imagine fighting to play my music the way I want to. I wouldn't want it to be a fight. But I can imagine it. And I'd do it."

For my part, I was most intrigued by Powell's first battle, the one long before Washington, D.C., the Colorado River, or Shiloh: his engagements with his stern, authoritarian father. His biographer, W. C. Darrah, describes a stormy, conflict-laden relationship. Joseph Powell, an itinerant Methodist preacher, named his first son John Wesley, expecting that he, too, would become a minister. Since his father refused to support his ambitions for a scientific education, John Wesley left home to pursue his career on his own. His father's letters were filled with angry attacks, chastising his son for being "undisciplined" and "irresponsible." Evidence for these charges included John Wesley's refusal to be satisfied with the limited curriculum at Illinois Institute, instead, creating his own science curriculum and studying independently.

He married the daughter of his mother's brother, his first cousin, despite the opposition of both sets of parents and the societal disapproval attendant upon such a scandalous act. When in 1865 he was discharged from the army with a "total and permanent disability," the couple returned home where his father advised him: "Wes, you are a maimed man. Settle down at teaching. It is a noble profession. Get this nonsense of science and adventure out of your mind."

This advice came four years before his first Grand Canyon expedition. Powell's life is a tribute to fatherly advice ignored, paternal hopes dashed, religious indoctrination overcome, and authoritarian control undermined.

Reports from men's workshops and support groups are filled with stories of sons who have painstakingly tried to win the approval of their fathers, only to find that approval, much less love, never came. I was reminded again of the anguished father-bashing that permeates so much of the men's movement, and acceptance of father-son conflict as natural and inevitable. I deny both. Nor do I find solace in accounts of late-in-life reconciliations: Bly's coming to understand his alcoholic father in the years just before his father's death or Powell's achievements ultimately recognized by his father; I even had a peaceful reunion with my father after years of battle, and Malcolm has reestablished contact with the father absent in his youth. But I take no comfort from such stories of eventual, modest reconnection. I want to avoid the need for reconciliation. I am sworn to battle against any societal scripting that accepts a thirty-year hiatus in father-son relationships as normal. Happy endings are all the more tragic when the middle years have been empty of connection.

But that night on Muav Saddle, these ideas were still just nascent feelings. When Malcolm had finished his rendering of Powell's accomplishments, I asked Brandon: "So how will you remember Powell? Warrior? Hero? Humanist? Renaissance man?"

Brandon scrunched up his face and shook his head in obvious rejection of my categories. "Powell was Powell," he replied.

"That's a tautology!" I reproached. "I can still remember getting back an essay on sociological theory with one word scrawled across it in red: TAUTOLOGICAL. I had committed the unforgivable sin in scholarly circles of failing to specify my independent and dependent variables in a way that they could be operationalized separately. It boiled down to my saying that what was requisite in society was essential. 'Powell was Powell' doesn't say any more."

Brandon grinned. "Are you saying Powell wasn't Powell?"

"It's redundant. Why would you say such a thing?"

"Because it's the truth," he asserted.

"But it's meaningless," I protested.

"Meaning is the stuff people make up," Brandon said, poking me in the ribs. "You taught me that. Powell was Powell. The canyon is the canyon. All else is made up."

"But—" I started, flabbergasted at Brandon's simplistic thinking. I looked to Malcolm. He shrugged and said, "Out of the mouth of babes."

"You're agreeing with him?!" I asked incredulously.

"It's hard to argue with the kid. The big hole is the big hole."

"Still—" I stammered, but Brandon stood up with his hands cupped over his mouth, shouting: "The canyon is the canyon."

He pulled Malcolm up. They stood over me and shouted it together, then grabbed me by my arms and pulled me up. Brandon stood face-to-face, his hands firmly on my shoulders, mouthing slowly as if teaching me to speak: "THE . . . CAN . . . YON . . . IS . . . THE . . . CAN . . . YON . . ."

"All right. All right," I said softly. "But let's keep it our little secret."

Brandon whirled around, his hands again cupped around his mouth. "Powell was Powell," he shouted turning north, east, south, and ending west, toward the glowing horizon. He then spun back toward us, waving his hands as if to direct an orchestra. Shaking my head, I finally yielded and joined his chorus, shouting: "THE CANYON IS THE CANYON."

Day Seven

33. Lost and Found

As we ascended Powell Plateau, we wondered why, since John Wesley Powell had his choice of all the Grand Canyon's magnificent monuments, he had selected this one place to bear his name. Eschewing any of the many distinctive formations since named as temples, castles, towers, buttes, and points, he chose a plateau shaped like a giant rooster's foot.

The answer may lie in comparing two maps. On the current topographical map of Grand Canyon National Park, Brandon counted 714 place names, Powell Plateau just one island in an ocean of canyon locations. Compare that to the first U.S. Geological Survey map of the Grand Canyon drawn by Lieutenant George M. Wheeler in 1873. At the center of Wheeler's map, in capital letters, Powell's Plateau stands out as the *only* prominent feature named *and* marks the beginning of the Grand Canyon. What is now the eastern canyon was then called Marble Canyon. And notice the possessive, absent from today's maps. Powell's Plateau thrusts south six miles from the North Rim forcing the Colorado River to make a twenty-mile detour before resuming its westward flow. Like the man who gave it his name, the plateau challenges the flow of the river.

We climbed the bald, rounded foundation of

Powell easily up the old CCC trail. Reaching the top, the trail ended and we entered a forest of large ponderosa pines. The flat terrain allowed us to walk three abreast. Pine cones crunched under our boots, warning wildlife of our approach. We stayed within sight of the eastern rim, traversing around thickets of gambel oak and thorny New Mexico locust that blocked a direct route. We marked our progress by identifying topographic points along Rainbow Plateau across Muav Canyon. Spotting a clearing on the rim that held the promise of a good view, we paused for a break. As we took off our packs, Malcolm noticed that Brandon's sleeping bag was missing.

Brandon looked dumbfounded at the place below his backpack where the bag should have been tied, sure he'd had it when we left the cabin. Since we hadn't been following a path, backtracking would be tricky. We spread out about fifteen yards apart and retraced our route all the way to the path down. I had led the way up with Brandon behind me. Malcolm, following Brandon, would surely have noticed if the bright-green bag had fallen down the sparsely vegetated hill.

We sat down to assess the situation. At 7,500 feet, the clear sky forecast a cold night, so the loss was far from trivial. But we each had one long-sleeved flannel shirt and rain gear. He'd have to make do wrapped up in all that. We left the trailhead and again spread out, this time even farther apart, as we made our way back out on Powell along our earlier route.

One might wonder why this incident merits reporting. Brandon lost the bag. We searched for it. We didn't find it. He expressed regret. We reassured him it could happen to anyone and continued on, having determined we had enough other things to get him through the cold night. That's all an observer would have seen, hardly noteworthy.

But in my head, my father was raving, his voice screaming out old, oft-played tapes. "How could you be so stupid? You'd lose your head if it wasn't attached. Brand new. $200. Gone, just like that. Easy come, easy go. And do you give a shit? No, because if you did, you wouldn't have lost it in the first place. And don't tell me you're sorry. 'Sorry' won't bring it back. I'm the one who's sorry. Sorry I ever had kids."

I listened with familiarity, as one who has been over the same path many times. His voice gave way to his father's voice, my grandfather screaming at my father. And then there were other voices, a long line of fathers berating their sons, all screaming to be heard, dependent for their survival on making me berate Brandon. Could I do it? Could I end the tradition of intergenerational disapprobation in my family line? Could I remain silent?

The voices became more subtle. No need to yell or even reprimand. I imagined little digs that would put him in his childish place like *Hey, Malcolm, from now on I think we'd better rope Brandon's backpack on so he doesn't lose that too.*

We arrived back at our break site on the rim collectively mystified at where the bag could possibly have fallen. Brandon remained silent, his shoulders and head drooping. I also stayed quiet, afraid of what might slip out as my father offered one cut after another that would shame Brandon. While they rested, I paced, finally urging them to their feet under the guise of getting to Dutton Point in time to photograph the afternoon colors. Only in motion could I distract myself from my father's exhortations. I was stunned by their vehemence and convinced that no amount of detox would silence him. Each of the next three nights, as we prepared Brandon's makeshift bedding, my father would surely be hovering, urging me to pass on a heritage of condemnation. I knew I would carry my father's voice with me always, but I vowed not to transmit it.

The sun shone directly overhead by the time we reached Dutton Canyon. We fought through thick, thorny brush down one side of the drainage and up the other. Tired from bushwhacking, we stopped for lunch on a rise near where the solitary remains of a charred pine stood. We had passed many such reminders of the 1989 lightning strike that became a wildfire. Below Swamp Point the whole hill had burned off, but on Powell the fire appeared to have jumped from place to place. This particular tree had burned three-fourths through, leaving what looked like the stretched hide of a deer suspended on one thin, charred leg. We were admiring this fire-carved sculpture when Brandon shouted, "Look!" A few feet beyond the tree he had spied a pair of antlers, freshly shed.

"If you didn't already have the bighorn, the deer could be your totem. Maybe they were meant for me," I joked.

"They're Brandon's all right," Malcolm replied seriously. "A person can have more than one totem."

"How many can you have?" Brandon asked.

"As many as you're given. Sometimes there's one primary totem—a major power ally—and several minor ones. In one American Indian spiritual system a person would acquire seven totem animals, one for each direction."

"How'd they get seven?" Brandon asked.

"The usual four plus Above, Below, and Within."

"That would seem to cover all the bases," he nodded, impressed. "How many do you have?"

"Just two—so far."

"What besides the raven?"

"The walrus."

"Did that become your totem before or after you started looking like one?" I asked.

Malcolm smiled. "I'd say at the same time."

Brandon secured the antlers as high up as he could in a tree. During lunch we kept glancing up at the strange sight of the antlers extending out on either side of the pine trunk like a stag ghost, invisible, except for his deciduous adornment.

"There's something strangely familiar about them," I mused, "an image of some kind. It'll come to me."

After lunch, as Malcolm and I were settling in for our afternoon siesta, Brandon said, "I'm going to see if I can find an open place to photograph Holy Grail Temple. I'll be back in—"

"I remember now!" I exclaimed sitting up. "In one of Joseph Campbell's books there's a picture of an ancient Roman monument that portrayed a muscular Apollonian figure with antlers holding a cornucopia in his lap. Combined in that one image Campbell saw human consciousness joined with animal wildness in harmony with the Grail."

"The Grail in Rome?"

"The cornucopia. The antlers, shed and regrown, symbolized for Campbell the mythos of natural cycles that undergird initiations."

"So then, Dad, you're now buying into the idea that the antlers could be, like, an initiation talisman?"

"He's still just reviewing the literature for you," Malcolm needled.

"I'm analyzing symbols, Dr. Gray, as is my sociological duty. Human beings are meaning-making animals. Much of the content of culture is expressed in symbols. They're shorthand ways of reminding us of things we value. I like what the antlers symbolize in reminding us of the cycles of nature. It's a long way from that scientific observation to attaching special talismanlike powers to a symbol. That's superstition. It's often born in serendipity. Consider our experience as a microcosm. You lose your sleeping bag and are kind of bummed out. Bad luck. Then you find something beautiful and meaningful. Ah-ha, change of luck. We hike on and have a great day. It would be easy to associate the good day and change of luck with finding the antlers. It's not far from there to attributing special luck-changing powers to the antlers. *Wham-bam-alacazam,* a talisman is created.

If you share your experience with others in your tribe, and they happen to have some good fortune in association with the antlers, you'd soon have a culture-shared superstition. Attach a story to it about why the deer has this power, say, the deer as a messenger from the gods, his antlers pointing in all directions to remind us of the omnipresence of the gods, and, *wham-bam,* you've got a myth."

"What do you think, Malcolm?" Brandon asked.

Malcolm laughed. "I think your old man needs some rock-lizard time to—how do you say it?—chill out."

"No, seriously. Do you really believe in talismans? And totems?"

"As I told you, I believe it's useful to have ways of reminding ourselves of our connection to nature and the cosmos. I believe that in times of trouble or when faced with a major decision, you could do worse than look inside yourself and think about the bighornlike qualities you have that you can draw on. Your dad's right that a lot of people get taken in by superstitions, like actually trying to live by reading tea leaves or astrology. But you can also rely too much on rationality. We have feelings and inner processes and spirit in human experience. And we have connections to larger traditions. Symbols, talismans, and totems are ways of being in touch with those things. You can make too much of them, to be sure. You can also make too little of them. You've got to find some balance."

"I would just add," I said, "that finding balance doesn't happen just once and then you've got it. Every time you have unusual good fortune, or experience some tragedy, serendipity will tempt you to make associations, not just as a way of honoring a memory, but to attribute causality. Athletes do it constantly, as do entertainers and politicians and everyday folks. A baseball player hits a grand-slam home run while wearing a new cap and wants to wear that cap forever, or wear a new cap every time the bases are loaded. Despite the scientific trappings of our culture, superstitions abound. I have some myself."

"Like what?"

"I believe that losing a sleeping bag calls forth the ghost of my father. I've felt his presence ever since you lost your bag. I've even heard him speaking to me."

"*Yebeday, ritzi bu.* That's a lot weirder than antlers, Dad. Why would you say that?"

"I suppose I could be talked into the hypothesis that my socialization includes strong associations with my father and the consequences of losing things. A behavioral psychologist might even expand that into a reward-punishment hypothesis. But if a person is predisposed to believe in ghosts . . . tell you what, I'll join Malcolm in a little rock-lizard time and see what my dreams reveal. Maybe James Randi will visit me and conjure up a rational explanation for the disappearance of your sleeping bag. Or maybe my father's ghost stole it to mess with my mind. I'll let you know what I find out."

34. Dutton Point

Nothing we had seen prepared me for Dutton Point. We followed the contour of the rim as far as it would take us east and south. There, we stepped out on a small, flat platform that was perfectly positioned to provide the best possible view in all directions. The point commands a 270° view of an arc from Fire Point north of Muav Saddle to the long line of the South Rim twelve miles west along Enfilade ridge. Dutton overlooks seven large topographical Amphitheaters—Hindu, Hotauta, Monadnock, Evolution, Aztec, Tapeats, and Shinumo—each its own complex geological system of side-canyon drainages displaying a unique array of formations and monuments, like stars clustered in constellations forming galaxies within the canyon universe. Through the center of this universe, connecting the constellations like a necklace of irregularly shaped precious stones, runs the Colorado River. We could see more of the river than we had ever seen at one time. We could distinguish rapids, turns, narrowings, and widenings. We could see fifteen miles east past the peaks of Confucius and Mencius Temples toward Horus Temple and the Towers of Ra and Set.

I soon found that the work of connecting

291

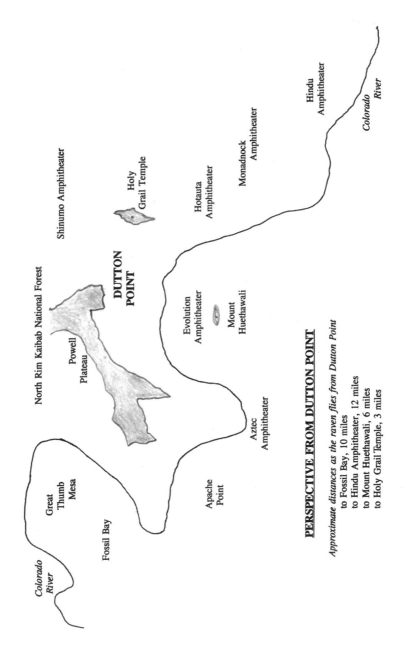

North Rim Kaibab National Forest

Shinumo Amphitheater

Holy
Grail Temple

Hindu
Amphitheater

Colorado
River

Monadnock
Amphitheater

Hotauta
Amphitheater

**DUTTON
POINT**

Powell
Plateau

Evolution
Amphitheater

Mount
Huethawali

Aztec
Amphitheater

Apache
Point

Great
Thumb
Mesa

Fossil Bay

Colorado
River

PERSPECTIVE FROM DUTTON POINT

Approximate distances as the raven flies from Dutton Point
        to Fossil Bay, 10 miles
        to Hindu Amphitheater, 12 miles
        to Mount Huethawali, 6 miles
        to Holy Grail Temple, 3 miles

distant points with names on the map distracted from contemplation. The horizon offered so many pinnacles, buttes, and monuments that I just wanted to take it all in as one complete landscape. Holy Grail Temple rose distinctly and dominantly at the center of Shinumo Amphitheater, the sloping terraces of its lower foundation draping outward like the delicately drawn lines of a pagoda in a Japanese woodcut, sculpted to accent the whole rather than call attention to itself.

I saw Mount Huethawali at once, but wanted to let Brandon discover it for himself. He sat with the map, working his way through the formations, calling out each one he identified. Dox Castle. Sagittarius Ridge. Fossil Mountain. Tyndall Dome. King Crest. Then: "There's Mount Huethawali! Does it look the same from this side of the river?"

"It's been a lot of years," I replied.

"And there's Apache Point!"

While Malcolm retraced for Brandon the route of our first canyon trek, I studied Mount Huethawali, observing how it rises from the brown Supai plateau like an onion-shaped mosque, the rounded white Coconino dome supported on a gradually sloping foundation of red Hermit Shale tipped by a column of gray Toroweap. The only formation on the flat, mile-in-diameter Darwin Plateau, it captivates as only stand-alone mountains can, not part of a range, not subject to contrast and comparison with nearby mounts, but dominantly solitary, like Mount Fuji. Below Huethawali projected Huxley and Spencer Terraces, the canyon's nod to science in the midst of mythology. Each a quarter-mile wide, they reached out four times that far toward the river like the outstretched legs of the Great Sphinx. Between these long terraces, the Supai walls fall away steeply, making it appear from Dutton Point that Mount Huethawali begins its rise, not just from the Supai, but from the Tonto Platform, a half-mile below its crown. The protrusion of Powell Plateau at Dutton Point reaches out to the great cradled opening of Copper Canyon below Mount Huethawali. I could see how they had once been connected.

"It's hard to take it all in," Brandon remarked. "Looking across at the river provides a kind of contrast that, you know, makes each more distinct in its own way. It's neat to look back and forth, near and far, across and down. The contrasts highlight what's unique about each area." He framed his hands together like a movie director framing a scene. "This view would make one hell of a background for a rock video."

Listening to Brandon compare perspectives gave me the idea that

Dutton Point could be the perfect place to celebrate his coming of age with a symbolic canyon gift. I had intended to wait until our final night back at Swamp Point to look through the things I had accumulated and decide which might most powerfully re-evoke some significant canyon place or moment. I had collected an item for each day: a charred sliver of wood from Swamp Point where we had gathered under a threatening sky to open the initiation; a small, flat slice of Redwall from our first day's descent; a vial of water from the hole beneath the alcove where we encountered the bighorn; a few pellets of rat shit from the cavelike formation we escaped to for rock-lizard relief on our thirsty return from the river; the cactus spine that Brandon fell on in Merlin Abyss; sand from the beach where we spent three nights at the confluence of Shinumo and White and where I paced in the night deliberating issues of Great Unconformity; a portion of root Brandon stepped on and broke climbing the Redwall, his boot right at my eye level on the steep ascent; a flattened remnant of tin can from the cabin on Muav Saddle that had rusted roughly into the shape of a clef; and a perfectly formed pinecone from Powell.

Each offered rich metaphoric potential as a coming-of-age gift. Metaphysically, I found myself most drawn to the rat shit, the pellets hard as precious stones. Rat shit: a secular humanist grounding in the real world. And a connection to Malcolm, reminding him not to become anal retentive. I could tell him about a Koanic exchange that I had kept on my wall to help me endure graduate school.

A monk asked Master Ummon, "What is the pure body of truth?"
  Master Ummon said, "A flower in bloom."
  Monk: " 'A flower in bloom'—what's it mean?"
  Master: "Maggot in the shit hole, pus of leprosy, scab over a boil."

I imagined the deeply intellectual conversations he could have with his friends. "Hey, Brandon, I got a car for my eighteenth birthday. What'd you get?"

But in the last day I had begun leaning toward giving him the whole collection: a Coming-of-Age Canyon Collage. Had a certain ring to it.

Then I experienced Dutton Point and decided that time, place, and object had come together.

Beyond the point where our senses could take in more of the view, like the feeling of saturated heaviness after a rich holiday feast, we retreated from the narrow precipice and found a clearing not far from the rim where we could camp. The area near the edge looked more like desert Tonto than the ponderosa forest we had hiked through all day. Malcolm explained that strong updrafts of warm air from below turn many rim points into arid zones. Thus, we found ourselves surrounded by old acquaintances from below: blackbrush, pinyon pine, a gnarled juniper, and an occasional cactus. Brandon was particularly taken with a large and impressive agave century plant near the edge. Its dry, once-flowering stalk rose more than ten feet high from a circular array of broad, thick, spiny-edged, and daggerlike leaves— the desert's version of a lotus. Malcolm described the plant's famed medicinal qualities: as a tea its leaves are used for treating indigestion and constipation; the sap serves as a salve for cuts and burns; and the root, fresh or dried, can be used as a soap or for relief from arthritis.

Brandon wanted to know about other medicinal plants in the canyon. Malcolm described Gambel's oak as *the* basic astringent among plants and first on the list of wilderness remedies for insect bites, stings, abrasions, diarrhea, and even toothaches. Boiled mountain mahogany twigs can be drunk as a laxative or to reduce an inflamed prostate gland. Manzanita has disinfecting qualities useful in treating urinary-tract infections, kidney inflammations, and menstrual discomfort. But, noting that we were about to reenter civilization, Malcolm called special attention to Mormon tea. In addition to relieving allergies, it is reputed to be an antidote to venereal disease and, as such, was served frequently in Nevada's houses of prostitution where it was supposedly introduced by one Jack Mormon during the gold rush.

After a dinner of freeze-dried pasta asparagus, we went back to our perch at Dutton Point. We sat quietly looking in different directions, Brandon gazing east at Holy Grail Temple, Malcolm looking west toward Apache Point, while I returned to Mount Huethawali. We could hear gusts of wind approaching from the distance well before they hit us, then follow the sound, like a retreating train, as the wind swept across the plateau. The intermittent light from the South Rim airport became visible, then more lights appeared across the river marking Grand Canyon Village. Before the lingering twilight had been fully embraced by night, Malcolm read an excerpt he had brought along from the 1882 report by Clarence Edward Dutton on the "Grand Cañon of the Colorado." He read slowly and softly, so that we had to lean toward him to hear above the wind.

It is never the same, even from day to day, or even from hour to hour. In the early morning its mood and subjective influences are unusually calmer and more full of repose than at other times, but as the sun rises higher the whole scene is so changed that we cannot recall our first impressions. Every passing cloud, every change in the position of the sun, recasts the whole. At sunset the pageant closes amid splendors that seem more than earthly. The direction of the full sunlight, the massing of the shadows, the manner in which the side lights are thrown from the clouds determine these modulations, and the sensitiveness of the picture to the slightest variations in these conditions is very wonderful.

Brandon spotted a hawk circling high overhead, distinctly visible against the glow of twilight. "He's riding the thermals," Malcolm explained, "but he's up kind of late."

"Let's give him a bedtime story," I suggested, making a not-very-subtle segue to "Iron John." I then read about the three-day festival the King sponsored in hopes of attracting the mysterious knight who had saved the kingdom. The boy, now a young man, sought Iron John's help so that he could catch the golden apple to be thrown amidst the competing knights each day by the King's daughter. The first day Iron John outfitted him in red armor on a reddish-brown horse. He caught the golden apple and galloped away. The second day Iron John gave him a white horse and white armor. Again he caught the golden apple and rode off. The third day the King laid a trap. When, in black armor on a black horse, he caught the golden apple, he was pursued by the King's men and wounded in the leg. Though he escaped, his helmet fell off, exposing his golden hair.

I looked up from reading to find Brandon grinning slyly.

"Red is passion. White is purity. Black is death."

"So you've got it all figured out?"

"What I figured out was that you'd ask me about the different colors of armor since they're obviously symbolic. I figure red usually means blood or fire or passion or anger, like seeing red. White's associated with pure ideals, you know, weddings, clouds, and angels. Black suggests mourning and death or sadness, maybe fear, sometimes evil."

"Impressive. You know your culture's colors," I congratulated.

"I told you I was culturally literate. So what's Bly say they mean?"

"He thinks young men should be allowed to show more red—anger and passion—that it's natural and healthy. He does a lot with the colors as stages of development and the implications of different sequences over one's lifetime. He suggests that male and female sequences may be different."

Malcolm tossed a pebble over the edge. "You could relate the colors to the canyon."

"You mean like the Redwall?" Brandon asked.

"Sure."

"So white would be Coconino and black would be the Vishnu."

"Right. Layers instead of stages."

"Layers? You go down through the Coconino first, so you start out in purity, then you encounter the challenge of the Redwall—it's dangerous and there are only a few ways through—and at the bottom you connect with the black Vishnu. Yeah, going down through layers feels better to me than putting on armor."

"Then the ascent."

"Right. So after some time at the river, you come back up through the Redwall and end on top of the white Coconino looking over the whole scene."

"Not bad," I said. "The boy did end up in white at the wedding, but on the third and final day of the festival, the day he wore black, he was wounded."

Brandon's eyes narrowed and he pointed his finger at me. "Didn't you say the King suffered a leg wound?"

"The King? No, the boy—"

"No, no," he interrupted, "I mean before, when you told about Perceval's Grail quest, he was supposed to ask some king how he got wounded or something and he didn't, so the king couldn't be healed."

"Right. The Fisher King. You remember well. Can you shed any light on the leg wound as archetype, Dr. Gray?"

"I'm not that expert on Jung, but in my experience the major work of individual therapy is healing childhood wounds."

"Bly agrees. He asserts that no one gets to adulthood without a wound that goes to the core."

"He's studied everyone in the world, has he?" Brandon scoffed.

"I take it as the observation of a poet, not a psychologist."

Malcolm nodded. "I suspect it's a generalization meant to comfort the many who do feel wounded to the core. Words like 'wounded' and 'core' describe metaphorically processes we understand only vaguely."

"Bly suggests that being wounded makes the warrior more compassionate," I added.

"Good in theory," Malcolm responded, "but those who are wounded tend to pass on their wounds."

"It's hard not to do," I affirmed, recalling again my father's raging voice. "But it's not inevitable, not absolutely scripted."

"Sure. But victims often become abusers, whether the abuse was physical or emotional. The people I see in therapy have buried their childhood wounds and repressed the pain. The wounds fester and, without their knowledge, sap their strength. Tribal initiations at least leave their wounds visible and attach value to them. Most tribes scar some part of the face or body to make the initiation wound a badge of pride."

"Well, we won't scar your face," I said, running my index finger along Brandon's cheek, "but you have had a leg wound."

"What wound?" Brandon asked.

I handed him a small velvet bag, dark green, with a black drawstring. "This is an Australian bag for safeguarding gold nuggets. Inside is . . ."

He peered into the bag and his face took on a puzzled look.

"You don't recognize it?" I asked.

"Should I?"

"That's the thorn that stuck in your thigh when you fell in Merlin Abyss."

Brandon examined the long thorn carefully. He pricked himself on the back of his hand, then his arm and his leg. He lifted his shirt and stuck his belly. He cleaned his front teeth with the point. He held it up in the breeze and pointed it like a weather vane. He used it to trace the life line on his hand. When he reached the edge of his palm, he pushed hard enough to draw blood, then looked up, grinning: "Does this thorn have any medicinal properties?"

"It wards off pointlessness," I laughed.

I took it and placed it in the center of his open right palm. "I've been thinking about what I have to pass on to you. Not impose, just offer." I made a sweeping gesture from horizon to horizon.

"It's all a matter of . . . ," he grinned and nodded.

"Precisely," I affirmed, squeezing his shoulder.

Malcolm took the cactus point and held it up in the fading light. "Just so I don't miss the point, it's all a matter of what?"

"Should I explain?" Brandon asked.

"I don't know. An initiate instructing an elder. Is that ever allowed, Malcolm? I wouldn't want to incur the anger of the gods."

"Don't think of it as instruction," he said to Brandon. "Think of it as a kind deed done for an old man."

"All right. In a class once we had to report on the thing a parent says most often," Brandon explained. He stood up on the narrow precipice and intoned deeply toward Darwin Plateau: " 'It's all a matter of perspective. You've got to have perspective.' "

"I'll never say it again," I promised.

"What'd you say yesterday, Malcolm? Something about fathers and lies?"

I took the thorn from Malcolm. "Well, this isn't a lie. Perspective isn't out there. You carry it within you. It's not what you see, it's how you look at what you see. The question is what will inform your perspective. Science? Religion? Mysticism? Reason? Emotion? End of sociological sermon."

"At least for tonight," Malcolm chided.

I took the bag from Brandon's knee, put the thorn back in, and held the bag out for him to take. Malcolm's hand flashed out and intercepted it. He held it close to his chest, slipped something into it and handed it back. Brandon gently moved the bag up and down, testing its weight and feel, now obviously heavier with whatever had been added. Then he felt the object through the bag without opening it. His eyes grew wide in recognition.

Brandon took out an arrowhead, holding it up for me to see. The mostly gray stone was roughly carved, jagged on one edge, straight on the other, revealing small ridges on its slightly rounded sides where chips had been knocked away. A couple of centimeters longer than the thorn, it came to a point no less sharp. "From the canyon?" I asked.

"Just over there near the rim. Probably Anasazi, the people who summered on Powell Plateau six or seven hundred years ago."

Brandon positioned the thorn and arrow point to point. "A point from nature and one from humans," he observed.

"And, if you choose," Malcolm said, "you can add the points from the deer rack. They're formed so as never to point all in the same direction at once."

"I don't think they'll fit in this little bag," Brandon laughed.

"I was speaking metaphorically," Malcolm added. "I'm afraid you can't keep the arrowhead in your little bag either. I'll show you where I found it and you can put it back."

"Did you know Dad was going to give me the cactus point?"

"No."

"So it's just coincidence that you both thought of giving me pointed things?"

"Not everything is coincidence, Brandon. In fact, not everything can be explained, period. Or needs to be explained. Some things just need to be accepted. This is not only a place of perspective. It's a place of power. A raven I was watching drew my attention to the arrowhead. It's a gift from the canyon. Accept it as that."

"Beware the allure of serendipity," I countered.

"*Bue düden,*" Brandon concluded. "It's all a matter of . . ."

We sat silently for a long time watching the sky turn orange and red, then gray. A cold wind rose as the sun set and darkness descended into the inner canyon. Dutton Point hovered above that inner darkness, but was never enveloped by it. The translucent glow on the western horizon faded, but never vanished. We seemed an island suspended above the abyss, a magnet point for light anywhere along either rim. Cold and weariness eventually drove us from the point, but had it only been a matter of having enough light to see, we could have stayed there all night.

Day Eight

35. Solstice

At first light I dressed and tried to rouse Brandon to watch the sunrise with me from Dutton Point. He hadn't slept well in his makeshift coverings and was cold, so I put my sleeping bag over him and went to the point alone.

I awaited the dawning of the first summer solstice I'd ever been awake for, the moment when the sun would rise above the eastern rim. The flat, gray light turned pink, then pale blue. An orange glow appeared to the northeast indicating where the sun would rise above Crescent Ridge. I fixed my gaze on that spot, saw the top of the bright orb appear, and traced the lines of the first rays. The piercing light fired between Holy Grail Temple and King Arthur Castle, crossed the Colorado, and struck Mount Huethawali. I turned slowly, full circle, letting the sun warm all of me. I saw my shadow on the cliff wall behind the point. I stretched my arms and extended up on my toes to cast a long, straight shadow pointing heavenward, holding this position rigidly until my arms and toes ached. Then I jumped and danced in perfect synchronicity with the shadow three times my size. As the sun rose higher, my shadow moved down the wall, as if descending into the canyon. Then it diffused and disappeared, leaving me again alone.

303

Brandon was stirring as I returned to our campsite. "Did I miss anything?" he asked.

"Just the usual epic struggle between day and night. Day prevailed, but night vowed to return. In celebration of day's victory I danced with my shadow until it descended into the canyon. Other than that you didn't miss anything."

"Danced? What, trying a bit of Bly's dancing warrior?"

"Not at all. Scientists dance too."

"Is there such a thing as solstice fever, Malcolm?"

"Danced with your shadow, huh? Very interesting."

"Don't give me any Jungian bullshit this early in the morning. The shadow I danced with was a real, visible, fully explainable, and empirically verifiable shadow, not a psychological metaphor."

"He has a double dose, Brandon: Solstice fever and shadow mania. We'd better keep a close eye on him today."

Over a breakfast of oatmeal and crackers, we interweaved Malcolm's stories of solstice ceremonies in ancient cultures with discussion of the physics of the sun's annual revolution. We then went out to Dutton Point for a farewell. We lingered a long time, watching the colors change, picking out points we had missed in the afternoon shadows that were now visible in the morning light, calculating the length of shadows in relation to the objects casting them, and trying again to find words for the beauty.

Malcolm showed Brandon where to return the arrowhead. Seeing the spot made it clear that the arrowhead, mostly buried, would be visible only to a trained and attentive eye, raven or no raven. Malcolm scattered some corn pollen and ground maize, then Brandon's "*Ritzi bu*" served as our benediction.

Our first destination proved elusive. We retraced the previous afternoon's route to retrieve the antlers Malcolm had lodged in a tree. Not only could we not find the antlers or the tree, we couldn't find the mound or clearing that had been so distinct the day before. We searched together at first, but soon disagreed about whether the spot was behind us or farther on. Malcolm remembered it near the rim; I thought we'd find it between shallow valleys somewhat away from the edge. Brandon admitted uncertainty. Using a large burned stump on a small hill near the rim as our meeting place, we set out in three directions. A half hour later we managed to reconvene more confused than ever about where the antlers could be.

"Wasn't meant to be," Malcolm concluded.

"What's that supposed to mean?" I gibed. "Might as well say it's like the Grail Castle."

"Your fever has you confused, Dad. We're looking for lost deer antlers. We know where Holy Grail Temple is."

"When Perceval was searching for the Grail Castle, he found it thirty miles from nowhere. When he awoke in the morning and found no one around, he left the castle and it disappeared."

"You're saying the antlers have disappeared?"

"I'll give you a choice of three explanations: One, it wasn't meant to be, a fatalistic perspective; two, Merlin's solstice magic, a mystical perspective; or third, we're three inattentive hikers who can't retrace their steps from one day to the next, an evaluator's perspective."

Malcolm, meanwhile, had taken out and was studying the map. "The spot may not have disappeared, but it's certainly not where it should be. Damn strange. Fascinating, actually."

We backtracked almost to Dutton Point. Nothing. We hiked back three abreast, just in sight of each other, search style, as we had done looking for the sleeping bag. When we arrived at Dutton Valley, we knew we'd missed it again.

"I guess the antlers will just have to stay up in the tree," Brandon concluded.

"Yeah," I agreed. "Imagine the mystical possibilities that await the next hikers who happen on that spot."

We had barely started hiking again when, bushwhacking through Dutton Valley, we startled three deer. As they crashed up the slope ahead of us, I yelled: "There go the lost antlers."

"Where?" Brandon yelled back, looking all around, as if he hadn't seen or heard the now vanished bucks.

A few minutes later Brandon claimed to spot a fox at the top of the ridge that neither Malcolm or I saw. Twice Malcolm pointed into the air at a raven he said was leading us to the far rim. Brandon and I never saw it. And so it went all afternoon as we played with each other's realities.

Sometime later I looked back and Malcolm wasn't there. I called ahead to Brandon and told him to wait. When Malcolm didn't show, we backtracked, carefully and anxiously, aware of our dismal record of retracing our steps. We found him in a clearing walking slowly around the outside of basketball-size gray and white stones, tracing a barely detectable rectangular border. "This is an Anasazi ruin," he explained as he removed his boots and socks and entered within. He walked slowly back and forth as if looking for something. When he squatted down and began feeling under one of the rocks, Brandon removed his boots and socks and joined him. By the time I joined them, also barefooted, Malcolm held a shard of pottery and was telling Brandon about the Anasazi.

"I've heard the name translated two ways," he explained. "It's a Navajo word meaning either 'Ancient Ones' or 'Ancient Enemies,' depending on who's doing the translating."

"Why can't they decide which it is?" Brandon asked.

"The meaning depends on context, so, stripped of original context, the meaning becomes ambiguous. Kind of like the word 'ancestor.' It can mean your actual blood forebears or just any people who came before you. If the Navajo who first discovered the ruins thought their forebears had lived here, the word would have meant 'Ancient Ones.' If they considered them non-Navajo, they might have meant 'enemies.' Either way, they acknowledged the remains of an ancient people."

"How ancient?" Brandon asked.

"Human artifacts in the canyon date back around five thousand years. The Anasazi habitation seems to have lasted from about two thousand to around seven hundred years ago as they evolved from basket makers to pottery makers. The Pueblo people emerged after that and thrived for about four hundred years, then abandoned the Grand Canyon."

"Why?"

"That's a matter of debate. Climate change. Drought. Overpopulation. Invasion. Disease. Probably a combination."

"Why would they have built here on Powell where there's no water?" Brandon asked.

"There could have been a spring back then. The canyon's always changing. More likely, this plateau provided safety. It's inaccessible except where we came up. They could have carried water from the seeping spring under the Coconino." He went to the thickest grouping of stones and inspected them.

"What are you looking for?" Brandon asked.

"Nothing. More like imagining."

"What?"

"That this might have been a *kiva*—a kind of ceremonial structure. Where these stones have collapsed was probably the rear wall. There's an entryway there, facing south. This looks like the fire pit. About halfway between that back wall and the fire pit I was imagining there might have been a *sipapu*."

"A what-who?"

"A *sipapu*—a hole representing where the ancestors emerged into this world from the one below, a conduit between the spirit world and this world."

Brandon looked pensive. "When you call the canyon the big hole, are you ever thinking of it as, like, a *sipapu*?"

Malcolm smiled, then squatted, looking meditative. After some moments of silence, he said softly: "This would be a powerful place to lament."

"Lament what?" Brandon asked.

"Black Elk said that any man can 'cry for a vision.' I've heard the Lakota phrase translated as 'lament.' Black Elk said that Crazy Horse received his power through lamenting. As I understand it, it's a combination of vision quest, meditation, supplication to the Great Spirit, and detox."

"The word 'lament' makes it sound sad," Brandon said.

"As I remember it from Black Elk, a man laments as a plea for mercy. He makes himself humble, like a child, and cries out to the Great Grandfather. My sense is it's more about connecting than grieving."

"Is it like praying? I mean, does he ask for something specific or just any vision?" We sat down, making a circle.

"I would guess that sometimes lamenting had a specific purpose, like getting ready for a hunt or a battle, or to seek direction in solving a problem. It could also be to just express thanks. Black Elk's lamenting brought him into oneness with the Earth and the universe. A boy laments to become a man. He undertakes a vision quest as a rite of passage."

"How long would one last?" Brandon asked.

"I'm not sure. Probably a few nights. Sometimes just one."

"What does a young man do during a rite-of-passage kind of lamenting?" I asked.

"The medicine man or holy man determines the appropriate ritual. It could be as simple as staying awake all night and watching, just listening and observing everything that happened."

"What could happen?" Brandon asked.

"His totem animal might visit or, if he didn't already have one, it might be revealed to him. Or he could have a vision about almost anything. Something important could happen that he wouldn't recognize, so my sense is that his primary task would be to stay alert, take in and remember everything that occurred, real or imagined, and then report what he experienced in great detail to the holy man and elders for interpretation."

"What if nothing happened?" Brandon asked.

"It wouldn't be like a test. I mean, it's not up to the boy or man what happens. What happens, happens. There's no shame in not getting a vision. It's enough to undertake the quest. And it's not a one-shot thing. Black Elk was only nine when he had his famous vision, but he did lamentings throughout his life."

Malcolm rooted around in the dirt and uncovered another pottery shard. "Probably several hundred years old," he estimated, handing it to Brandon. He went to his pack, got his small pouch of maize from Supai, and sprinkled some at the center of the ruin.

Brandon handed me the piece of pottery. Studying the roughly triangular, thumbnail-sized shard, a white glaze with black markings, I asked Brandon, "You interested in trying a lamentation here tonight? See what it's like?"

Brandon scowled. "I'll pass."

"A final night alone. Just stay awake and see what happens."

"Why?"

"Just to do it. To have the experience."

"Have you ever done a lamenting?" Brandon challenged.

"I've done a solo."

"Because someone told you to?"

"Yeah," I laughed. "Malcolm told me to."

"In the canyon?"

"No, in the Gila Wilderness as part of the program Malcolm ran. We each did a one-night solo."

Brandon turned to Malcolm. "Have you done a lamenting?"

"Not exactly."

"Or a vision quest?"

"Not formally."

"But you've done a solo?"

"Many times."

"Where you stayed awake all night?"

"No."

"Just no food or water?"

"Just no food."

He turned back to me, his manner calm and determined. "I'd like to do a solo sometime, but not tonight. I'll do it if you really want me to, but it would be for you, not me. As for lamenting, I don't like the idea of dabbling in sacred Indian ways. I'm not Indian. Seeking a vision sounds religious. I'm not religious. It would be like going to a Catholic church and taking communion without knowing what it really meant or believing it. It doesn't feel right."

"Where does he get these sacrilegious views?" I wondered aloud.

Malcolm ignored me. "Supposedly Black Elk shared his vision so that it would be available to all peoples, not just Indian people. Catholics might object to your taking communion, but not sitting in a cathedral meditating. It would be sacrilegious to smoke the sacred pipe without the instruction of a holy man, but, in my mind, the wilderness is our real cathedral. It would not be disrespectful to meditate here. However, the Lakota never required anyone to lament. When he felt ready, a boy went to the holy man and asked for instruction in undertaking a vision quest."

Malcolm looked directly at Brandon and spoke slowly and authoritatively. "The Bighorn has offered himself to you as a totem. You have received a talisman gift and a medicine pouch, if you choose to view them that way. It appears your path leads to college. Your direction over the next few years has some prescriptive qualities to it. This may not be your time for a vision quest. But, if your cactus needle ever points you in the direction of a wilderness solo, or even a vision quest, come find me. I'm not a holy man, but I can take you to one. I'll help prepare the site. I'll sit with you afterward if he offers you his interpretation. I might even offer you mine. And I'll listen to yours." He smiled. "It won't be a test or initiation. It will be a man's lamenting."

Malcolm turned back to me. "Brandon knows the lament is available to him if ever he feels the need. There's nothing more to be done here. Let's get to the rim for sunset."

"Just a minute," I said. "I appreciate what you've offered to Brandon and the spirit in which you've offered it. I mean that. One of my hopes for this trip was that the two of you would connect and that Brandon would experience your perspective on the canyon—and the world—and see you as a resource to him in the future. So I intend no disrespect when I add my own offer to yours." I turned to Brandon. "At any time, if you're wanting to explore more deeply alternative perspectives on the world, I would sponsor you for a pilgrimage to the Center for Inquiry in Amherst, New York, or the

Western Center in Los Angeles, where you could interact with scientists on the cutting edge of investigating mystical claims. Just as scientists dance, they also meditate and reflect."

"This has gotten a little heavy," Brandon said. "I'm not sure what to say. I mean, my thanks to both of you. Really. I won't forget. And, umm, as long as we're on the subject, like, there is a pilgrimage I wouldn't mind doing, I mean, as long as, you know, you're offering. Either of you have any connections to Paul Simon?"

36. Ironic John

It began innocently. Huge ponderosa pines had dropped their carpet of large pinecones all around our campsite. Brandon was using a stick to clear a place for the stove. He began throwing the pinecones up and hitting them as if they were baseballs. I made a disparaging comment when he missed one, so he challenged me to do better. Soon we were playing home run derby, taking turns hitting, pitching, and fielding. As the competitive juices flowed, animated disputes arose over foul lines, strikes and balls, illegal bats, spit cones, and what constituted a home run. Brandon supplied the broadcast commentary:

"Old man Patton pitches a feeble knuckler to the elder Gray. He swings and—what a stroke! Broke the bat. Brandon makes a magnificent catch in left. One out. A brief delay, folks, while Gray searches for a new bat. Now he's got something that looks more like a hockey stick than a baseball bat, but the ump allows it. M-Q-P throws his best fastball, about 2 miles per hour, and Gray takes a mighty swing, and—what a fantastic swoosh of air! They'll feel that at Grand Canyon Village."

Brandon pulled out a one-run victory in the third and final inning. At the end the diamond

311

was littered with broken branches and smashed pinecones. We agreed that the winner won the privilege of restoring the area to its precompetition naturalness while the losers cooked a postgame repast of macaroni and tuna.

Being on the western side of the plateau gave us an hour more light than we'd had in the inner canyon. After dinner, with coffee and hot chocolate, we settled at the rim to enjoy the sunset. We weren't sure exactly where we were on Powell—somewhere above Bedrock Canyon—but it didn't matter. We hadn't set out with a precise destination in mind. I had never before appreciated the difference between not being sure where you are and being lost.

The view to the west looked dramatically different and felt unfamiliar, as it was. At Dutton Point, our attention had always been drawn to prominent buttes, pinnacles, temples, and castles. Here, the broad expanse of Great Thumb Mesa on the South Rim reached out as if wanting to rejoin Powell, but the panorama displayed mostly gently sloping terraces framing wide drainages. The effect was more open and less complex than we were used to. No monument stood out to divert our attention from the slow descent of the enormous red sun.

We watched in silence from the moment the sun began to disappear until the solstice denouement was complete. In the red afterglow I said, "It's time to do the same with 'Iron John.' "

I reread the final segment in which the King's daughter confirmed her suspicion that the boy was really the great knight who had won the three golden apples at the tournament and the rescuer who had turned the tide of battle when the kingdom was attacked. Before the King, she pulled off his tarboosh and exposed his golden hair. He then revealed that he was a prince and asked to marry the King's daughter. She agreed. At the great marriage ceremony, attended by his astounded parents, Iron John appeared at the head of a rich procession. He explained that he had been freed from an evil enchantment by the boy's valor and pledged his wealth to the boy.

"Three kingdoms combined in one marriage," Brandon observed. "Not a bad day's work."

"Quite a golden-haired boy," Malcolm chuckled.

"Yeah, but I'm kind of surprised his hair stayed golden," Brandon remarked. "I don't know why. I guess I thought the gold would wear off."

"I wondered about that myself," Malcolm affirmed.

"It seems important because, to me," Brandon continued, "the hair turning gold stands out as major. It's how Iron John knew the boy failed the test that led to his getting banished from the forest. His hair got him in trouble with the King when he tried to hide it. It's what attracted the King's daughter to him. And, let's see, what else? It gave him away at the tournament and it's how she proved who he was to the King. The gold hair seems pretty significant."

"Signifying . . . ?" I asked.

Brandon looked pensive. "The boy's hair turned gold when he leaned close to the pool to see his reflection and his hair touched the water. It's like he saw himself for the first time. That changed him, but he wasn't sure how to handle it so he tried to hide it. His triumph came when he was able to let everyone else see how he'd changed."

"You're on a roll," I said. "Bring it on home."

"You mean make it a lesson. All right, what the hell? The first big change is seeing yourself as you really are. Then you have to deal with how the world sees you. The place to get to, I guess, is accepting who you are and letting the world take it or leave it. It wasn't enough for the boy that his father was a king. He had to prove himself to himself before he could let the world know him."

"Impressive," Malcolm lauded.

"Very," I added, as Brandon bent forward in a mock bow. "Way beyond mere cultural literacy. But, would you have liked it better if his hair had changed back to its original color?"

"No, the story's right. Once you've seen yourself you can't go back to the innocence of not seeing yourself. It had to be a permanent change. The main tension in the whole story, really, is between how the boy sees himself and how others see him. He's constantly trying to hide who he is."

"And it's the daughter who shows the world who he is," Malcolm added. "He's not able to do it alone. She sees who he is, accepts him, loves him, and reveals to others what she sees."

"Is that a family-systems lesson?" Brandon asked, grinning.

"It's a lesson about how we're always part of some larger system and our perceptions of who we are depend partly on how others see us. People who saw the boy's golden hair and great deeds were attracted to him. Many of the people I see in therapy have received so much negative feedback about who they are that they want to hide. They never want the tarboosh to come off. They want to make it bigger—a robe with a hood to cover all of them."

"So how do you help?" Brandon asked.

"Everybody doesn't have a whole head of golden hair, but everyone has at least some part that's golden. I really believe that. The process involves helping them find the golden part. First, you remember, the boy's finger turned gold, then one hair, then his whole head. Healing starts with finding a golden fingertip or one golden hair."

"How do you find that starting point?" Brandon asked.

"By listening to family stories, helping them hear and understand each other's stories as well as their own, then helping them script the future direction of the story."

Brandon furrowed his brow.

"Give an example," I suggested.

"I'm seeing a mother and daughter now. Daughter's your age, Brandon. She's attractive and thoughtful, and appears, on the surface, to have a lot going for her, but she's developed some pretty self-destructive tendencies, especially hooking up with real losers for boyfriends."

"What do you mean, 'losers'?"

"That's her term. Drug users. Abusers. Jerks. She's repeating her mother's pattern with men. Since her parents split-up, her mother's had a series of relationships with what her mother also calls 'losers.' I wanted to help them both feel more worthy, especially if it led to attracting men who would treat them better. In other words, changing the story line. I asked the mother if she watched Westerns growing up. She did, like I did and your dad did"—I nodded—"because that's about all there was. I asked if she remembered the movies where a young Indian brave would ride in with a string of ponies to show himself worthy of the chief's daughter. I told the mother she'd been settling for one-pony men. She needed to insist on more ponies—deserved more ponies."

"Did she understand?" Brandon asked.

"Whenever she meets a new man now, we talk about how many ponies he's brought to her. She's moving the number up. But the daughter has never seen any of those movies."

"So what do you tell the daughter?"

"The daughter was molested by one of the mother's one-pony men—actually, a no-pony man. The mother denied it at first. Her father and brothers refused to believe it. Even her boyfriend at the time refused to deal with it. I told her she needed a champion, that she deserved a champion, someone who would believe her and honor her. But she didn't really respond to the idea, didn't seem to get it. So I told her about the knights of the Round Table and chivalry. I reminded her that knights behaved in exactly the opposite manner of her brothers and boyfriends. A knight was pledged to defend his lady's honor even if, as in the case of Lancelot and Guinevere, the knight knew the lady to be guilty. Her brothers and boyfriends not only didn't support her, they abused her, so she has trouble believing that anyone would honor and champion her, and she settles for losers. She goes looking for them."

"According to the Iron John story," Brandon interrupted, "she needs golden apples to attract a winner."

"She has golden apples. But, you're right, she has to realize it and, in her case, learn to value them."

"And if she finds she really doesn't have any golden apples?"

"Then we'll have to start with a fingertip or a simple strand of hair and create some gold."

"You're a New Age version of a medieval alchemist," I teased. "Therapy is alchemy."

"And the process of transmutation is looking at oneself like the boy did," Malcolm continued unabashed, "then learning to value who you are and letting others see it. When it works, and it doesn't always, but when it works, it's . . ." His face broke into a broad smile. "In a session just recently, I asked her how her search was going. She said she'd stopped searching for someone else to champion her. She'd decided she had to champion herself. I thought we were still working on her finger, but she grabbed the brush and painted her whole body golden."

"It just occurred to me," Brandon said, his voice excited, "there were really two incompatible tests: the Wild Man's test and Iron John's. The Wild Man told the boy not to look at himself or touch the water in any way. If he had obeyed, he would have remained innocent and wild—a forest creature. When he looked at himself—and failed the test because of it—he gained self-knowledge, lost his innocence, and had to leave the place of nature, *but* by doing so he ultimately freed Iron John."

"And that's the other system connection," Malcolm said, his voice also excited. "Everything the boy does affects others. What he does determines whether Iron John is set free. How he serves the King affects the cook and the gardener. How he fights affects the whole kingdom. How he does at the tournament affects the daughter. He appears to be acting for himself, but he's really part of a complex system. It's a great systems story."

"So, Dad, is that how Bly interprets it?"

"It doesn't matter."

"I know, but now you can tell us what Bly said without limiting our own interpretation."

"Bly doesn't really do much with . . . I'm trying to remember. He does more with the boy's wound than with the happy ending. He certainly doesn't note that an extended family system has been created with the marriage. Quite the contrary, he sees a need to free ourselves from what he calls 'family cages.' I think Bly considers all families dysfunctional—inevitably so."

"Dysfunctional how?" Brandon asked.

"Dysfunctional for the individual. He used the story to explore the roles available to men, so he interpreted the boy's experiences as stages in the journey to manhood. The sequence varies, but all the stages are desirable, perhaps even necessary. His happy ending, I suppose, is that the boy becomes a man, not that he's openly part of a new extended family system. I'd say Bly has a developmental rather than a systems perspective. You'll have to do your own book, Malcolm: *Iron John from a Systems Perspective.*"

"Do it, Malcolm!" Brandon exclaimed. "But you'll need a better title, like . . . I've got it: *Inside the Wild Man's Matted and Tangled Hair.*"

"You're giving a whole new meaning to 'hair systems for men,' " I said, running my hand through my thin and depleted crop.

"And you should do a book, too, Dad. Let's see: *Skeptically Inquiring into Iron John: Scientific Explanations for Hair Turning Gold in the Woods.*"

"And you can compose the soundtracks to the movie versions," Malcolm added. "But before we leave the story, I do have one last comment. It strikes me as ironic that the story is titled 'Iron John.' Even though it concludes with Iron John's liberation, that's a minor theme. The heart of the story is the boy's development. Yet he never has a name! Even at the end, as a man, he still doesn't have a name. To be an initiation story he should end up with a name and adult identity."

"Maybe we should give Brandon a new name," I suggested, standing up. "How about—"

"No!" Brandon shouted. "No way. I already have four names. I appreciate the thought, but—"

"Then how about we just knight you, Sir Brandon?"

"You can't knight me because you're not knights. You can't lead me in a vision quest because you haven't done one. And that's all fine with me. You've shared with me what you know and given me this *buedeniferous* canyon. You don't have to make up new stuff. You're working too hard at this initiation thing. We've finished 'Iron John.' Let's relax and celebrate."

Malcolm's canyon-sized laugh reverberated into the darkening sky. He slapped Brandon on the back. "Well said, Brandon. You're right, we are finished with Iron John. He's been an interesting companion but I think we've gotten what we can from him. You comfortable with that, Michael?"

"Completely," I said.

The red sky turned gray. A faint glow lingered on the horizon as a cold wind drove us to our sleeping gear, but not before agreeing that the title for Malcolm's systems book should be *Ironic John.*

Day Nine

37. Lancelot Point

We were packed and ready for our final full day in the canyon. "Where's Malcolm?" Brandon asked. "He said he was going to take a whiz, but that was a while ago."

I stood behind him vigorously rubbing his shoulders.

"He's most likely on the rim, gazing into the big hole."

After a while, Brandon, impatient to hike, went off to find him. He returned a short time later. "He's at the rim, all right, just sitting there."

"He'll be along when he's ready."

Brandon's fidgeting finally got to me, so I set off to stir him. I found him on the rim, leaning forward, arms resting easily on his knees, a stalk of grass in his mouth and his maize pouch on a rock beside him. I turned back, recognizing from past canyon treks his wistful gaze, understanding for the first time that this was Malcolm's form of lamenting, the sad kind. He was mourning the inevitable separation from the canyon. Only the final ritual of returning to Grand Canyon Village and having a sumptuously disappointing meal in the Lodge's magnificent dining room would restore his sense of folly and return him to laughter. Until then he would grieve.

He finally showed up. In silence we shouldered our packs. We hiked north along the western rim, admiring the sequence of long pointed terraces separated by deep canyons that gave the impression of sculptured bear claws extending out and supporting Powell Plateau. We could see along the length of the plateau from Arrowhead Terrace at the northwestern end to Spencer Terrace off the southwestern tip of Thompson Point. Interestingly, the longest terrace—a great scorpion claw reaching out for the river—bore no name.

We left our packs where the plateau narrowed back toward Muav Saddle and bushwhacked through about a mile of dense brush and forest savannah to the northernmost point of Powell, out on a narrow buttress overlooking Steamboat Mountain. Beyond was the great expanse of Tapeats Amphitheater set off by distinct promontories on the distant North Rim: Crazy Jug Point, Parissawampitts Point, and Monument Point. Directly below us Arrowhead Terrace pointed to Deubendorff Rapids in Middle Granite Gorge. A flock of swifts played in the wind currents and downdrafts formed by the atmospheric convergences at the tip of Powell. We settled on a shady ledge just large enough for the three of us to cluster around our last canyon lunch: a can of sardines, cracker crumbs, and generous globs of mustard.

"It's not hard to see why Steamboat got its name," Brandon observed. He compared the long, triangular formation below us to the map. "This side is too steep, but it looks like the other side could be climbed." When neither of us responded he went on, describing how other notable land formations compared to the map, speculating on the meaning of names, and trying vainly to draw his solemn companions into conversation.

Malcolm had a far-off look in his eyes. He had hardly spoken all morning.

I tried to tap into Brandon's energy and enthusiasm as he speculated on what a great adventure it would be to do a loop hike all the way around Powell Plateau. I managed a few short responses, clearly unsatisfactory. The more withdrawn we seemed, the more animated he became, as if determined to do battle with our melancholy vibrations. I felt as inwardly focused as Malcolm looked. Brandon's chatter wasn't really annoying, but having to respond was. At length I said, "Let's just listen to the canyon for awhile. Okay?"

"Sure," he agreed. Then, a moment later: "I can hear—"

My scowl stopped him. He retrieved his journal from the daypack in which we had brought our lunch. Malcolm and I exchanged wise, knowing glances.

"I saw that," Brandon said. "I know you want me to shut up. Consider it done. But don't think my not working on a bummer means I care less. It just means I'm still into being here. You two are acting like you've already left." And he settled back against the cliff wall to write.

Malcolm and I looked at each other. I shook my head and he raised his eyebrows in acknowledgement. We looked away and down, then back at each other, and burst out laughing, giggling really, like teenagers caught mimicking their parents and suddenly embarrassed to find those very parents were watching them in amusement. I made a fist and hit Brandon hard on the arm. "Don't be so goddamn wise," I reproached.

"Would you two please be quiet?" he said solemnly. "I'm trying to write something depressing here."

That set us off again, beyond giggling—full, belly-deep, body-shaking laughter. Brandon studiously ignored us, which only made us laugh harder. At length he gave up pretending to write, slammed his journal down, and said, "You two are acting very immaturely. You've completely spoiled my meditation." Which set us off again, joined at last by our suddenly laconic companion.

Brandon led us in planning several possible future trips: up Steamboat, through Surprise Valley, around Powell, and along Conquistador Aisle. We were unrestrained by details like where to find water or how to get through the Redwall. The implicit message was that we weren't leaving the canyon; we were just going out for awhile to resupply.

After some requisite rock-lizard time, we bushwhacked back to our packs and picked up the trail down to Muav Saddle. At the cabin we discussed where to spend our last night.

"Sleeping with the Mercedes and possibly other hikers and vehicles at Swamp Point isn't very appealing to me," I said, "although it would close the loop to end where we began. But we've seen the view there. I'd like to truck up to Swamp and drive to where we can bushwhack out to Lancelot Point."

Malcolm spread out the map and we huddled over it, calculating distances with twigs, speculating on the terrain, estimating how long it would take, and otherwise working up enthusiasm for one last adventure. Success would hinge primarily on two factors: figuring the right place to leave the car—we calculated 4.5 miles from Swamp Point—and finding a way through what was likely to be two or more miles of dense underbrush and prickly thickets, especially at the bottom of Big Spring Canyon, which we'd have to traverse before cutting west to the promontory named Lancelot.

Cuts on every bare appendage, clothes torn, packs looking like a collector's display of North Rim spindly vegetation, and spirits high, we made it. Bird songs filled the air as the singers searched for sleeping crevices along the cliff walls in the dwindling light. We were faced with the same challenge, though we did so without song. We settled for a sloping area under a large oak between two steep ravines away from the jagged and undulating rim. We'd dine and sleep there, but in between time we'd pass our final evening on a narrow ledge directly above the territory framed by Merlin and Modred Abysses, in full view of Elaine, Guinevere, and King Arthur Castles. What mattered most to me was that we could see Galahad Point from our position somewhere along the edge of Lancelot's ridge.

It took some study to get oriented to this new perspective on Shinumo Amphitheater. The panorama offered several nameless buttes and distinctive formations on this side of Rainbow Plateau that had been hidden from view on Powell. Brandon was particularly intrigued by a thousand-foot-tall, free-standing column that looked like it had once been a long, narrow ridge connected to the rim. The top had eroded into a series of uneven knobs and misshapen blocks that gave the impression of a human procession. Suspended above the distant canyon floor, the procession looked as if it had been caught unaware, captured in motion, and petrified in some cataclysmic instant, leaving the pilgrims freeze-dried, some with one foot stepping forward, many with heads bowed and shoulders hunched, as if bearing heavy loads. In size and caricature the procession suggested Snow White's seven dwarfs, though that cartoonish association felt like it lacked the appropriate dignity for the monument. Hard as we tried, we couldn't make them out as knights of the Round Table; they just didn't have the right bearing. Brandon suggested what we eventually agreed was the best name: Canterbury Column. He drew the formation in his journal while Malcolm and I prepared our final feast of rice and beans.

Afterward, we sat on the rim and watched the stars come out. I found myself lost in the hugeness of the night sky. I watched as one light after another emerged. Captivated. Transfixed. Finally beyond thought. No voices in my head. No past or future. Suspended in the moment. Detoxed.

At length, it felt like time to add our own dim lights to the celestial display. I set out the three votive candles we had lit on Swamp Point nine nights earlier. I lit one and passed the matches to Brandon. He lit one, then Malcolm. As we watched the flames, Malcolm asked, "Have you selected the proper sociological benediction?"

"I think we can dispense with sociology tonight. If I haven't gotten deep into Brandon's subconscious by now, I never will."

"Subconscious!" Malcolm looked shocked. "You would use that word? You recognize that it exists?"

"As a working hypothesis. What it is and whether it exists is certainly a matter of scholarly debate. We could, however, test its cognitive content right now. Ask Brandon how much organizational sociology he remembers."

Brandon scrunched up his face.

"You don't remember?"

He looked pensive, then his eyes brightened. "I've seen the photo but, no, can't say I remember. Sorry."

"Remember what?" Malcolm asked.

"When Brandon was but a mere babe, I taught a graduate course in organizational sociology with him *on my back*. He would peer over my shoulders at the students. From the time he was a few months old until several months after his first birthday he accompanied my every step as I paced back and forth expounding great sociological insights."

"Must have been a short course," Malcolm baited.

"Short for Brandon, anyway. He'd fall asleep as soon as I started lecturing. Having him there did seem to keep the students awake though. At any rate, word got around and the campus newspaper put the story on the f ont page. That's the photo Brandon remembers. The *Minneapolis Tribune* picked it up from whence it made its way to that pinnacle of journalism, the *National Enquirer.* In 1974 it was apparently newsworthy that a father was caring for his son. We were featured right there alongside reports on alien sightings, exotic weight-loss techniques, and unfaithful Hollywood stars."

"Didn't you get some letters after that?" Brandon asked.

"A lot, and from around the country, most of them warning about the damage I was doing. They let loose their imaginations on the varieties of harm that could result from exposing an infant to such subliminal rantings as they assumed were contained in my lectures. My favorite came from a woman who threatened she was going to contact her congressman to advocate legislation banning children under age twelve from university classrooms."

"How'd other faculty react?" Malcolm asked.

"I don't remember any reactions from male colleagues, but the females—they wanted to be supportive, at least in principle, but a couple were quick to point out that only a male could get away with what I was doing because it was new and 'cute,' especially keeping Brandon in my office all morning after class. They were sure that, if a woman did the same thing, it would be detrimental to tenure and promotion."

"I wish I remembered," Brandon said.

"It ended somewhat badly, I'm afraid. You eventually began staying awake and babbling—if you can imagine!—given how quiet you've become in old age. I was clearly losing the competition for student attention. I got an anonymous note that insinuated you made every bit as much sense as I did. When a bottle or graham crackers would no longer silence you, I had to start you in day care."

"Well I may not remember those backpack trips, but I'll never forget this one."

"I suspect not," Malcolm nodded. "But to help etch the memory a little deeper I've got something for you." The trip to and from his pack offered just enough time for Brandon to fix the wick on the one candle that was flickering badly. We watched for a moment as the relit flame took hold, then Malcolm continued.

"At the end of an initiation, it is customary to celebrate with gifts. I want to give you a book by Scott Momaday called *The Way to Rainy Mountain*. It's about the Kiowa people. Rainy Mountain's in Oklahoma, not far from where I grew up, so it's always had special meaning for me. It's a book about connections to ancestors and former times."

He placed the book in front of Brandon.

"What Momaday says about his people's journey to Rainy Mountain captures, for me, our canyon journey. The Kiowa journey, he wrote, was an 'evocation of three things in particular: a landscape that is incomparable, a time that is gone forever, and the human spirit, which endures.' "

Brandon fingered the book. "Thank you, Malcolm."

"And I want to give you these." He took Brandon's hand and placed something in it. Brandon held his open palm near a candle. The light revealed six small objects of different colors, shapes, and textures. "The white pebble is from the Coconino. The flat black piece is Vishnu Schist from along the River. The round red one is from the Redwall. The gray pebble is from the Tonto. The jagged orange quartz is from near Bass Camp and the tiny piece of charcoal is from what was once a huge ponderosa pine on Powell. They come from different strata and therefore from vastly different periods of time. I hope they will evoke for you this journey through an incomparable landscape, through time gone forever and the human spirit, which endures."

"I won't forget, Malcolm. *Bue düden.*"

We sat silently for a few moments, Brandon gazing intently at Malcolm's gifts. The glossy white-covered Momaday book rested in his lap, reflecting the flames and illuminating his face. His countenance blended with the soft light of dusk. A gentle luminescence enveloped us from the inner canyon.

Brandon closed his fist around the rocks. I reached for his other hand, held it palm up and gently formed the fingers and thumb into a bowl. I did the same with the hollow of my hand and placed it alongside his, two dippers, equal in size, flesh against flesh. I cleared my throat, looked at him, his eyes encouraging, understanding. He pressed the side of his hand against mine.

I cupped my hand under his, feeling his bony knuckles. The short hairs on the back of his hand were thick, like I knew mine to be. I stroked them to experience their softness and felt a vein yield to my pressure. I placed my other hand on top, and found myself pressing hard, as if I could make our flesh one. His muscles firmed, not resisting, but asserting themselves, emanating strength. I relaxed my hold, lifted the covering hand, and dipped my finger into the space formed by his fingers as if testing the firmness of gelatin. The consistency felt perfect.

"When I cup my hand like this and look into it, I am anchored in canyon space. Your cactus needle or pebbles may be lost like the antlers that disappeared on Powell, but this space in the hollow of your hand cannot be lost or taken away. Malcolm said anything can be a totem. I offer you this, then, as a totem: Nothing. Which is to say, space. And openness."

I took my finger from the hollow of his hand and pointed. His eyes followed my gesture to the vastness beyond the rim. "Out there is space for your bighorn to roam. Here," I dipped back into the space of his cupped hand, "is also space for your bighorn to roam. Freedom to inquire."

I stood, pulled him up, and we embraced. Malcolm rose and hugged Brandon. Then we interlocked arms and stood silently in a circle looking up into the night sky. At length, as we disentangled, Brandon bent down, picked up a candle, held it over the rim, and let the wind extinguish the flame. Malcolm and I did likewise. As the candle light vanished, the surrounding darkness deepened its luminescence. I looked out and saw the big hole.

At that very instant, my knees gave way under the unexpected weight of all that had happened. At least that's how Malcolm recounted the story. I just remember this heavy object on my back screaming, "One more ride, Daddy. Come on. One last ride."

Day Ten

Epilogue
Reflections on Coming of Age:
A Humanist Perspective

Reentry rituals followed our night on Lancelot Ridge. My notes from that last day convey only mild resistance to the inevitability of retox.

Returned to Grand Canyon Village amidst bus fumes and a marauding horde of strangers. Walked at sunset out to Bright Angel Point past parents trying vainly to restrain running children; young couples holding hands, enraptured more by each other than the immensity surrounding them; international visitors pointing this way and that, a barrage of staccato phrases shooting off their tongues; and camera shutters chattering to the stony silence of Deva, Brahma, and Zoroaster Temples. A sumptuous dinner in the great dining hall of Grand Canyon Lodge left us praising the incomparable taste of quickly cooked ramen at the end of a hard day hiking. Our table, next to the towering windows overlooking the Ottoman Amphitheater, offered only a view of mood-matching darkness. But gradually, the ritual Malcolm insisted on took hold. A stream of toasts turned our last canyon dinner together into a celebration: To youth. To age. To human connections. To the Mercedes. To

331

descending before ascending. To the Redwall. To Merlin. To detox. To retox. To the Big Hole. To forever becoming.
    Then Brandon's benediction: Bue düden.

◆   ◆   ◆

This epilogue derives from my inclination to make sense of things. To analyze. Not everyone bears that affliction, I know. Those who prefer reading stories unencumbered by an author's post hoc ruminations might do well to stop at this point, all the better to let canyon images linger.[1] What follows imposes a conceptual framework on the story's meaning. And that may be alienating to those who prefer the feel of the Redwall to analysis of that feeling. I find I like and need both, the one as a father, the other as a social scientist.

In effect, drawing on the traditions of phenomenology and qualitative research,[2] the story becomes a case study of a humanist rite of passage. The inductive analysis in this chapter has grown out of and remains grounded in the story. Yet, to have a more general significance, both the story and analysis must ultimately transcend particularities of the Grand Canyon, the characters who lived the story, and the myths, rituals, and stories that informed it.[3]

I'm not sure when the notion first took hold of me that articulating alternative coming-of-age paradigms might help elucidate our canyon experience. Before formally conceptualizing contrasting paradigm dimensions, I experienced them as conflicting feelings that emanated from my struggle to sort out what I wanted Brandon's initiation to be, while also grappling with defining my role in the process. I suppose the idea of alternative paradigms first emerged the second night as I paced the narrow beach where White Creek intersected Shinumo and pondered the Great Unconformity as metaphor for the gap between tribal approaches to initiation and coming of age for contemporary youth. In the weeks and months after our canyon experience, far from languishing in the throes of retox as I expected, the idea of contrasting paradigms stayed with me, as did the canyon experience. I started listing themes and matching them with incidents and turning points along the way. The sequence of incidents became this book and the contrasting themes became the basis for this closing chapter, a way for me to figure out how what started out as an initiation become a humanist coming-of-age celebration.

Stated more formally, this final chapter extracts themes from Brandon's Grand Canyon Coming-of-Age story and connects them with principles and practices of humanism.[4] In so doing, I'll use some dominant (though certainly not universal) themes of traditional tribal initiations for contrast. Placed alongside each other, the opposing themes align as alternative coming-of-age paradigms: the traditional initiation paradigm versus the celebration paradigm of humanism. Table 1 summarizes the dimensions of comparison in paradigmatic opposition.

Table 1. Coming-of-Age Paradigms

Dimensions of Comparison	Traditional Initiation Paradigm	Humanist Celebration Paradigm
Value Base	1. Tribal tradition; religious beliefs	1. Humanism
Outcome	2. Tribe-based identity: assimilation	2. Personal identity: independent sense of self
Dominant Process	3. Controlling/indoctrinating	3. Freeing/questing/discovering
Focus	4. Dogma/answers: elders all-knowing	4. Perspective/questions: all searching
Foundation	5. Mystical	5. Rational: skeptical inquiry
Authority	6. Deities/gods	6. Reason
Experience	7. Suffering/fear	7. Affirming/understanding
Approach	8. Standardized	8. Individualized
Identity	9. Becoming a man/woman	9. Becoming a complete person
View of Childhood	10. Temporary: exit childhood forever	10. Keep the child alive throughout life
View of Life Passages	11. One-time transition from child to adult	11. Multiple passages over a lifelong journey
Territory	12. Tribal territory	12. Earth: global community
Ancestry	13. Creation myth	13. Evolutionary story of humankind
Relation to Parent	14. Separation	14. Adult to adult bonding

Portraying these themes in opposition is a heuristic device that will inevitably oversimplify, first, in that what I'm calling "traditional tribal" themes are abstract overgeneralizations and, second, in that differences are emphasized while areas of congruity are correspondingly underanalyzed. I offer this, not as a finished framework, but as a source of dialogue in exploring how to support and celebrate modern youth's coming of age.

Tribe-based Identity versus Personal Identity: Assimilation versus Independent Sense of Self

A primary purpose of traditional tribal initiation was to move a youth from family-identity to tribal-identity. Becoming a man meant becoming a member of the tribe. Initiation ceremonies developed as a way of assuring assimilation into the tribe and, therefore, tribal survival.

During our evenings in the canyon, we related to Brandon stories about initiation rites in several tribal societies. For example, the Pitjandjara conduct what may be the most severe initiation in the world, what they call the "ceremony of man making." Anthropologists hypothesize that the difficulty of an initiation is directly proportional to the harshness of the tribe's environment. Thus, the unforgiving Australian outback gave rise to a harsh initiation process. For the tribe to survive, the individual had to learn to survive. Once a Pitjandjara boy passed the initiation tests, he could face any fear, endure any pain, and suffer any deprivation.[5]

Poet Robert Bly, among other prominent figures in the contemporary New Age "Men's Movement," has lamented the modern loss of initiation tests and ceremonies of man making.[6] He has focused selectively on the strength of identity that results from surviving the initiation tests. However, passing the test didn't just make the boy a man, it made him a *tribal man.* Only on the surface, it seems to me, does the identity that emerges from traditional tribal initiations resemble the self-aware, independent-thinking, and reflective ideal of humanism. The indoctrinating nature of the typical tribal initiation process effectively bent the will of the young under the authority of tribal elders, crushing any display of independent thought and action.

A humanist coming-of-age process would have quite a different result, not only because survival of the tribe is not a central issue for postindustrial society, but more fundamentally because humanists seek to nourish reason and compassion, deplore efforts to control thought, reject subservience to authoritarian elites, and foster learning in the place of dogma. A humanist coming of age paradigm would celebrate the uniqueness, dignity, and worth of each human being, and seek to support all persons in fully realizing the best and noblest of which they are capable.

The identity messages of the alternative paradigms, then, are quite different and distinct, as shown in Table 2. Tribal-initiation results in tribal identity. In contrast, a humanist coming-of-age celebration reinforces a strong personal identity and individual sense of self.

Table 2. Identity Messages Embedded in Initiation Processes

Tribal* Identity Messages	**Humanist Celebratory Messages**
• You are first and foremost a member of the tribe.	• You are first and foremost a person in your own right.
• Your status and importance derive from and are dependent on the tribe.	• Your status and importance derive from your own sense of who you are, your inner sense of worth.
• The tribe will tell you how to live your life, what paths are open to you, and what to believe.	• You must make your own choices, find your own path, and take responsibility for the consequences.
• You serve the tribe and the tribe will take care of you.	• You choose what community to be part of and how to serve that community out of a shared sense of mutuality.
• Tribal values are the only values. They are not open to question, discussion, or individual adaptation.	• You live by values of moral decency and normative standards developed rationally in relation to others, freely chosen, freely lived by, and tested by their consequences.

*One can substitute church, military, or fraternity for tribe and often find the messages of control in the left hand column to be essentially or fundamentally the same. The differences are typically matters of degree, not kind.

To contrast these messages in this way is not to criticize either the tribal messages or the rites that carried those messages. Understood in context, within a specific ecological-cultural milieu, these rituals and their embedded messages stand on their own. My complaint is with those who romanticize tribal initiations and recommend their reintroduction as a solution to problems of identity formation in modern societies.

Control versus Freedom:
Dogma/Answers versus Perspective/Questions

Tribal initiation ritualizes an indoctrination process; religious initiation does likewise. In the first case tribal elders act as authorities indoctrinating the young in the truths of the tribe; in the second case the clergy take on the trappings of authority, infusing young minds with the catechism of religious belief. What's common to these initiations is that the young are told what's real. No questioning. No doubt. The Pitjandjara bull-roarer, the initiates are told, *is* the voice of a spirit. The African elder dancing in a leopard mask is said to *become* a leopard spirit. The Oceanic elders, costumed as sea monsters who attack and terrorize initiates, are portrayed as *real* monsters. Explanations come in stories and myths and the initiates are told what the stories mean, how to behave, and what to think. Modern catechisms leave out the drama, but not the thought control and fear of Satan.

A humanist coming of age, in contrast, centers on inquiry. Young people become inquirers into their own belief systems and active participants in constructing their own knowledge. What they are offered, then, are the tools of inquiry—reason and scientific methods. In the Unitarian coming-of-age ritual in which Brandon participated, he joined other youths in studying various religions and traditions, and reflecting on issues of theology, philosophy, and morality. At the end of their inquiry, each youth made a formal and public declaration of personal beliefs before the assembled congregation. No minister or church elder questioned their right to state their beliefs based on wherever their inquiry had led them. Humanism offers the young ways of discovering truth for themselves by posing questions and offering perspective. Ancient "truths" are offered as perspectives to be considered, reviewed in light of available evidence and personal experience, and adapted as needed to contemporary circumstances.

During Brandon's canyon experience, an opportunity for inquiry emerged at the confluence of Merlin and Mordred Abysses when I offered him a choice of routes. Brandon chose Merlin, saying he wanted to hike to the waterfall. We began a shared inquiry into alternative explanations, mystical and scientific, for why he expected to find a waterfall where the map showed none and the guidebooks we had were quiet on the subject. Likewise, in reading and discussing the initiation story of "Iron John," Brandon was free to offer his interpretations. Malcolm and I, as elders, told the tales. The canyon provided a setting to have experiences. And Brandon ultimately decided what it all meant. Instead of giving him explanations and dogma, we offered an opportunity for inquiry, time for reflection, and some principles for arriving at his own conclusions.

The differences in orientation between what I'm calling here the traditional tribal paradigm versus a humanist paradigm of celebration derive from dramatically contrasting societal and cultural conditions. In subsistence communities the future of the tribe was always uncertain, so control was essential for survival. With small numbers of genetically related people, the tribe had to carefully control who married whom. Subject to periodic famines, the tribe controlled the sharing of scarce food. In the face of threats from other tribes, slave traders, and colonizing armies, the tribe had to guarantee the commitment of warriors to die in defense of the tribe. Given the unpredictability of the gods, the shaman needed ways of controlling the willingness of tribal members to sacrifice in order to appease and cajole temperamental deities. The benefit of all this control was tribal survival. The individual gained a place of security and defined status in the tribe. The cost to the tribe was loss of flexibility in the face of changed conditions. It would overstate the reality to suggest that individuals somewhat consciously exchanged freedom for security and a sense of belonging; personal choice was a luxury subsistence societies could not afford and a pain individuals did not seek.

In contrast, a contemporary coming-of-age process that is a dialogue about perspectives rather than the imposition of truth would not threaten the survival of society. In today's rapidly changing world, multiple perspectives and new ways of looking at things are our hope for adaptation and survival. Ancient times may have required that the young bend to the will of the group. Modern times demand young people who can move society in new directions by applying their intellects and creativity.

Mystical versus Rational

Consistent with wanting Brandon to make up his own mind and engage in his own inquiry, I wanted him to be exposed, up close, to mystical belief and the alternative, skeptical inquiry.[7] Brandon had long since rejected organized, institutional religion as having anything of value to offer him. Malcolm's gentle form of wilderness spiritualism and cosmic mysticism offered a perspective more likely to be alluring. Examples of New Age mysticism include the following beliefs:

- Certain spiritual dimensions of the human experience lie beyond scientific understanding.

- A Jungian collective unconscious unites us as a human community.

- Nonordinary powers of mind exist, extrasensory capabilities, that can be developed if one is open to them.

- Sacred places exist where one can experience unexplainable power and a connection with the universe; the Grand Canyon is such a place.

- Certain animals, totem animals, have special roles and powers to guide humans open to their guidance and protection.

- Certain objects, talismans, contain powers that physics cannot test or explain.

- Things are as they are meant to be; the universe is unfolding as it should under some teleological purpose; we simply have to be open and align ourselves with cosmic karma.

- Ancient systems of belief from Native Americans, Africans, and Asians are closer to real truth than is science because they have endured and are grounded in humans' ancient experience of the Earth and cosmos.

A majestic and awe-inspiring environment like the Grand Canyon, laying bear the oldest exposed rock on earth, invites mystical connection. During ten days hiking the canyon one can be sure that unexpected things will occur that, serendipitously, offer the allure of karmic connection. By interpreting coincidental occurrences through the mystic lens of synchronicity, that is, without regard for verifiable causal linkages, one can reexperience how mystical beliefs have emerged throughout human history.

The humanist's skeptical response is straightforward: *Extraordinary claims require extraordinary evidence.* But it's one thing to discuss such rationality in a classroom, familiar urban setting, or laboratory. It's quite another to inquire into extraordinary claims where extraordinary rock formations, animals, and plants abound; where seemingly extraordinary occurrences happen daily; and in the presence of one who believes in mystical explanations.

The first day hiking I got separated from Brandon and Malcolm, and came close to sliding off an edge of the Hermit Shale. Was this, as Malcolm later hinted, an omen from "the canyon," or just my inattention and inexperience? The second day a bighorn came close and appeared to make intense and lengthy eye contact with Brandon: a totem for Brandon, or an animal routinely checking out intruders in his territory? The third day our water filter clogged at the river and we had a thirsty hike back to camp: a "reminder from the canyon that we should honor water and the river," or a simple mechanical malfunction? The fourth day Brandon chose to hike Merlin Abyss "to see the waterfall" without identifiable prior knowledge that a waterfall existed there: a cosmic intuition and parapsychological premonition, or a reasonable guess and hope verbalized as seeming knowledge? And so it went. The Grand Canyon became a laboratory for Brandon to experience how mysticism emerges and to consider the skeptical inquiry admonition to examine carefully ordinary evidence and explanations before seeking extraordinary evidence and explanations.

At the waterfall in Merlin Abyss I recounted to Brandon the scene from Mark Twain's *A Connecticut Yankee in King Arthur's Court* in which Merlin and Twain's twentieth-century hero compete to see who can repair a well that has ceased to provide water. Merlin's magic failed; Twain's hero repaired the well much as Malcolm and I would later repair the Mercedes, with logic and empirical study. Later, on our next to last day in the canyon, when we couldn't find the antlers Brandon had placed in a tree, we examined how such an event could appear cosmic and mystical to the superstitious. Finding the antlers was "good luck"; losing them was "bad luck." It's not far from there to attributing special luck-changing powers to the antlers, and from there to viewing the antlers as a talisman. Attach a story about why the deer has this power, say, the deer as a messenger from the gods, and you've got a myth, all from the serendipity of finding and losing some antlers in the forest.

What we can learn from tribal initiations is that the coming-of-age process should be *experiential*. Tribal elders didn't just lecture young initiates about tribal beliefs. The initiates experienced those beliefs. Papuan elders construct a monster called Kaiemunu and force the petrified initiates to enter its belly to experience ritual death and rebirth surrounded by terrifying sounds. In Brandon's humanist coming of age, he experienced events and objects that could be interpreted mystically or rationally. He lived the experience of skeptical inquiry.

Deities/Heaven versus Humanity/Here and Now

Tribal polytheism and modern monotheism share the belief that humans must look beyond themselves, to gods or God, to be complete, and must look to another time and place for ultimate peace and comfort. Humanism, in contrast, honors human intelligence and directs us to live in this world, here and now, enjoy life as it unfolds, and look to ourselves and each other for answers as we engage in shared inquiry, not await revelations from elsewhere.[8]

When Brandon and I became pooled out on our descent down Merlin Abyss, we found ourselves in a potentially life-threatening situation. We didn't appeal to higher power for direction and protection, nor did we take comfort in the belief that, if the worst happened, we would be rejoined in some other world. We analyzed our options as best we could decipher them, looked to ourselves for solutions, and took responsibility for the consequences of our actions. In that moment, and in many other canyon moments, Brandon lived the humanist approach to encountering the world and solving problems—an empirical, this-world, use-your-reason, and take-responsibility-for-your-actions paradigm. No deity to bail you out. No heaven to compensate for poor choices made in this world. This is your one shot. When Brandon plunged over the waterfall to an unknown landing below, that was how he went. And that's how I followed.

Suffering/Fear versus Affirming/Understanding

Tribal initiations routinely include suffering and fear. Enduring pain is at the core of ritual circumcision, tooth evulsion, scarring the face, snakebites, and deprivation of food and sleep. Fear includes not only fear of pain, but of shame, disgrace, humiliation, failure, and even death. Religious initiations have often involved mutilations by self and/or others, and always invoke the fear of God. Military and fraternity initiations involve hazing, some of which can be quite painful and frightening, examples of which I shared with Brandon in the canyon as I told him for the first time of my own degrading initiation into a college fraternity.

Inflicting pain and inducing fear, we now know, are classic brainwashing techniques. These are mechanisms for controlling and indoctrinating the initiates, thereby circumventing reason and guaranteeing that the initiates will not dare to question authority or investigate the mystical explanations they are given. Enduring pain and overcoming fear have been romanticized as desirable characteristics of manhood by some who would reintroduce in contemporary society the rituals of tribal initiation.

The humanist alternative offers affirmation rather than testing, nurturing rather than infliction of pain, intellectual inquiry rather than indoctrination, and compassion rather than fear. Instead of imposing standards on youth from a position of authority, the humanist ideal seeks to help young people develop moral standards and norms for behavior by examining their consequences.

All-knowing versus Acknowledging Uncertainty, Mutual Exploration

Humanism allows us, as parents and elders, to admit what we don't know, acknowledge uncertainty, and recognize that moral guidance requires situational application and interpretation. In this regard, Brandon was keenly interested in what kinds of dilemmas I felt I had faced as a parent. The canyon hike gave us time to explore such questions in some depth. He had typically experienced me as confident, knowledgeable, and certain. Had I had doubts? Certainly. And still did. It felt liberating to share openly my uncertainties, not to have to pretend to be an all-knowing father figure or tribal elder.

Standardized versus Individualized

Tribal and organizational initiations take the form of standardized rituals. Their essential sameness from person to person, and from time to time, carry part of the message: Your individuality is subsumed to the group. The power of tradition and the import of ritual are the comfort and authority they carry regardless of, indeed, over and above, the individual.

Brandon's coming-of-age celebration was designed especially for him and with his participation. The process affirmed his uniqueness as a person. The coming-of-age celebration for Brandon's younger brother, Quinn, though it took place in the canyon by *his* choice, was significantly different, but no less special. Their sister's coming-of-age celebration will likewise be unique and special, affirming and celebrating Charmagne's unique personhood.

The canyon's geology came to symbolize for me the relationship between individuality and conformity. Our ancestral past, dependent on group conformity, was like the ancient Vishnu Schist, formed by 75,000 pounds per square inch of tectonic pressure and named for the Hindu god, the Preserver. The black schist is the floor, the foundation, of the canyon. The river has cut through the canyon rock, all the way down to and including the Vishnu. In that vein, humanism offers a contemporary coming-of-age journey that recognizes ancient foundations of human experience, but refuses to be contained or completely restricted by that foundation. Humanism cuts, like the Colorado, through conformity by offering principles to inform an individualized and liberating coming-of-age process, one that does not require the societal equivalent of 75,000 pounds per square inch of pressure to assure acquiescence—to guarantee subjugation of the individual to the tribe, whatever form the tribe may take.

Gender Identity versus Personhood

Tribal initiations are founded on a clear, once-in-a-lifetime, permanent break between childhood and adulthood. This age- and gender-based change in status, prescribed by tradition, is dramatic, with major implications for every aspect of the initiate's life, including place of residence, responsibilities, primary activities, and prospects for marriage.

In contrast, adolescence in modern society has become an equivocal stage located ambiguously between childhood and adulthood. Status differences based on age and gender are being challenged in some arenas, like academic achievement and employment opportunity, even as they are accentuated in other arenas, like sports and entertainment.

Tribal initiations in older times and the Men's Movement in modern society focus on what it means to be a man. Female rites of passage and the feminist movement focus on what it means to be a woman. Humanism focuses on what it means to be a fully mature adult and self-actualized, moral person, regardless of gender. Humanism aims to wean people from dependence on gender, or any other ascribed characteristic, as the primary basis for identity.

Humanists are committed to transcending artificial and divisive groupings of human beings based on race, religion, class, sexual orientation, ethnicity, or gender. This does not mean ignoring the impact of these categories or pretending that they lack power to affect people's lives. Quite the contrary, the commitment to transcend such parochial thinking derives from recognizing the injustices that have stemmed from category-based discrimination. In this respect, humanism is person-centered rather than status-centered. This supports coming-of-age processes that are personalized and individualized.

Views of Childhood, Youth, and Life Passages

Because humanists believe in enjoying life here and now, the childhood capacity for play, spontaneity, and creativity can be nurtured and honored throughout life. Unlike Paul the Apostle, who took pride in asserting that, once he became a man, he put away "childish things," humanists can enjoy and participate in life's comedies and games while also attending to life's work and tragedies.[9]

Visiting Bass Camp at the bottom of the canyon and reading about the boy's encounters with work in the "Iron John" fable gave us occasion to talk about work and play, childhood and adulthood. We talked about my own father's somber life of work and duty, his anger and violent temper, and his intolerance for things "childish," even among children. In contrast, we celebrated Brandon's energy, creative spontaneity, and capacity for play, and affirmed that acknowledging his adulthood did not imply in any way abandoning those qualities.

We also talked about lifelong learning and development, involving multiple life transitions, rather than a single, onetime movement from childhood to adulthood. Malcolm and I, each in our own way, were experiencing transitions of middle age. Our time in the canyon became a chance to reflect on and celebrate those midlife transitions as a complement to Brandon's coming of age.

Territory: Tribalism versus Global Community

The chapter on the Great Rift opens by acknowledging two kinds of roots: place roots and people roots. Ancient initiation ceremonies attended to both. Initiation made the young man part of the tribe—people roots—and heir to the tribe's territory—place roots. One mechanism for rooting was retelling creation stories. These myths had to account for two things: creation of the earth and creation of the earth's inhabitants. These two are universally and intrinsically connected. Without a place there can be no people. Without people, place has no significance.

I grew up without a strong sense of either place or people roots. How does a father pass on to his son that which he does not possess? Humanism took me beyond this question to a sense of being part of humanity—my territory the earth, my sense of community, global. Humanism seeks to transcend nationalism and parochialism, instead advocating that people work together for the common good of humanity.

This perspective informed how we dealt with territory and community during Brandon's coming of age in the canyon. I recounted my visit to Oldavai Gorge in Africa's Great Rift Valley, site of the discovery of *Zinjanthropus boisei* and *Homo habilis* by the Leakeys—our evolutionary ancestors.[10] The geology of the Grand Canyon told the story of the Earth's history and evolution. Science gave us all the sense of place roots and people roots we needed.

Separation versus Bonding

Tribal initiation rites function to psychologically separate children, especially sons, from parental domination. Traditional initiations are conducted by the tribal elders to symbolize the death of the child and the rebirth of a new member of the tribe—a full adult.[11] That's why the father can't initiate his own son, because the son's actually being separated from his parents and brought into the tribe. Sometimes that involves literally tearing a terrified child from his mother's skirt or kidnaping him while he sleeps. When the boy returns to the village from the initiation camp, he doesn't return to his parents' hearth. This separation appears to serve a crucial psychological function. Because parents and children will live their entire lives within the same territory and interact within the prescribed roles of the extended family, some mechanism for psychological independence had to be provided for the children to become fully functioning adults. Initiation was that mechanism.

In contrast, modern society provides just the opposite challenge: bonding rather than separation. Our children are separated from us by day care, schools, music, television, peer groups, divorce, and easy geographic mobility. Society has evolved multiple mechanisms for detachment. Parents and children today are subjected to unprecedented centrifugal forces. The challenge now is to connect with each other and stay connected.

During our evenings in the canyon, we told Brandon initiation stories and fables from many cultures, most of them depicting father-son conflict. What humanism brings to the interpretation of such tales is recognition and celebration of the human capacity for reason and, in that capacity, the potential to discover, agree to, and act on new normative standards. Tales of father-son conflict, both ancient and modern, do not script us. They hold no power to predetermine our fate. They provide insights into historical patterns and warnings about the consequences of following old scripts. But humanism, grounded in social-science research and thoughtful analysis, offers a reasoned path to create new modes of connection. On that basis, a humanist father can dare to participate actively in his own son's coming-of-age ritual and can work with him to maintain a new, healthy adult relationship thereafter. That's what Brandon and I did, and what this book has told the story of.

Conclusion

The Statement of Humanism's Principles affirms: "We are deeply concerned with the moral education of our children. We want to nourish reason and compassion." The question is how best to do this. While the focus here has been on the time when a youth comes of age, no initiation ritual, no matter how meaningful, will be more important to a young person than the experiences and socialization that occur throughout childhood. Examining how humanist principles can inform a coming-of-age celebration is really a microcosm of how they can constitute the foundation for a parent-child relationship throughout the years of childhood. Brandon's coming-of-age celebration was no more or less grounded in humanism than was his entire childhood. His coming of age, then, was a gradual, developmental process over eighteen years, the canyon celebration being simply the culmination and marking of that longer, more important journey.

Modern youth deserve a coming-of-age journey for *this* epoch, one that recognizes past traditions of human experience, but is separate and distinct in accordance with the great human potential in our times; a process individually designed for each young person instead of standardized by tradition; rituals of affirmation and confirmation rather than categorization and control; and a process grounded in and honoring rational, scientific thought rather than mysticism and otherworldly spirituality. All in all, a participatory and celebratory process, not a dictatorial, fear-inducing, and authoritarian one. And, of special import to me, a process of intergenerational bonding rather than separation. In all this, humanism offers the opportunity to create our own rituals and make new traditions, or avoid rituals and traditions altogether for those who so choose, guided by affirmative principles and a sense of our common humanity. For we share a vision of a world into which we want youth to come of age:

> *We believe in optimism rather than pessimism, hope rather than despair, learning in the place of dogma, truth instead of ignorance, joy rather than guilt or sin, tolerance in the place of fear, love instead of hatred, compassion over selfishness, beauty instead of ugliness, and reason rather than blind faith or irrationality. We believe in the fullest realization of the best and noblest that we are capable of as human beings.*[12]

Notes

1. This caution comes courtesy of Jeanne Campbell, writer, editor, research colleague, and, not incidentally, my wife, who liked and helped greatly with the rest of this book, but who prefers stories without analytical epilogues, and who I know speaks for many when she expresses particular loathing for the word "paradigm," used often in this chapter. For my part, I stubbornly refuse to abandon a perfectly good and, in this case, I think, altogether appropriate term, just because it's been popularized and overused, all of which makes for stimulating dinner-time conversation.

2. Michael Quinn Patton, *Qualitative Evaluation and Research Methods* (Newbury Park, Calif.: Sage Publications, 1990).

From a research perspective, this Grand Canyon story is a qualitative case study based on participant observation. As a literary genre, however, given distinctions current in literature, this book can be classified as creative nonfiction. The "creative" part derives from the fact that I have recreated the experience as a story, imposing order and sequence on events and conversations that occurred more chaotically than reported here. I have reconstructed dialogues and interactions to capture their essence, as I remember them. Given the strenuous nature of the hike, I took just enough field notes to permit reasonably accurate reconstruction and elaboration afterward.

3. That what occurred during our Grand Canyon experience might be of general significance beyond what it meant to our family derives from a classic sociological distinction between purely personal concerns and larger societal issues. Sociologist C. Wright Mills put the matter thusly:

Issues have to do with matters that transcend the local environments of the individual and the range of his inner life. They have to do with the organization of many such milieux into the institutions of an historical society as a whole.

C. Wright Mills, *The Sociological Imagination* (New York: Oxford University Press, 1959), pp. 8–9.

4. References throughout this chapter to the Principles of Humanism refer to "The Affirmations of Humanism: A Statement of Principles," Council for Secular Humanism, P.O. Box 664, Amherst, NY 14226-0664.

5. See John Greenway, *Down Among the Wild Men* (Boston: Little, Brown and Company, 1972).

6. Robert Bly, *Iron John: A Book About Men* (Reading, Mass.: Addison-Wesley Publishing Company, Inc., 1990). For more on the argument that modern men need traditional initiations, consult James Hillman, Michael Meade, and Malidoma Somé, *Images of Initiation* (Pacific Grove, Calif.: Oral Tradition Archives, 1992), audiotapes of a gathering of men.

7. Skeptical inquiry is the application of reason to any and all ideas. Skeptical inquiry is based on the scientific method and the premise that evidence must be brought to bear on claims, beliefs, and hypotheses before they are accepted, even provisionally or temporarily pending new data. For more on skepticism see *Skeptical Inquiry: The Magazine of Science and Reason,* published by the Committee for the Scientific Investigation of Claims of the Paranormal, and *SKEPTIC,* the quarterly magazine of the Skeptics Society.

8. For skeptical-inquiry tales and fables that could be used in coming-of-age processes, see Michael Martin, *The Big Domino in the Sky* (Amherst, N.Y.: Prometheus Books, 1996).

9. For a discussion of the differences between viewing life as comedy instead of tragedy, see Joseph W. Meeker, *The Comedy of Survival* (Los Angeles: Guild of Tutors Press, 1980).

10. See Donald Johanson and James Shreeve, *Lucy's Child: The Discovery of a Human Ancestor* (New York: Avon Books, 1989); and Mary Leakey, *Disclosing the Past* (Garden City, N.Y.: Doubleday & Co., 1984).

11. Mircea Eliade, *Rites and Symbols of Initiation: The Mysteries of Birth and Rebirth* (New York: Harper & Row, 1958).

12. From "The Affirmations of Humanism: A Statement of Principles," Council for Secular Humanism.

Bibliography

Grand Canyon Bibliography

Abbey, Edward. *Desert Solitaire*. New York: Ballantine Books, 1968.

Ambler, J. Richard. *The Anasazi*. Flagstaff, Ariz.: Museum of Northern Arizona, 1989.

Annerino, John. *Hiking in the Grand Canyon*. San Francisco: Sierra Club Books, 1986.

Beus, Stanley S., and Michael Morales, eds. *Grand Canyon Geology*. New York: Oxford University Press, 1990.

Brand, John. *In the Desert We Do Not Count the Days*. Duluth, Minn.: Holy Cow Press, 1991.

Brian, Nancy. *River to Rim*. Flagstaff, Ariz.: Earthquest Press, 1992.

Butchart, Harvey. *Grand Canyon Treks*. Glendale, Calif.: La Siesta Press, 1970.

———. *Grand Canyon Treks II*. Glendale, Calif.: La Siesta Press, 1975.

———. *Grand Canyon Treks III*. Glendale, Calif.: La Siesta Press, 1984.

Collier, Michael. *An Introduction to Grand Canyon Geology*. Grand Canyon, Ariz.: Canyon Natural History Association, 1980.

Crumb, Kim. *A River Runner's Guide to the History of the Grand Canyon*. Boulder, Colo.: Johnson Books, 1994.

Darrah, William Culp. *Powell of the Colorado*. Princeton, N.J.: Princeton University Press, 1951.

Dawson, John, and Charles Craighead. *The Grand Canyon: An Artist's View*. Salt Lake City, Utah: Haggis House Publications, 1996.

Euler, Robert C., and Frank Tikalsky. *The Grand Canyon: Intimate Views*. Tucson: University of Arizona Press, 1992.

Evans, Edna. *Tales from the Grand Canyon: Some True, Some Tall*. Flagstaff, Ariz.: Northland Press, 1953.

Fishbein, Seymour L. *Grand Canyon Country: Its Majesty and Its Lore.* Washington, D.C.: National Geographic Society, 1991.

Fletcher, Colin. *The Man Who Walked Through Time.* New York: Vintage Books, 1967.

Fowler, Don D., Robert C. Euler, and Catherine S. Fowler. *John Wesley Powell and the Anthropology of the Canyon Country.* Geological Survey Professional Paper 670. Washington, D.C.: Geological Survey, 1969.

Fradkin, Philip L. *A River No More: The Colorado River and the West.* Tucson: University of Arizona Press, 1968.

Grand Canyon Natural History Association. *The Mountain Lying Down: Views of the North Rim.* Grand Canyon, Ariz.: Grand Canyon Natural History Association, 1979.

Granger, Byrd H. *Grand Canyon Place Names.* Tucson, Ariz.: University of Arizona Press.

Hamblin, W. Kenneth, and Joseph R. Murphy. *Grand Canyon Perspectives.* Provo, Utah: Brigham Young University Geology Studies, Special Publication No. 1, 1980.

Heaton, Timothy. "A Young Grand Canyon?" *Skeptical Inquiry* 19, no. 3 (1995): 33–36.

Hoffman, John F. *The Grand Canyon: Horrid Abyss, Wondrous Titan of Chasms.* Casper, Wyo.: National Parkways, World-Wide Research and Publishing Company, 1977.

Houk, Rose. *An Introduction to Grand Canyon Ecology.* Grand Canyon, Ariz.: Grand Canyon Associations, 1997.

Hughes, J. Donald. *In the House of Stone and Light: The Human History of the Grand Canyon.* Grand Canyon, Ariz.: Grand Canyon Natural History Association, 1978.

Jones, Anne Trinkle, and Robert C. Euler. *A Sketch of Grand Canyon Prehistory.* Grand Canyon, Ariz.: Grand Canyon Natural History Association, 1990.

Kolb, Ellsworth L. *Through the Grand Canyon from Wyoming to Mexico.* New York: Macmillan Company, 1946.

Krutch, Joseph Wood. *The Desert Year.* Tucson: University of Arizona Press, 1951.

———. *Grand Canyon: Today and All Its Yesterday.* Tucson: University of Arizona Press, 1952.

Lamb, Susan, ed. *The Best of Grand Canyon Nature Notes.* Grand Canyon, Ariz.: Grand Canyon Natural History Association, 1994.

Martin, John F. *The Havasupai.* Flagstaff: Museum of Northern Arizona, 1986.

Maurer, Stephen G. *Solitude and Sunshine: Images of a Grand Canyon Childhood.* Boulder, Colo.: Pruett Publishing Company, 1983.

Moore, Michael. *Medicinal Plants of the Mountain West.* Santa Fe: Museum of New Mexico Press, 1979.

Nash, Roderick. *Wilderness and the American Mind.* New Haven: Yale University Press, 1967.

O'Connor, Letitia Burns. *The Grand Canyon.* Los Angeles: Hugh Lauter Levin Associates, Inc., 1992.

Percy, Walker. "The Loss of the Creature." In *The Message in the Bottle,* 46–63. New York: The Noonday Press, 1990.

Phillips, Arthur M., III. *Grand Canyon Wildflowers.* Grand Canyon, Ariz.: Grand Canyon Natural History Association, 1979.

Powell, J. W. *The Exploration of the Colorado River and Its Canyons.* New York: Dover Publications Inc., 1961.

Pyne, Stephen J. *How the Canyon Became Grand.* New York: Viking, 1998.

Schmidt, Jeremy. *A Natural History Guide: Grand Canyon National Park.* Boston: Houghton Mifflin Company, 1993.

Spangler, Sharon. *On Foot in the Grand Canyon: Hiking the Trails of the South Rim.* Boulder, Colo.: Pruett Publishing Co., 1989.

Stanton, Robert Brewster. *Down the Colorado.* Norman: University of Oklahoma Press, 1965.

Steck, George. *Grand Canyon Loop Hikes I.* Evergreen, Colo.: Chockstone Press, 1989.

Stegner, Wallace. *Beyond the Hundredth Meridian.* New York: Penguin Books, 1953.

Stephens, Hal G., and Eugene M. Shoemaker. *In the Footsteps of John Wesley Powell.* Boulder, Colo.: Johnson Books, 1987.

Stevens, Larry. *The Colorado River in Grand Canyon.* Flagstaff, Ariz.: Red Lake Books, 1983.

Whitney, Stephen. *A Field Guide to the Grand Canyon.* New York: Quill, 1982.

General Bibliography

Adams, Gerald R. et al., eds. *Adolescent Identity Formation.* Newbury Park, Calif.: Sage, 1992.

Adler, Jerry. "Drum, Sweat and Tears: What Do Men Really Want?" *Newsweek*, June 24, 1991, 46–53.

Alexie, Sherman. "White Men Can't Drum." *New York Times Magazine*, October 4, 1992, 2–3.

Andrews, Ted. *Animal-Speak: The Spiritual and Magical Powers of Creatures Great and Small.* St. Paul, Minn.: Llewellyn, 1993.

Arcana, Judith. *Every Mother's Son: The Role of Mothers in the Making of Men.* London: Women's Press, 1983.

Avalos, Hector. "Is Faith Good for You? Examining Whether Unjustified Beliefs Are Really the Best Medicine." *Free Inquiry* 17, no. 4 (Fall 1997): 44–46.

Bly, Robert. *Iron John: A Book About Men.* Reading, Mass.: Addison-Wesley Publishing Company, Inc., 1990.

———. *The Light Around the Body.* New York: HarperPerennial, 1959.

———. *The Man in the Black Coat Turns.* New York: HarperPerennial, 1981.

———. *Sleepers Joining Hands.* New York: HarperPerennial, 1973.

Brown, Joseph Epes, ed. *The Sacred Pipe: Black Elk's Account of the Seven Rites of the Oglala Sioux.* Norman: University of Oklahoma Press, 1953.

Byers, Kenneth. *Man in Transition: His Role as Father, Son, Friend, Lover.* La Mesa, Calif.: Journeys Together, 1990.

———. *WWTMMA? (Who Was That Masked Man Anyway?).* La Mesa, Calif.: Journeys Together, 1993.

Cable, James, trans. (author unknown). *The Death of King Arthur.* Middlesex, England: Penguin, Ltd., 1971.

Campbell, Joseph. *Historical Atlas of World Mythology, Volume I: The Way of Animal Powers, Part 2, Mythologies of the Great Hunt.* New York: Perennial Library, 1988.

———. *Historical Atlas of World Mythology, Volume II: The Way of the Seeded Earth, Part 1, The Sacrifice.* New York: Perennial Library, 1988.

———. *Transformations of Myth Through Time.* New York: Harper & Row, 1990.

Campbell, Joseph, with Bill Moyers. *The Power of Myth.* New York: Doubleday, 1988.

Christian, Catherine. *The Pendragon: The Glorious Life and Death of Arthur, King of Britain, recounted by Bedivere, His Friend Since Boyhood, His Fellow Knight and Companion-in-Arms.* New York: Alfred A. Knopf, 1978.

Council for Secular Humanism. "The Affirmations of Humanism: A Statement of Principles." *Free Inquiry* 15, no. 4 (1995): 68.

Cowan, James. *Messengers of the Gods.* Sydney: Vintage, 1993.

Dalby, Gordon. *Father and Son: The Wound, the Healing, the Call to Manhood.* Nashville, Tenn.: Thomas Nelson, 1992.

D'Antonio, Michael. *Heaven on Earth: Dispatches from America's Spiritual Frontiers.* New York: Crown, 1992.

de Troyes, Chretien. *The Story of the Grail.* Translated by Robert White Link. Chapel Hill: University of North Carolina Press, 1952.

Eliade, Mircea. *The Forge and the Crucible: The Origins and Structures of Alchemy.* Chicago: University of Chicago Press, 1962.

————. *Myth and Reality.* New York: Harper Books, 1963.

————. *Rites and Symbols of Initiation: The Mysteries of Birth and Rebirth.* New York: Harper & Row, 1958.

Feder, Kenneth. "Indians and Archaeologists: Conflicting Views of Myth and Science." *Skeptic* 5, no. 3 (1997): 74–80.

Fossum, Merle. *Catching Fire: Men Coming Alive in Recovery.* San Francisco: A Harper/Hazelden Book, 1989.

Freeman, Derek. "Paradigms in Collision: Margaret Meade's Mistake and What It Has Done to Anthropology." *Skeptic* 5, no. 3 (1997): 66–73.

Gardner, Martin. "Extreme Credulity." *Skeptical Inquiry* 19, no. 5 (1995): 29.

————. "Science vs. Beauty?" *Skeptical Inquiry* 19, no. 2 (1995): 14–16.

————. *Science: Good, Bad and Bogus.* Amherst, N.Y.: Prometheus Books, 1990.

————. *Weird Water and Fuzzy Logic.* Amherst, N.Y.: Prometheus Books, 1996.

Gilliam, Richard, Martin H. Greenberg, and Edward E. Kramer, eds. *Excalibur.* New York: Warner Books, 1995.

Greenway, John. *Down Among the Wild Men.* Boston: Little, Brown and Company, 1972.

Grimm, Jacob W., and Wilhelm K. Grimm. *The Complete Grimm's Fairy Tales.* Translated by Margaret Hunt and James Stern. New York: Pantheon Books, 1972.

Haught, James A. "The Honest Agnostic: Battling Demons of the Mind." *Free Inquiry* 17, no. 2 (1997): 8–9.

Heinrich, Bernd. *Ravens in Winter.* New York: Vintage Books, 1989.

Hill, Tom, and Richard W. Hill Sr., eds. *Creation's Journey: Native American Identity and Belief.* Washington, D.C.: Smithsonian Institution Press, 1994.

Hillman, James, Michael Meade, and Malidoma Somé. *Images of Initiation.* Pacific Grove, Calif.: Oral Tradition Archives, 1992. Audiotapes of a gathering of men.

Horowitz, Anthony. *Myths and Mythology.* New York: Simon & Schuster, 1985.

Johanson, Donald, and James Shreeve. *Lucy's Child: The Discovery of a Human Ancestor.* New York: Avon Books, 1989.

Johnson, Robert A. *HE: Understanding Masculine Psychology.* New York: Harper, 1989.

———. *Transformation: Understanding the Three Levels of Masculine Consciousness, Masculine Psychology.* San Francisco: HarperCollins, 1991.

———. *WE: Understanding the Psychology of Romantic Love.* San Francisco: Harper, 1983.

Jung, Emma, and Marie-Louise von Franz. *The Grail Legend.* Boston: Sigo Press, 1970.

Keen, Sam. *Fire in the Belly: On Becoming a Man.* New York: Bantam, 1991.

Keyes, Ralph, ed. *Sons on Fathers.* New York: HarperCollins, 1992.

Kurtz, Paul. *Eupraxophy: Living Without Religion.* Amherst, N.Y.: Prometheus Books, 1989.

———. *The Humanist Alternative.* Amherst, N.Y.: Prometheus Books, 1973.

———. *In Defense of Secular Humanism.* Amherst, N.Y.: Prometheus Books, 1983.

———. "Is John Beloff an Absolute Paranormalist?" *Skeptical Inquiry* 19, no. 5 (1995): 28.

———. *The New Skepticism: Inquiry and Reliable Knowledge.* Amherst, N.Y.: Prometheus Books, 1992.

———. *Philosophical Essays in Pragmatic Naturalism.* Amherst, N.Y.: Prometheus Books, 1992.

———. *A Secular Humanist Declaration.* Amherst, N.Y.: Prometheus Books, 1981.

———. *A Skeptic's Handbook of Parapsychology.* Amherst, N.Y.: Prometheus Books, 1985.

Lacy, Norris J. *The Arthurian Encyclopedia.* New York: Peter Bedrick Books, 1986.

Lanier, Sidney, ed. *The Boy's King Arthur: Sir Thomas Mallory's History of King Arthur and His Knights of the Round Table.* New York: Charles Scribner's Sons, 1917.

Larrington, Carolyn, ed. *The Feminist Companion to Mythology*. London: Pandora, 1992.

Leakey, Mary. *Disclosing the Past*. Garden City, N.Y.: Doubleday & Co., 1984.

Leakey, Richard. "Homo Erectus Unearthed." *National Geographic* 168, no. 5 (November 1985): 624–29.

Lee, John. *At My Father's Wedding: Reclaiming Our True Masculinity*. New York: Bantam, 1991.

Lévi-Strauss, Claude. *Myths and Meaning*. New York: Schocken Books, 1978.

———. *The Raw and the Cooked, Mythologies*. Vol. 1. Chicago: University of Chicago Press, 1969.

———. *Totemism*. Boston: Beacon, 1962.

Loevinger, Lee. "The Paradox of Knowledge." *Skeptical Inquiry* 19, no. 5 (1995): 18–21.

Machel, Hans G. "A Geologist's Enlightened Notes on 'Crystal Power.' " *Skeptical Inquiry* 24, no. 4 (1996): 59–60.

Malone, Tom. "So, What Do You Teach Your Kids?" *Free Inquiry* 14, no. 3 (1994): 19–20.

Malory, Thomas. *The Book of Sir Galahad*. Philadelphia: George W. Jacobs & Co., n.d.

Martin, Michael. *The Big Domino in the Sky*. Amherst, N.Y.: Prometheus Books, 1996.

Mason, Marilyn. *Seven Mountains: The Inner Climb to Commitment and Caring*. New York: Dutton, 1997.

Meeker, Joseph W. *The Comedy of Survival*. Los Angeles: Guild of Tutors Press, 1980.

———. *Minding the Earth*. Alameda, Calif.: Latham Foundation, 1988.

"Men: It's Time to Pull Together. The Politics of Masculinity." *Utne Reader* (May/June 1991): 66–87.

Meyer, Kathleen. *How to Shit in the Woods*. Berkeley, Calif.: Ten Speed Press, 1989.

Mills, C. Wright. *The Sociological Imagination*. New York: Oxford University Press, 1959.

Minnich, Elizabeth K. *Transforming Knowledge*. Philadelphia: Temple University Press, 1990.

Momaday, N. Scott. *The Way to Rainy Mountain*. Albuquerque: University of New Mexico Press, 1969.

Monaco, Richard. *Parsival or a Knight's Tale*. New York: Macmillan, 1977.

Morrow, Lance. "The Child Is Father of the Man: How Robert Bly Transformed His Struggle with an Alcoholic Dad into a Strange, Mythicized Phenomenon of Celebrity and Mass Therapy." *Time*, August 19, 1991, 52–54.

Moustakas, Clark. *Being-In, Being-For, Being-With*. Northvale, N.J.: Jason Aronson Inc., 1995.

Nerburn, Kent. *Letters To My Son: Reflections on Becoming a Man*. San Rafael, Calif.: New World Library, 1993.

Ode, Kim. "Robert Bly: A Man's Man Rethinks His Role." *First Sunday Magazine*, February 2, 1992, 4–11.

Osherson, Samuel. *Finding Our Fathers*. New York: Fawcett Columbine, 1986.

Paton, Lucy Allen, trans. *Sir Lancelot of the Lake*. New York: Harcourt, Brace & Co., 1929.

Patton, Michael Quinn. *Qualitative Evaluation and Research Methods*. Newbury Park, Calif.: Sage Publications, 1990.

———. *Utilization-Focused Evaluation*. 3d ed. Thousand Oaks, Calif.: Sage Publications, 1997.

Pratt, Minnie Bruce. *Crime Against Nature*. Ithaca, N.Y.: Firebrand Books, 1990.

———. *S/HE*. Ithaca, N.Y.: Firebrand Books, 1995.

———. *We Say We Love Each Other*. Ithaca, N.Y.: Firebrand Books, 1985.

Radin, Paul. *The Trickster: A Study in American Indian Mythology*. New York: Schocken Books, 1956.

Randi, James. *The Faith Healers*. Amherst, N.Y.: Prometheus Books, 1989.

———. *Flim-Flam! The Truth About Unicorns, Parapsychology, and Other Delusions*. Amherst, N.Y.: Prometheus Books, 1982.

———. " 'Psychic Healing' and Alternative Medicine." *Free Inquiry* 14, no. 1 (1993/94): 15–18.

———. " 'Twas Brillig Fairies, Frauds, & Fuss." *Skeptic* 5, no. 3 (1997): 10–11.

Rhŷs, John. *Studies in the Arthurian Legend*. Oxford: Clarendon Press, 1891.

Rutledge, Don, with Rita Robinson. *Center of the World: Native American Spirituality*. North Hollywood, Calif.: Newcastle Publishing, 1992.

Sams, Jamie, and David Carson. *Medicine Cards: The Discovery of Power Through the Ways of Animals*. Santa Fe, N.M.: Bear & Company, 1988.

Schlegel, Alice, and Herbert Barry III. *Adolescence: An Anthropological Inquiry*. New York: Free Press, 1991.

Silverstein, Olga, and Beth Rashbaum. *The Courage to Raise Good Men*. New York: Viking, 1994.

Stewart, R. J., ed. *The Book of Merlin*. Poole, England: Blandford Press, 1987.

Tallmadge, John. *Meeting the Tree of Life*. Salt Lake City: University of Utah Press, 1997.

Tennyson, Alfred, Lord. *The Holy Grail and Other Poems*. London: Strahan and Co., 1870.

———. *Idylls of the King*. London: Penguin Books, Ltd., 1983.

Thom, Laine. *Becoming Brave: The Path to Native American Manhood*. San Francisco: Chronicle Books, 1992.

Tolstoy, Nikolai. *The Coming of the King: A Novel of Merlin*. New York: Bantam, 1989.

Twain, Mark. *A Connecticut Yankee in King Arthur's Court*. New York: Penguin Classics, 1990.

———. "Letters From the Earth, Letters II and III." *Free Inquiry* 17, no. 4 (Fall 1977): 50–52.

von Eschenbach, Wolfram. *Parzival*. New York: Random House, 1961.

Weaver, Kenneth. "Stones, Bones, and Early Man: The Search for Our Ancestors." *National Geographic* 168, no. 5 (November 1985): 560–623.

Weiner, Bernard. *Boy into Man: A Father's Guide to Initiation of Teenage Sons*. San Francisco: Transformation Press, 1992.

Weston, Jessie L. *From Ritual to Romance*. Gloucester: Peter Smith, 1957.

———. *The Legend of Sir Perceval*. London: David Nutt, 1909.

Weston, Jessie L., trans. *The Legend of Sir Gawain*. London: David Nutt, 1987.

White, T. H. *The Book of Merlyn*. Austin: University of Texas Press, 1977.

———. *The Once and Future King*. New York: Ace Books, 1987.

"Wild Men and Wimps." *Esquire,* Special issue, October 1991.

Zipes, Jack. " 'Genuine Masculine' Reinforces Male Elitism." *Minneapolis Star Tribune*, August 7, 1993, 15A.

About the Author

M ichael Quinn Patton has been hiking the Grand Canyon since 1978. He is a lifetime member of the Grand Canyon Association and a member of the Grand Canyon Trust. In between hikes he has written five major books on program evaluation and research methods, including *Utilization-Focused Evaluation* (1997) and *Qualitative Evaluation and Research Methods* (1990). He also edited *Culture and Evaluation* and served as editor of the *Journal of Extension* for three years. He has been president of the American Evaluation Association and is the only scholar to have received the field's two highest honors: the Gunnar and Alva Myrdal Award from the Evaluation Research Society "for outstanding contributions to evaluation use and practice" and the Paul F. Lazarsfeld Award for "advancements in evaluation theory" from the American Evaluation Association.

After earning a doctorate in sociology from the University of Wisconsin, Madison, he taught and conducted research at the University of Minnesota for eighteen years, including five as director of the Minnesota Center for Social Research. He received the University's Morse-Amoco Award for Outstanding Teaching. He continues to pursue his dedication to teaching research methods as a faculty member with The Union Institute's Graduate College of Interdisciplinary Arts and Sciences, a national, nontraditional doctoral program. He is an associate member of the Committee for the Scientific Investigation of Claims of the Paranormal.

About the Illustrations

Illustrations are reproductions from Mimbres pottery transcribed by New Mexico artist and potter Barbara Campbell-Moffitt. For information on pottery with these designs write to P.O. Box 775, El Rito, NM 87530.

359